CW00722807

The Sunday Assembly and Theologies of Suffering

This book draws on a study of the Sunday Assembly—a "godless congregation"—to reflect on how the Church might better deal with suffering, lament, and theodicy. Against a backdrop of a shifting attitudes towards religion, humans are now better connected than ever before. It is no exaggeration to suggest that we carry the suffering of the world in our pockets. In the midst of these intersecting issues, the Sunday Assembly provides insight into how meaning making in times of trauma and crisis is changing.

Drawing on practical theology and using ethnographic tools of investigation, this book includes findings from interviews and observation with the Sunday Assembly in London and Edinburgh. It explores the Sunday Assembly's philosophy of "celebrating life" and what this means in practice. At times, this emphasis on celebration can result in situations where suffering is "passed over" or only briefly acknowledged. In response, this book considers a similar tendency within white Protestant churches to avoid explicit discussion of difficult issues.

This book challenges churches to consider how they might resist the avoidance of suffering through the practice of lament. The insights provided by this book will be of particular interest to scholars of Religious Studies, Practical Theology, Secularism, and Atheism/Non-religion.

Katie Cross is Christ's College Fellow in Practical Theology at the University of Aberdeen, Scotland.

Explorations in Practical, Pastoral and Empirical Theology

Series Editors: Leslie J. Francis, Jeff Astley, Martyn Percy and Nicola Slee

Theological reflection on the church's practice is now recognised as a significant element in theological studies in the academy and seminary. Routledge's series in practical, pastoral and empirical theology seeks to foster this resurgence of interest and encourage new developments in practical and applied aspects of theology worldwide. This timely series draws together a wide range of disciplinary approaches and empirical studies to embrace contemporary developments including: the expansion of research in empirical theology, psychological theology, ministry studies, public theology, Christian education and faith development; key issues of contemporary society such as health, ethics and the environment; and more traditional areas of concern such as pastoral care and counselling.

Ecclesial Leadership as Friendship
Chloe Lynch

Poetry, Practical Theology, and Reflective Practice
Mark Pryce

Tragedies and Christian Congregations
The Practical Theology of Trauma
Edited by Megan Warner, Christopher Southgate, Carla A. Grosch-Miller and Hilary Ison

Disclosing Church
An Ecclesiology Learned from Conversations in Practice
Clare Watkins

The Sunday Assembly and Theologies of Suffering
Katie Cross

For more information and a full list of titles in the series, please visit:
www.routledge.com/religion/series/APPETHEO

The Sunday Assembly and Theologies of Suffering

Katie Cross

Routledge
Taylor & Francis Group

LONDON AND NEW YORK

First published 2020
by Routledge
2 Park Square, Milton Park, Abingdon, Oxon OX14 4RN

and by Routledge
52 Vanderbilt Avenue, New York, NY 10017

Routledge is an imprint of the Taylor & Francis Group, an informa business

© 2020 Katie Cross

The right of Katie Cross to be identified as author of this work has been asserted by her in accordance with sections 77 and 78 of the Copyright, Designs and Patents Act 1988.

All rights reserved. No part of this book may be reprinted or reproduced or utilised in any form or by any electronic, mechanical, or other means, now known or hereafter invented, including photocopying and recording, or in any information storage or retrieval system, without permission in writing from the publishers.

Trademark notice: Product or corporate names may be trademarks or registered trademarks, and are used only for identification and explanation without intent to infringe.

British Library Cataloguing-in-Publication Data
A catalogue record for this book is available from the British Library

Library of Congress Cataloging-in-Publication Data
A catalog record for this book has been requested

ISBN: 978-0-367-27699-7 (hbk)
ISBN: 978-0-429-29847-9 (ebk)

Typeset in Sabon
by Apex CoVantage, LLC

In memory of Christina "Chris" Clunie, whose love and faith and humour played no small part in bringing me here.

Where can I go from your spirit?
Or where can I flee from your presence?
If I ascend to heaven, you are there;
if I make my bed in Sheol, you are there.
If I take the wings of the morning
and settle at the farthest limits of the sea,
even there your hand shall lead me,
and your right hand shall hold me fast.
                    Psalm 139:7–10

Contents

Acknowledgements

First and foremost, I would like to thank the members of the Sunday Assembly in London and Edinburgh. In particular, I am very grateful to Sanderson Jones for accepting me with open arms and for allowing me to conduct interviews and observations in both places. Thank you to each one of the 30 people who agreed to be interviewed by me, and the many more who shared their thoughts in other ways. It's hard not to be fond of the Sunday Assembly when its members are so kind and welcoming.

This book (as many others do!) began its life as a PhD project at the University of Aberdeen. I was supervised by the inimitable Chris Brittain, and I am very grateful to him for helping me to complete not only my PhD, but this work. Thanks, Chris, for your curiosity and good guidance. My work on the Sunday Assembly was supported by the Scottish Graduate School for the Arts and Humanities (which, in conjunction with the AHRC Doctoral Training Partnership for Scotland, funded my doctoral project in its entirety). A very special thanks to all SGSAH for their continued friendship.

I'd also like to thank my colleagues at the University of Aberdeen for their support. A lot of the issues explored in this book have been the subject of a course I teach at the University of Aberdeen called *Atheism and Atheisms*. I'm particularly grateful to the students who took this class in the Winter term of 2019 for shaping and testing my ideas in our class discussions. I want to thank them for their generosity, patient encouragement, and good humour.

The practical theological community in the UK (and beyond!) has been so generous in welcoming me into its ranks as a young scholar. In particular, I'm indebted to John Swinton and Elaine Graham, who examined my PhD thesis and gently aided and emboldened its transformation into this book.

My family and friends are deserving of endless praise for listening to me talk about this project for five years! To my parents, Christine and Nicos, and my brothers, Andrew and Peter, for their unconditional love; Jacqui, Charlie, Esther, Ben, and the rest of the Cross Clan; Conor Fegan and Colin Bennie, for all the red wine nights and convincing me to (finally) get a dog; Leila Evans, for looking after me in London; Cara Dutfield, Amy Sykes, and Heather Bates, for making me laugh and keeping me sane; Clare Radford,

Karen O'Donnell, Leah Robinson, Nicola Whyte, Kait Dugan, and the rest of the theological "sisterhood" that has kept me afloat in the past few years; Callum Pearce, for everything in my first year at Aberdeen; Joshua Bullock, for being a Sunday Assembly expert, fieldwork friend, and generous advice-giver; my friends at BIAPT and SST for wise counsel and for big ideas hatched over whisky; and my church family in Cardross for their years of care, and for reminding me to always "look forward in faith."

Finally, to my husband, Peter, who married me in the middle of all of this: for humouring me, supporting me, challenging me, and loving me . . . thank you so, so much.

Introduction

It was a bright sort of morning in London, though the air was chilly. Bundled up against the frigid January wind, I walked briskly through Holborn, making for a silver-grey bricked building tucked in the corner of Red Lion Square. I could hear voices spilling out from inside before I'd even touched the door handle. Through the doors, the hallway was teeming with activity. Green-shirted volunteers with name-badges wound their way across the foyer, shepherding new arrivals towards the main hall. I followed behind a knot of people shuffling slowly through a set of double doors. Once inside the hall, I took a seat at the back and watched as the room began to fill.

At the front of the room was a stage, and on it were instruments: a guitar, a violin, and a piano. On the right sat the choir, who had already assembled. Above the stage, emblazoned in green lettering, were the words "To thine own self be true." Upbeat music filtered through the sound system. The noise level increased significantly as more and more people streamed through the door, breathing an air of excitement into the room. Friends greeted one another with hugs and bumping of fists. The majority were young, white, and well-dressed, albeit casual; they wore jeans, jumpers, printed dresses, knitted cardigans. They held takeaway coffee cups. Expensive-looking watches circled their wrists.

Not everyone who entered the room seemed to be familiar with it. Some moved hesitantly, scanning the hall, before taking a seat at the back. After about ten minutes, a slightly dishevelled looking middle-aged man, wearing a crumpled shirt and carrying a clipboard, approached me. He asked if it was my first time there and told me that he was responsible for looking after people who had come on their own. I assured him that I was quite happy.

Shortly before 11, the rows of seats downstairs were almost full. Before long, a young woman with dark curly hair had claimed the seat to my right. She looked to be in her mid-twenties—about the same age as me. Turning towards me, sloshing coffee from a paper cup and dropping croissant crumbs down her blue floral-patterned dress, she offered me her hand. "I'm Jackie," she said, through mouthfuls of breakfast. "First time?" I nodded. She grinned. "You'll like it here," she told me, taking another sip of coffee. "You look just the type. I'm sure you'll make lots of friends."

Her final few words were interrupted by the arrival of the charismatic leader on-stage. He was strikingly tall, with long strawberry-blonde hair and a bushy, unkempt beard. He smiled widely. The leader's presence was magnetic. As soon as he appeared, every head in the room was turned towards him. At his prompting, the band struck up the opening chords of the first song. All across the hall, people leapt to their feet; a little off-pace, I joined them. Most clapped along, many swayed in time to the music. Some, seemingly enraptured, raised their hands in the air. The leader jumped up and down, holding his hands high, his face flushed and contorted as he roared along to the opening anthem. There was a palpable energy in the room.

As the song ended, the cheers from the 300-strong congregation were almost deafening. The leader's introductory address was met with clamorous applause. He introduced, first, a reading. Then came a homily: a longer talk, delivered by a member of the congregation. During the next song, a blonde-haired woman in purple dungarees, seated further along the row to my left, lifted her arms in response. She sang along with her eyes closed, dancing and twirling to the music in an almost transcendent way.

In a haze of tumultuous applause from the congregation, the leader appeared again, shouting hoarsely over the crowd. Calming them just enough to be heard, he invited everyone to sit for a moment of contemplative reflection. For two minutes, a fitful silence fell across the hall, punctuated by the occasional jarring phone alert and murmur of quiet conversation.

The leader announced that a collection would be taken; chatter broke out across the hall, as jute bags were passed hand to hand, and steadily filled with money. We were called to order one last time. An older woman with short grey hair ascended to the stage, where she delivered the intimations. Then the leader delivered his closing oration. With boundless energy, and in perfectly quotable idiom, he spoke about that which had influenced his spiritual journey, and his determination to "get the most out of life." The leader's relentless positivity seemed to span out across the room with every upward motion of his arms. The congregation listened, seemingly transfixed, as he evangelised about the overwhelming "awesomeness" of life and the wonders of human existence. Once more, he called us to our feet. The room swelled with life as congregants sang, clapped, and swayed their way through the closing song.

The Sunday Assembly

The Sunday Assembly is a church like no other. In this "church," there are no sermons; instead, there are short, informative, TED-style talks, covering a range of topics from particle physics to mindfulness. Rather than hymns, the congregation sings songs by Queen, Fleetwood Mac, David Bowie, and the Beatles. In place of scriptural readings are poems, limericks, and sometimes literary extracts. The congregation does not draw together in prayer but pauses for moments of silent, contemplative reflection. The collection is not for the work of the church but for the furtherance of a worldwide congregational movement, which has described itself (varyingly) as an "atheist church,"[1] a "non-religious gathering,"[2] and a "godless" or "secular" congregation.[3] While the Sunday Assembly claims to constitute a non-religious expression of community, its leaders do not deny that it draws on the institutions and structure of the Church. The shape of the liturgy is "analogous to a low-church service."[4] Indeed, *Guardian* journalist Esther Addley suggests that "a church goer who stumbled through the wrong door would find much they recognised."[5] Jackie, who sat next to me at my first Sunday Assembly explained that "Anyone who has ever been to church would relate to the feeling of being at Sunday Assembly."

As a theologian, this organisation has intrigued me since its inception in 2013. Even a simple description of the Sunday Assembly and its intended remit is enough to elicit endless theological queries, spanning in various disciplinary directions. In ecclesiological terms, how might such a "church" function? What sort of doctrine do its members follow? What do they "worship" there? As a practical theologian, my concern is first and foremost practice based. In some ways, this does not immediately narrow the possibilities for theological study of this organisation! I was, however, intrigued about one particular set of practices in the Sunday Assembly. I wanted to find out how the organisation would respond to suffering. So began the very journey that has brought me to writing this book.

Theologies of suffering

Why suffering? For one, it would (of course) be impossible to address all of the theological quandaries raised by the Sunday Assembly in a single work. But centrally, I chose to consider suffering because it a universal aspect of the human experience; an ever-present shadow on the fabric of human life, which has intrigued theologians for centuries. Suffering provokes time-worn questions: "How can there be a God when there is so much suffering in the world?" or "How could a loving God allow this to happen?" Theologically speaking, the process of thinking through and responding to trauma and disaster is both a painful and an arduous task. It implicates speech about the brokenness of the human condition, the hopelessness of unrestrained suffering and the apparent failure of the gospel message. Christian teachings on the all-knowing and all-loving nature of God are fiercely challenged by such cries of anguish and distress.

Historically, theologians have sought to answer questions about suffering by drawing on the practice of theodicy. Theodicy emerged as a theological attempt to defend the love and goodness of God in a world of constant evil and suffering. While theodicy remains prevalent within contemporary theological discourse, intended to reflect upon a concrete, all-pervading and thoroughly human set of problems, it can be problematic in its abstraction of suffering, undermining the problem of evil and minimising human suffering. Rather than addressing the question of divine culpability, theodicy can turn the blame for suffering on the communities and individuals at the very centre of tragic events. As a result, while theodicy is the most influential philosophical approach to the problem of evil, it holds the potential to become dangerous when communicated at a human level.

Theological speech about suffering is further complicated in our current context, as fewer and fewer people in Britain are familiar with Church language and tradition. Proponents of secularisation theory, including philosopher Charles Taylor,[6] historian Callum Brown,[7] and sociologist of religion Steve Bruce,[8] claim that the influence of traditional religions in the industrial world is in terminal decline. To support their assertions, they cite surveys and polls, which appear to return a vote of no-confidence in Christianity.[9] In the 2017 British Social Attitudes Survey, 53% of British adults described themselves as having "no religion."[10] Others challenge the straightforward nature of these assertions, contesting that the situation is more complex. Sociologists Paul Heelas and Linda Woodhead have suggested that religion is not necessarily disappearing, but that its function is shifting from public to private.[11] Woodhead points to the growth of a "middle ground" between religion and non-religion and argues that those who neither identify as belonging to a religion, or as atheist ("none's") could comprise as much as 50% of the UK population.[12] Public theologian Elaine Graham notes that religion continues to occupy a place of social importance within Western democracies and "compelling and vibrant signs of religious activism" that are still to be found within the United Kingdom.[13] Whether secularisation theory is correct, or an overly simplistic presentation of the current landscape of belief and unbelief in Britain, it is clear that habitual Christian practice can no longer be taken for granted.

Within this tension, the darkness of the human experience does not relent. Suffering is continually present, and a lack of faith in God does little to dispel the bleakness of human tragedy. In the twenty-first century, instantaneous methods of communication allow for pictures of mass-shootings, terror attacks, and natural disasters to be beamed directly to phones, tablets, and other devices. With current technology, it is no exaggeration to suggest that one is able to carry the suffering of the world in within their pocket. Yet human beings still seek affirmation and explanation for their existence, and the search for answers in times of tragedy does not dissipate. Candle-lit vigils and meditative gatherings are held,[14] and questions of life's meaning are asked.[15]

How, then, are such questions discussed in the contemporary context? In particular, how are these addressed in British society, which is experiencing a changing relationship with religion? This particular convergence of thought is ripe for theological investigation, and the Sunday Assembly, which inhabits a curious space between faith and unbelief, provides a unique point of reference through which these questions might be explored. It is home to an unforeseen brand of godlessness, one that claims to stand in contention to the acute (and often vitriolic) rhetoric of New Atheism. Its members exhibit a Christian "cultural memory"[16] and continue to engage with vestiges of Christian life and practice.[17]

In this book, I seek answers to several key theological questions. Beginning with the premise that theodicy is a problematic practice, I turn to the Sunday Assembly to ask what measures are being used to respond to suffering. In doing so, I find that the Sunday Assembly itself does not necessarily practice theodicy. Instead, it responds to large-scale global events and instances of individual trauma by placing emphasis on the "celebration of life."[18] From this finding, I seek to reflect critically on the practices of the Church[19] and to question how the Church might respond to suffering in light of the issues with classical theodicy.

Approaching this work

This work is centred on a group which calls itself a "secular congregation." It will engage with those who have left the Church and with the opinions of people who no longer (or perhaps never did) term themselves Christians. Yet, this is also work of practical theology. On what basis might a practical theologian engage with such a movement, in ways which are both critical and constructive yet faithful to her theological roots? Why approach the topic of suffering in this particular way, and why listen to voices from outwith the Church?

First, it is worth considering exactly what practical theology entails. Practical theology is a "rich and diverse,"[20] "intricate and complex" discipline within the study of theology.[21] It is difficult to provide a single definition of practical theology, given that it spans theological denominations and contains within its ever-shifting boundaries a wide range of approaches and methodologies.[22] The complexities and varying dynamics of practical theology are noted by some of its key proponents. Bonnie Miller-McLemore describes it as "a term with loaded and over-lapping meanings,"[23] while Eric Stoddart claims that practical theology is binary, and that no two people engaged in the discipline will respond to the multi-directional conversation between doctrine and practice "in exactly the same way."[24] Nonetheless, as Miller-McLemore points out, "both extremes . . . either declaring practical theology undefinable as a discipline or easily defined" are problematic.[25] While practical theology *does* concern the relationship between beliefs and practices, these "abbreviated mantras," commonly the preserve of scholars, do "leave much unsaid."[26] Practical theology seeks to engage critically with theological knowledge, challenging what constitutes "wisdom" and striving towards a theological vision "for the masses."[27] It explores the dissonance between theology and lived reality, looking to test the authenticity of doctrinal claims against the lives of real people. It is, for Don Browning, "descriptive" because of its close attention to the particular.[28] It is also interpretive, asking "why" the particular event or practice is taking place. Finally, it is pragmatic, and it looks to respond in ways which are "transformative."[29]

Browning adds that practical theology should involve:

> some description of the present situation, some critical theory about the ideal situation, and some understanding of the processes, spiritual forces, and technologies required to get from where we are to the future idea, no matter how fragmentarily and incompletely that idea can be realised.[30]

I begin this book by acknowledging the present situation; one wherein theodicy, although potentially becoming displaced as a central response to the question of evil remains a problematic component of Christian theology, and one which is divorced from the lived realities of suffering. Increasingly, the Church falters in its ability to respond to the on-going trauma scarring the globe on a daily basis, while scepticism and unbelief grows, in part by way of reaction to poor theodicy. The central goal of this study is to examine this current situation, in which all of the previous considerations are interwoven. Overall, this study seeks new ways of thinking, which are at once both faithful to the roots of theology, attentive to experience, and aware of the problems of academic theology and theodicy as remote and removed. As such, the intentions of this study are quite clearly aligned with Browning's description of the dynamic movement of practical theology from the present to the ideal.

John Swinton and Harriet Mowat understand that the locus of practical theology does not simply "encompass the practices of the church and the experiences of Christians."[31] Rather, "the theological reflection that is practical theology also embraces the practices of the world."[32] This point is especially salient for this book, which considers the opinions of those who, while attending a pseudo "church-like" congregation, also consciously locate themselves outside the Christian faith. Swinton and Mowat identify some space for nuance, recognising that some perceive and acknowledge the work and movement of God, and some do not. However, drawing on the Doctrine of Creation, they add that: "because we live in God's creation, all human beings, implicitly or explicitly, participate in the unfolding historical narrative of God."[33] British practical theologian Alistair Campbell is consistent with this stance in his own work:

> The actions of Christians are celebrations of and attestations to God's reconciling work in the world which begins and ends in Jesus Christ. The relationship of these actions to non-Christians is one of both similarity and difference. The similarity is that all human actions both participate in and fall short of the purpose of God.[34]

Campbell argues that the practices of the church and the practices of the world are not ontologically separate, since both occur within God's creation.

A logical next step would, therefore, be to include of the lives, habits, and rituals of those who exist outwith the church (i.e., the Sunday Assembly) in practical theological reflection. Stoddart argues that "every practice—within and beyond the ministries of Christian caring organised by the church—can be explored theologically."[35] He refers to this idea as a "stunningly basic realisation," and one which is "fundamental to the discipline" of practical theology.[36]

It is worth noting Swinton and Mowat's caution that there are "radical dissimilarities" between the church and the world. The church "notices and seeks to live out the significance of residing in a world which we recognise as creation."[37] In other words, the church and those in it (theoretically speaking) respond to the world around them as God's creation. More crucially, though, is the locus of Christian faith. Faith in Jesus Christ separates Christians from non-Christians, since "the Church recognises who Jesus is, and seeks to live its life in the light of this revelation," while "the world does not."[38] For Swinton and Mowat, this is hugely significant. Jesus Christ is the pinnacle of Christian belief, and the outworking of God's revelation. Further, the church's emphasis on Christ has "radical implications" for its work and mission.[39] The practices that it engages in are intended to faithfully embody a recognition of Christ as God made flesh. As such, the church has a different "telos" to the world.[40]

Thus, to Swinton and Mowat at least, practical theology simultaneously recognises the practices of both the church and the world, yet it cannot be separated from its primary locus of faith in Christ. As explained earlier, this investigation is bound to Christian practice in that it is centrally concerned with questions pertaining to theodicy, a fundamentally theological act. In examining the Sunday Assembly within this book, I do not intend to ignore the clear differences between the ultimate aims of this group, which fall along the lines of gathered community, shared learning, and the celebration of life, and the Church, which is centred on the revelation of Christ. In the sense of its fundamental direction and purpose, the church *should*, therefore, practically speaking, be radically dissimilar to the rest of society. Nevertheless, with regards to the discourse contained in this book, I do question the absolute existence and implementation of a clear divide between the church and the world. While the Church appears to have the tools to respond to evil and suffering, drawing on a rich tradition of lament, the redemptive power of the gospels, and eschatological hope of the cross, it is clear that, in the practice of theodicy, the church has, at times, abandoned its grounding in Christ. Indeed, this book explores some of the ways in which the church has fallen silent in the face of suffering or has otherwise been complicit in creating a culture of blame. Where the church has engaged in theodicy with damaging consequences, I argued that it has shifted away from its grounding in the love, goodness, forgiveness, and hope found in the incarnation and resurrection of Jesus Christ. Where it has done this, the church has not embodied the "radical dissimilarity" with the world which Swinton and

Mowat impress. In addition, such reactions to suffering are, in many ways, profoundly human, and as such, affect those who call themselves Christians in much the same way as they affect everyone else. Indeed, Swinton and Mowat realise that, in a creation which is profoundly fallen and broken, all human beings fall short of God's good purposes. Significantly, they include the Church in this.

In his 2012 monograph, *Faith in the Public Square*, Rowan Williams traverses public debates concerning religion in an increasingly non-religious British context. He discusses the complexity and fluidity of the term "atheism," suggesting that: "a number of intellectual and spiritual policies involve, or at least accompany, the denial of certain versions of the divine."[41] In other words, all positions of faith involve aspects of atheism, or at least the rejection of some specific doctrines, systems, theologies or perspectives. In fact: "most major religious discourses require and cultivate unbelief."[42] When considering atheism theologically, therefore, Williams argues that one must begin by asking "what it is about some particular piece of speech about God that is causing trouble, and whether [this] is in fact essential to a religious tradition's understanding of what it means by God or the divine."[43] It is crucial, he argues, to explore areas in which these points of strain are felt, not so that Christians might evangelise or engage in missional activity or conversion, but so that "convictions may be tested and if possible, reinforced."[44,45] The challenge of atheism and unbelief, therefore, is theologically constructive. For Williams, it has the potential to "deepen whatever is said about [Christian] commitments," or at the very least, encourage theological reflection on what the most important parts of belief and practice are. Indeed, the intention of this book is not simply to reflect on the Sunday Assembly but to critically engage with theologies of suffering and to better understand how the Church might respond to it without invoking theodicy.

The contents of this book

In the opening chapters of this book, I lay the ground for my investigation. In Chapter 1, I explore the theological grounding of this enquiry. In order to understand some of the limitations of theodicy, I examine its historical formation through classical strains of thought, including the Irenaean and Augustinian traditions and their contemporary developments. I then discuss in greater detail some of the problems related to theodicy in practice, paying particular attention to the way in which it can undermine the realities of evil and become inapplicable in the midst of real suffering. I also make the case that theodicy can be too all-encompassing in nature, and that it can be used to perpetuate a culture of blame. I argue that theological attempts to "re-imagine" theodicy are not satisfactory. As such, I suggest that creative and practical solutions are required to help communities in the wake of suffering. Finding a possible solution for Church practice therefore becomes the leading task of this work.

Because the Sunday Assembly self-identifies as a "secular congregation" or "atheist church," it is instructive to consider contemporary public and academic discourse surrounding unbelief, in order to understand why this particular movement has been able to emerge in recent years. In Chapter 2, I therefore frame the leading conversations in philosophical and atheistic literature regarding unbelief. I outline a recent shift, away from the dominance of New Atheist writings, which characterised much of the public debate around unbelief at the turn of the twenty-first century. I suggest that the increased prevalence of what I term "temperate atheism" in recent years is has created a climate of thought in which religion is held more sympathetically, allowing the Sunday Assembly to draw on Church structures and practice and to grow rapidly. Chapter 3 introduces the Sunday Assembly in more detail. I outline the group's history and beliefs and identify some of key features of its ethos, including its calls to "live better," "help often," and "wonder more," in addition to its emphases on "radical inclusivity" and the "celebration of life."

In Chapter 4, I turn to the field research that underpins this work, presenting an account of the qualitative processes used to guide my investigation. I discuss the rationale behind using qualitative methodologies within a theological study before presenting some reflexive considerations relating to my place within the research as a white Christian woman. I then describe my Sunday Assembly fieldwork, referring to interviews, observation, and other ways that I collected data in the London and Edinburgh congregations.

The third part of this book relates to the findings of the research. In Chapter 5, I gather the "threads" of my research together, and in doing so, note the key finding of this investigation. The Sunday Assembly does not have any particular way of responding to suffering, in an official sense. However, the language of "celebrating life" is pervasive and recurring. The vernacular of "celebration" relates to suffering inasmuch as it appears to constitute a way of responding to it; the Assembly reverts to celebration in times of suffering. In particular, I argue that the culture of the Sunday Assembly is prone to what I term "passing over" suffering and turning quickly back to its central ethos of "celebrating life." Circumstances which are difficult are used as tools for self-improvement and to help community members to more deeply appreciate the meaning of life. The act of celebrating life is not in itself wrong; nonetheless, it is clear from data gathered within this investigation that the movement's acute emphasis on "celebration" has practical implications for its ability to deal with suffering.

The final section of this book constitutes a theological response to the key finding from my research data. In Chapter 6, I employ the works of Rowan Williams and Shelly Rambo, who work in different ways to resist theologically the "passing over" of suffering, instead suggesting (and in some cases, creating) spaces in which suffering might be acknowledged and grieved over longer than momentarily. I examine whether the Church, too, might be prone to "passing over" suffering. Relaying my own experience of the Church during the writing of this book, in addition to John Swinton's account of attending his local church in the aftermath of the Omagh bombing, I note the tendency of white Protestant churches (in particular) to engage in the denial and avoidance of suffering in worship.

In Chapter 7, I respond briefly to the Sunday Assembly before concentrating my efforts on a set of practical suggestions for the Church in light of my research findings and my argument that the Church is also prone to "passing over" suffering. In particular, I discuss the importance of community and the creation of a "culture of lament" in order to practically resist the denial and avoidance suffering. The "culture of lament" might look different depending on where in what Christian denomination it is adopted. However, it is intended to be put in place either by the inclusion of songs or words of lament during worship and should be there to draw upon and invoke when times of individual or communal suffering arise.

Conclusion

Overall, this book begins with a sense that theodicy is a difficult and problematic discipline and looks thereafter to a particular movement of people outwith the Church, to see how they engage in, and practice responding to, the on-going realities of suffering. What is learnt from this investigation is that the Sunday Assembly "passes over" suffering and turns instead back towards a pattern of celebration. Yet the Church, too, can be a space in which human beings struggle to acknowledge and respond to suffering. As such, I suggest the practical step of constructing a Church culture in which lament becomes a central and integral practice, whether communicated through liturgy, song, or spoken word.

To engage in lament is to avoid responding too quickly, with a problematic explanation grounded in theodicy. Lament also calls Christians to resist "passing over" suffering quickly, something which both the Sunday Assembly and the Church are found to be capable of. Lament is a centuries old endeavour and often suggested by theologians looking to respond to suffering in their writings.[46] Nonetheless, this work reaches such conclusions in yet uncharted ways. It engages with a new movement and holds the Church in dialogue with a changing world; one in which its traditions are no longer found so compelling, and in which human suffering is amplified beyond measure by modern technology. In such a world as this, in which suffering is so constant, the adoption of lament practices is arguably more important than ever before.

Notes

1 The Sunday Assembly, "Frequently Asked Questions": https://sundayassembly.online/faqs/ (accessed 7th January 2020).
2 Robert Pigott, "Doing Church without God," *BBC News*, 1st November 2013: www.bbc.co.uk/news/uk-24766314 (accessed 7th January 2020).

3 The Sunday Assembly, "Frequently Asked Questions."

4 Andrew Watts, "The Church of Self-Worship: Sunday Morning with the Atheists," *The Spectator*, 22nd February 2014: www.spectator.co.uk/2014/02/so-tell-me-about-your-faith-journey-sunday-morning-at-the-atheist-church/ (accessed 7th January 2020).

5 Esther Addley, "'Not Believing in God Makes Life More Precious': Meet the Atheist Churchgoers," *The Guardian*, 2nd February 2013: www.theguardian.com/world/2013/feb/03/atheist-church-sunday-assembly-islington (accessed 7th January 2020).

6 Taylor notes that: "We no longer live in societies in which the widespread sense can be maintained that faith in God is central to the ordered life we . . . enjoy." See Charles Taylor, *A Secular Age* (Cambridge: Harvard University Press, 2007), 531.

7 Brown argues that the decline of religion has occurred in an abrupt fashion: "really quite suddenly . . . something very profound ruptured the character of the nation and its people, sending organised Christianity on a downward spiral to the margins of social significance." For Brown, secularisation is evident in the "unprecedented numbers" of British people who have "stopped going to church, have allowed their church membership to lapse, have stopped marrying in church and have neglected to baptise their children." From a historical perspective, Brown cites the 1960s and the latter half of the twentieth century as being the time from which Britain has undergone a "sudden plunge into a truly secular condition" as a result of shifting social attitudes. See Callum Brown, *The Death of Christian Britain: Understanding Secularisation 1800–2000*, Second Edition (London: Routledge, 2009), i–ii.

8 See Steve Bruce, *Religion in the Modern World: From Cathedrals to Cults* (Oxford: Oxford University Press, 1996), *Choice and Religion: A Critique of Rational Choice* (Oxford: Oxford University Press, 1999), and *God Is Dead: Secularization in the West* (Oxford: Blackwell, 2002).

9 In the latest British Social Attitudes Survey (2017), 53% of respondents said they had "no religion." This figure represents a 5% decrease in figures from 2015. For full data, see Nat Cen Social Research, "NatCen's British Social Attitudes Survey: Religious Affiliation among Adults in Great Britain": www.natcen.ac.uk/media/1469605/BSA-religion.pdf (accessed 7th January 2020).

10 Ibid.

11 See Paul Heelas and Linda Woodhead, *The Spiritual Revolution: Why Religion Is Giving Way to Spirituality* (London: Wiley-Blackwell, 2004).

12 Woodhead refers to this group as "none's." "None's" are "not straightforwardly secular." As Woodhead explains, "they reject religious labels—but they reject secular ones as well." See Linda Woodhead, "The Rise of 'No Religion' in Britain: The Emergence of a New Cultural Majority," *Journal of the British Academy*, (4), 2016, 249.

13 In particular, Graham points to faith-based organisations which help to deliver welfare and other public services. In addition, she notes that religion "continues to be a potent force in many aspects of global and civil society." See Elaine Graham, *Between a Rock and a Hard Place: Public Theology in a Post-Secular Age* (London: SCM Press, 2013), xiv.

14 Countless examples of candle-lit vigils as expressions of grief are available. A series of impromptu, contemplative vigils were held worldwide in the wake of the Paris attacks of November 2015. See Joe Daunt, "Paris Attacks: Candlelight Vigils Held across the World for Victims of French Massacre," *The Telegraph*, 14th November 2016: www.telegraph.co.uk/news/worldnews/europe/france/11996358/Paris-attacks-candlelight-vigils-held-across-the-world-for-victims-of-French-massacre.html (accessed 7th January 2020).

15 In 2004, in the wake of the Indian Ocean earthquake and tsunami, Rowan Williams, who held the office of Bishop of Canterbury at the time, wrote a piece for the *Telegraph*, in which he pointed to the continuing prevalence of theodicy-like questions in the public sphere: "The question: 'How can you believe in a God who permits suffering on this scale?' is . . . very much around at the moment, and it would be surprising if it weren't." See Rowan Williams, "Of Course This Makes Us Doubt God's Existence," *The Telegraph*, 2nd January 2005: www.telegraph.co.uk/comment/personal-view/3613928/Of-course-this-makes-us-doubt-Gods-existence.html (accessed 7th January 2020).

16 Former Archbishop of Canterbury Rowan Williams notes the relatively strong Christian cultural presence and memory apparent in British society. See Andrew Sparrow, "Britain Is Now 'Post-Christian', Says Ex-Archbishop Rowan Williams," *The Guardian*, 27th April 2014: www.theguardian.com/uk-news/2014/apr/27/britain-post-christian-says-rowan-williams (accessed 7th January 2020).

17 In an article for *Practical Theology*, I outline some of the "vestiges" of Christian life and practice apparent in the Edinburgh congregation of the Sunday Assembly. The term "vestiges" here "refers centrally to aspects of Christianity, whether ritualistic, identity-driven, or otherwise, which are carried over, unconsciously retained, or actively incorporated into a secular perspective, even where faith in a divine being is not." See Katie Cross, "The Sunday Assembly in Scotland: Vestiges of Religious Thought in a Secular Congregation," *Practical Theology*, 10 (3), 2017, 253. Examples of religious memory within the Sunday Assembly in both London and Edinburgh, which will be explored within the body of this work, include pastoral care, funerals and "life celebrations," and church-like organisational structures, such as an annual Synod.

18 In Sunday Assembly vernacular, the terms "celebration of life," "celebrating life," and "celebrating being alive" are used interchangeably to describe the same idea. As such, they are used interchangeably throughout this book in reference to the Assembly's particular conceptualisation of celebration.

19 It should be noted that, in this book, references to the "Church" are not tied to any one denomination. Later, illustrative examples from the Church of Scotland will be used. However, suggestions contained within this book for Church practice (i.e., the "culture of lament") are intended to be more widely applicable. Since I am not discussing ritual or preaching, it is possible that the "culture of lament" could be adapted for use in different Christian traditions and could feasibly incorporate liturgical or non-liturgical elements. Further, mentions of the Church in this book, while referring primarily to the British context, might also be relevant within other Western societies experiencing similar shifting attitudes towards religion. However, it should also be noted that white Protestant churches are later identified as the communities where a renewal of lament practice is most acutely required.

20 Bonnie Miller-McLemore, *Christian Theology in Practice: Discovering a Discipline* (Grand Rapids: Wm. B. Eerdmans, 2012), 157.

21 John Swinton and Harriet Mowat, *Practical Theology and Qualitative Research*, Second Edition (London: SCM Press, 2016), xi.

22 Ibid. xi.

23 Bonnie Miller-McLemore, "Five Misunderstandings about Practical Theology," *International Journal of Practical Theology*, 16 (1), 2012, 20.

24 Eric Stoddart, *Advancing Practical Theology: Critical Discipleship for Disturbing Times* (London: SCM Press, 2014), xii.

25 Miller-McLemore, "Five Misunderstandings about Practical Theology," 19.

26 Ibid.

27 Ibid.

28 See Don Browning, *A Fundamental Practical Theology: Descriptive and Strategic Proposals* (Minneapolis: Fortress Press, 1996).
29 Ibid. 2.
30 Don Browning, "Practical Theology and Political Theology," *Theology Today*, 42 (10), 1985, 20.
31 Swinton and Mowat, 7–8.
32 Ibid. 8.
33 Ibid.
34 Alistair Campbell in Duncan Forrester (ed.), *Theology and Practice* (London: Epworth, 1990), 16.
35 Stoddart, 13.
36 Ibid.
37 Swinton and Mowat, 8.
38 Ibid.
39 Ibid.
40 Ibid. 9.
41 Rowan Williams, *Faith in the Public Square* (London: Bloomsbury, 2012), 283.
42 Ibid. 281.
43 Ibid.
44 Ibid. 284.
45 At this juncture, it is worth noting that the aim of this work is not to engage in apologetics: a branch of Christian theology intended to present reasoned and evidential bases for Christianity, defending it against outside objection. While scholars such as Elaine Graham (see Graham, *Between a Rock and a Hard Place*, 2013) suggest that contemporary theology should return to an approach involving apologetics in its public conversations regarding faith, this particular work is concerned with a critical examination of theological practice and the development of new ways in which the Church might approach suffering in the current context. As such, while engaging with non-religious participants, it is not intended to communicate with them on a missional or apologetic level. Instead, their answers and insights will be used to critically reflect upon the Church, and the theological practice of theodicy. Because of this, apologetics is not something I will engage in in this particular work.
46 In Chapter 7, in order to underline the importance of the practices of lament, I engage with the writings of Emmanuel Kantongole and Chris Rice, John Swinton, Nancy Duff, Walter Brueggeman, and Soong-Chan Rah, all of whom advocate a greater emphasis on lament in Christian Churches.

References

Addley, Esther. "Atheist Sunday Assembly Prepares for First 'Synod' as Expansion Continues." *The Guardian*. 29th April 2014. www.theguardian.com/world/2014/apr/29/atheist-sunday-assembly-first-synod

Brown, Callum. *The Death of Christian Britain: Understanding Secularisation 1800–2000*. Second Edition. London: Routledge, 2009.

Browning, Don. S. *A Fundamental Practical Theology: Descriptive and Strategic Proposals*. Minneapolis: Fortress Press, 1991.

———. "Practical Theology and Political Theology." *Theology Today*. 42 (10), 1985: 15–33.

Cross, Katie. "The Sunday Assembly in Scotland: Vestiges of Religious Memory and Practise in a Secular Congregation." *Practical Theology*. 10 (3), 2017: 249–262.

Daunt, Joe. "Paris Attacks: Candlelight Vigils Held across the World for Victims of French Massacre." *The Telegraph*. 14th November 2016. www.telegraph.co.uk/news/worldnews/europe/france/11996358/Paris-attacks-candlelight-vigils-held-across-the-world-for-victims-of-French-massacre.html

Graham, Elaine. *Between a Rock and a Hard Place: Public Theology in a Post-Secular Age*. London: SCM Press, 2013.

Heelas, Paul and Woodhead, Linda. *The Spiritual Revolution: Why Religion Is Giving Way to Spirituality*. London: Wiley-Blackwell, 2004.

Miller-McLemore, Bonnie. *Christian Theology in Practice: Discovering a Discipline*. Grand Rapids: Wm. B. Eerdmans, 2012.

———. "Five Misunderstandings about Practical Theology." *International Journal of Practical Theology*. 16 (1), 2012: 5–26.

Pigott, Robert. "Doing Church without God." *BBC News*. 1st November 2013. www.bbc.co.uk/news/uk-24766314

Sparrow, Andrew. "Britain Is Now 'Post-Christian', Says Ex-Archbishop Rowan Williams." *The Guardian*. 27th April 2014. www.theguardian.com/uk-news/2014/apr/27/britain-post-christian-says-rowan-williams

Stoddart, Eric. *Advancing Practical Theology: Critical Discipleship for Disturbing Times*. London: SCM Press, 2014.

The Sunday Assembly. "Frequently Asked Questions." https://sundayassembly.online/faqs/

Swinton, John and Mowat, Harriet. *Practical Theology and Qualitative Research*. Second Edition. London: SCM Press, 2016.

Taylor, Charles. *A Secular Age*. Cambridge: Harvard University Press, 2007.

Watts, Andrew. "The Church of Self-Worship: Sunday Morning with the Atheists." *The Spectator*. 22nd February 2014. www.spectator.co.uk/2014/02/so-tell-me-about-your-faith-journey-sunday-morning-at-the-atheist-church/

Williams, Rowan. *Faith in the Public Square*. London: Bloomsbury, 2012.

———. "Of Course This Makes Us Doubt God's Existence." *The Telegraph*. 2nd January 2005. www.telegraph.co.uk/comment/personal-view/3613928/Of-course-this-makes-us-doubt-Gods-existence.html

Woodhead, Linda. "The Rise of 'No Religion' in Britain: The Emergence of a New Cultural Majority." *Journal of the British Academy*. (4), 2016: 245–261.

1 Theological roots

The evils of theodicy

The realities of human trauma are long established. "History shudders," writes theologian Rebecca Chopp, "pierced by events of massive public suffering."[1] Now, as in centuries past, that which Christopher Brittain refers to as "ground zero" events pose a challenge to Christian configurations of divine benevolence.[2] Now, as then, raw pain galvanises hard questions. The frequently heard exclamation, "How can God allow so much suffering?" confronts theologians with a particular issue: is it possible to hold that God is good, loving, and wants the best for the world, even when confronted with evidence of suffering which suggests otherwise? As in ages past, this question continues to present a robust challenge to belief in God.

The practice of theodicy has maintained a central place within Christian thought for centuries. It has been required to placate concerns about the existence and personhood of God against a backdrop of continuous suffering. Nevertheless, I argue that theodicy in the classical sense, which seeks to justify the divine in sight of on-going suffering in the world, is problematic. The attempts of theologians to produce explanations that justify divine goodness in response to radical suffering are, in John Swinton's words, both "theologically questionable" and "pastorally dangerous."[3] Theodicy is often bound up in overly abstracted philosophical dialogue, and thus undermines the realities of evil. All too often, theoretical renderings of theodicy are inapplicable to human experience, pass over the particularities of suffering, and perpetuate a culture of blame. In sum, theodicy can hold greater potential for hurt than for healing.

Theodicy: a history

Augustinian theodicy

Augustinian theodicy, named for Aurelius Augustinus or St. Augustine of Hippo (354–430), a fourth- and fifth-century philosopher and theologian, constitutes a classical Christian response to the problem of evil.[4] Twentieth-century philosopher John Hick identifies a number of variations of this theodicy throughout history. In his 1966 text, *Evil and the God of Love*, Hick distinguishes Augustine's theodicy and its subsequent developments as "Augustinian." Augustinian theodicies commonly assert that evil is a privation of good, and the result of human misuse of free will. Accordingly, God is not held to be directly responsible for evil, and thus, divine goodness and benevolence is upheld.

Augustine develops his key ideas regarding suffering in his two major works, *Confessions* and *City of God*. In *Confessions*, he begins his theological response to the problem of evil, drawing on the opening chapters of Genesis and the writings of the Apostle Paul. In *City of God*, he develops his theodicy further, situating it within the wider framework of human history. Centrally, Augustine proposes that evil cannot exist within God, and that it cannot be created by God. As such, evil is a by-product of God's creativity, and a lack of goodness, which exists as a result of human misuse of free will. Augustine assumes that human beings were created in possession of free will, which provides conditions of self-determination. Because of this, humans are presented with the choice to discern and choose between good and evil. The blame for evil and suffering is, therefore, passed on to humans. Augustine draws on the creation narrative in Genesis and argues that instances of evil in the world occur as a result of Adam and Eve's original sin. This is true of all evil, whether it is moral (involving human wrongdoing), or natural (involving natural disaster or disease). The evil will present in humans is, within his understanding, a corruption of the conditions of free will given to human beings by God.

Within the Augustinian account, suffering is held to be a consequence of sin but also a means of its gradual extirpation. To Augustine, the purpose of suffering is to gradually destroy sin over time. In soteriological terms, suffering therefore has a "positive purpose." Ultimately, Augustine rests upon an eschatological argument: that suffering will finally be justified in the consummated purposes of God. It is because of this that Augustine's work has widely been referred to as constituting a "free will defence."

Important though Augustine was in the world of his day, G. R. Evans suggests that his impact on theological and philosophical discourse has been "still greater in the . . . years which came after."[5] Thomas Aquinas (c.1225–1274), a thirteenth-century scholastic philosopher and theologian, was heavily influenced by Augustine's works, writing a form of Augustinian theodicy in his *Summa Theologica*. For R. Douglas Geivett, "Aquinas believed that the presence of evil in the world is the basis for the most threatening argument against the existence of God."[6] As such, his theodicy begins with five arguments for the existence of God, known also as the "Five Ways." Thereafter, Aquinas attests that "God, being good, must have a morally sufficient reason for permitting the existence of evil."[7] He approaches the question of theodicy by arguing that all goodness in the world must exist perfectly in God, and that since God exists perfectly, God must therefore be perfectly good. As such, there is no inherent evil in God. Building on the Augustinian concept of evil as a privation of good, Aquinas links the existence of evil to human free will and argues that the possibility of sin is necessary for a perfect world. Like Augustine, he sees individuals as responsible for their own sin, and thus, their own suffering. Eleonore Stump considers Aquinas to have a positive view of suffering, inasmuch as he finds evil acceptable and justifiable because of the good that comes from it. However, she also draws attention to his emphasis on the doctrine of heaven:

> [I]n order not to see the acceptance of suffering or the justification of God's allowing suffering as senseless, it is essential to include the doctrine that human beings are capable of everlasting union with God in the afterlife.[8]

In other words, as Stump points out, Aquinas sees suffering as legitimate because human beings have the option to choose "good" and therefore reach a perfect afterlife, where no pain or evil exists. The eschatological nature of Aquinas" approach points away from current anguish, towards that which is yet to come. Later in this chapter, a particular critique, stemming from the work of Fyodor Dostoyevsky, will be applied to this reasoning.

German philosopher Gottfried Leibniz (1646–1716) was the first to use the term "theodicy" in his 1710 text of the same name.[9] In his writings, Leibniz, seeking to defend the goodness of God against the accusation that divine goodness is incompatible with the realities of human suffering, draws upon the Augustinian tradition. *Théodicée* is a direct response to the writings of Pierre Bayle, a French philosopher, who rejects philosophical attempts to solve the problem of evil on the basis that there can be no rational solution to it.[10] From Bayle's perspective, the co-existence of God and evil can be proven, given that it is prevalent throughout the Bible. Ultimately, Bayle concludes that there is no defensible, rational solution to the problem of why God permits evil. As such, he does not conceive of evil as a problem to be solved but rather a state of affairs which should simply be acknowledged, and ultimately accepted.[11]

In contrast, Leibniz, like Augustine and Aquinas before him, argues that God is infinitely perfect. As such, God must have created a world which contains the best possible balance of good against evil. Leibniz posits that God chose the present world from an infinite number of "possible worlds" that were present as ideas in God's mind. Because God wills what is best, this world is therefore the "best of all possible worlds."[12] Leibniz also presents his own theodicy; he argues that there are three central and distinguishable forms of evil, including moral (sin), physical (pain), and metaphysical (limitation). Building on Augustine's renderings of the free will defence, Leibniz suggests that God permits moral and physical strains of evil for the "greater good." Metaphysical evil is an unavoidable consequence of the existence of the world, since any created world must necessarily fall short of God's absolute perfection.

In contemporary discourse, Alvin Plantinga (1932–), an American analytic philosopher, has paid tribute to Augustine's renderings of the "free will defence" in his own work. Plantinga does not consciously present his work as *theodicy*; he is not interested in presenting a justification for God's actions. Rather, he intends to demonstrate the logical possibility for an omnibenevolent, omnipotent and omniscient God to create a world that contains moral evil. Nevertheless, as Alistair McGrath points out, since Plantinga himself identifies as a Christian, and seeks to reconcile the existence of suffering with the existence of God, his work could feasibly be construed as a classical form of theodicy. Indeed, Plantings reasoning is "deeply rooted in the Christian tradition," and has, as such, been widely accepted within Christian and theological circles as a legitimate theodical explanation for the existence of suffering.[13]

Plantinga asserts the importance of free will thus:

> A world containing creatures who are significantly free (and freely perform more good than evil actions) is more valuable, all else being equal, than a world containing no free creatures at all.[14]

In other words, Plantinga suggests that the "value" of free will is that it allows human beings to choose to love God freely. That being the case, God can (and did) create free creatures. However, God cannot "cause or determine them to do only what is right."[15] If God were to intervene, and force humans to choose good over evil, then they would not be "significantly free" after all and would "not do what is right *freely*."[16]

In order, therefore, to create creatures who are capable of making good choices, God must also allow for humans to be capable of moral evil; God cannot "give these creatures the freedom to perform evil and at the same time prevent them from doing so."[17] Inevitably, these conditions have allowed some humans to go "wrong" in the exercise of their freedom. This, says Plantinga, "is the source of moral evil."[18] Nonetheless, the fact that human beings enact evil and cause suffering counts neither against God's omnipotence or goodness, since God could only have prevented evil by also removing the possibility of freely chosen acts of good.

The work of British philosopher Richard Swinburne also falls within an Augustinian framework. Swinburne expresses his theodicy as follows:

> The central core of any theodicy must, I believe, be the "free-will defence", which deals—to start with—with moral evil. . . . The free-will defence claims that it is a great good that humans have a certain sort of free will which I shall call free and responsible choice, but that, if they do, then necessarily there will be the natural possibility of moral evil. . . . A God who gives humans such free will necessarily bring about the possibility, and puts outside his own control whether or not that evil

occurs. It is not logically possible . . . that God could give us such free will and yet ensure that we always use it in the right way.[19]

For Swinburne, suffering stems directly from God's decision to grant human beings free will, which is then, inevitably, abused. The presence of evil in the world is compatible with a good God, since:

> [a] good God would have reason to create a world in which there were men [sic] with a choice of destiny and responsibility for each other, despite the evils which would inevitably or almost inevitably be presented in it, for the sake of the good which it contained.[20]

In other words, Swinburne suggests that God chose to create a world in which evil was a possibility, in order to allow human beings moral autonomy. In this framework, God is not held to be directly responsible for evil.[21] If God were to intervene in human wrong-doing and prevent it, the state of free-will, given out of divine love, would be compromised. Later, I question the pastoral implications of Swinburne's suggestions.

Irenaean theodicy

A second prominent and influential strain of theodicy can be found in the works of Irenaeus (c. 130–c.202).[22] As with the Augustinian tradition, this approach emphasises the place of free will in relation to evil. By contrast, while Augustinian theodicy is held to be "soul-deciding" (i.e., it emphasises the human role in evil and suffering and the ability for human beings to ultimately choose good over evil), the Irenaean tradition views the world as a "vale of soul-making" (a term taken from the English poet John Keats). In other words, evil and the experiences of suffering cannot be controlled by human beings, and are instead held to be necessary prerequisites for spiritual growth and development

Irenaeus, a second-century philosopher and early Church Father, developed a theodicy based upon the idea that human beings are created by God with the potential for growth towards maturity. Within his thinking, creation consists of two stages, with human beings existing both in the image of God and in the likeness of God. While the former stage is complete, the latter is still in progress:

> God made humanity to be master of the earth. . . . Yet this could only take place when humanity had attained its adult stage. . . . Yet humanity was little, being but like a child. It had to grow and reach full maturity. . . . But humanity was a child; and its mind was not yet fully mature; and thus humanity was easily led astray by the deceiver.[23]

For Irenaeus, human nature is a potentiality; he adheres to an evolutionary perspective, which emphasises the future of the human condition. In order for humans to achieve moral perfection, there must be free choice of action, with the possibility of choosing to do evil. Additionally, in order for humans to exist under conditions of free will, Irenaeus proposes that God must be at an epistemic distance. Growth towards maturity can only take place in a world which contains experiences of good and evil, if truly informed decisions are to be made. The Irenaean tradition of theodicy thus views the world as a place in which souls are forged, and in which encounters with evil are necessary prerequisites for spiritual growth and development.[24]

In the early nineteenth century, Friedrich Schleiermacher (1768–1834), a German Protestant theologian, constructed a theodicy which Hick later identified as Irenaean in nature. Schleiermacher's theodicy is critical of the Augustinian argument that a perfectly created world went wrong, since this implies that evil created itself from nothing. For Schleiermacher, it would be illogical for a perfect creation to go wrong. Either the world could not be made perfect to begin with, or evil stems from God. As such, suggests Schleiermacher, evil must have been created by God for a good reason. He explains that:

> the measure in which sin is present is the measure in which evil (*Übel*) is present, so that, just as the human race is the proper sphere of sin, and sin the corporate act of the race, so the whole world in its relation to man [sic] is the proper sphere of evil (*Übel*), and evil the corporate suffering of the race.[25]

In other words, Schleiermacher holds that the evil suffered by humankind is a direct punishment for sin. He does not necessarily mean that God sends suffering specifically in response to evil acts, but that evil stems from a corruption of God's good world, and human sinful ways of responding to it. Within Schleiermacher's conceptualisation, sin is an obstruction to humanity's dependence on God. Eschatologically, humans cannot overcome sin; but Christ, as a sinless man, with consciousness of God unobstructed, is able to do this on behalf of humanity. This reasoning ultimately leads Schleiermacher to a theological perspective of universalism, wherein he argues that it is divine will that every person be "saved."

Later, the concepts of Irenaean theodicy found a more modern exponent in the aforementioned John Hick, whose work stems directly from the Irenaean tradition. Hick is particularly noted for his contribution to "soul-making" theodicy and makes an explanatory attempt to account for the conceptual and empirical problems of suffering. His perspective is underpinned by a set of theological presuppositions. He identifies these thus: that God is good and limitlessly powerful, and that human beings are on a "pilgrimage" towards betterment. Hick's approach is primarily eschatological, in that he believes that human beings can become the perfected persons whom the New Testament calls "Children of God." Nonetheless, he holds that "they cannot be created ready-made as this."[26] As such, Hick suggests that humans become perfected through a process of "soul-making" or, alternately, "person forming." This occurs over time, as goodness is built up throughout human history:

> I suggest then, that it is an ethically reasonable judgement, even though in the nature of the case not one that is capable of demonstrative proof, that human goodness slowly built up through personal histories of moral effort has a value in the eyes of the Creator which justifies even the long travail of the soul-making process.[27]

For soul-making to be a possibility, Hick suggests that human beings must be free; his model entails a degree of autonomy and self-will. His perspective also necessarily requires a degree of epistemic distance from God, without which humans would not be fully free. Nature must also have a degree of autonomy. Further, the world has to be relatively stable and consistent place, in order for human beings to engage in the pilgrimage, in order to make moral choice and pursue knowledge. This particular configuration of suffering and evil may be attractive, on account of its emphasis on human freedom. Yet Hick's approach may be critiqued for the way in which it appears to lend some semblance of dignity to suffering. Later, some pastoral considerations of Hick's view will be examined where other aspects of traditional theodicy are also subjected to scrutiny on account of their lack of application in practice.

Theodicy as problematic

The previous outline constitutes a brief history of the development of two major strands of theodicy. Because suffering is such an unrelenting aspect of the human experience, theodicy has enjoyed a long history of prominence within theological thought. However, in more recent years, theologians have increasingly pushed back on attempts to reconcile the existence of God and the lived realities of atrocity. In the following, I explore some of the key problems with classical strains of theodicy. None of these critiques are necessarily new, and that the idea to abandon the enterprise of theodicy is well established in theological discourse (as will become evident). Nevertheless, it is important to make these arguments in the following pages, since this is the theological basis from which I begin my study; on the grounds that theodicy is problematic, and that new, practical, approaches to suffering which do not require theodicy are required. The criticisms of theodicy outlined in the following are multi-layered, and the issues contained within are intrinsically linked to one another. Woven together, these create a fuller picture of the failings of theodicy in application and practice. Given that this particular piece of work is consciously located within the sphere of practical theology, which deals centrally with the human experience, my criticisms of theodicy are largely concerned with the harm that they might cause to individuals and communities rather than the intellectual failings of such views.

Theodicy undermines the reality of evil

As theologian Mark Scott ascertains, "Reflection on the problem of evil has operated at a high level of abstraction in contemporary philosophy and theology."[28] His words points to a key issue with traditional theodicy, concerning the particular contemplation of issues surrounding suffering within the academic context. Theodicy has long been engaged with primarily on an academic level. Within such boundaries, the problem of evil is written about in advanced technical jargon, placed out of reach from the general populous, who are distanced from taking part in or influencing the process. Methodologically, the practice of theodicy has presented suffering as an intellectual problem which must be solved. It has defended the logic of a "just" God, and works to release God from culpability for the existence of evil,[29] using subtle and sophisticated analysis to demonstrate that God is not directly responsible for human suffering.[30] This divergence between theory and practice has occurred as a result of the historical development of theodicy. Historically, the Enlightenment shift towards reason and logic tilted many philosophical pursuits, including theodicy, towards a preoccupation with solving the problems of human experience logically. This includes questions that are theodical in nature, regarding God's relation to suffering. Approaches to suffering within this framework have a tendency to sterilise the human aspects of suffering in order to reach neat conclusions about divine providence. As a result, the human experience is displaced, and the full extent of pain and trauma is overlooked and undermined.

To Scott, this approach is "cold, dispassionate and overly-abstracted."[31] In his own work, Swinton echoes a similar concern, pointing out that intellectual accounts for the problem of evil eschew accountability for the realities of human suffering:

> Theodicy . . . assumes responsibility for producing convincing answers to the complex problem of evil, but it need not be responsible for reflecting on the actual impact of evil on the lives of real people or for developing active ways to resist evil and deal compassionately and faithfully with suffering.[32]

In other words, theologians and philosophers have largely accounted for the problem of evil without considering the experiential ramifications of their work. For Swinton, the approach and assumptions of the philosophical questions associated with theodicy often stand "in stark contrast to the experiences of most of the world's population."[33] Human beings do not experience suffering as a philosophical problem to be solved, but as something real, near, and affecting.

The abstraction of theodicy from lived human experience is not only problematic, but inherently dangerous. Swinton presents a theoretical example of the way in which philosophical renderings of theodicy, divorced from the realities of suffering, might operate in ways which are both insouciant and cruel. He imagines the harsh predicament of the mother of a starving baby in Sudan. Intellectual configurations of the problem of evil might suggest to the mother that her baby's impending death is part of the "greater good"; an event from which she will learn "valuable" lessons.[34] Swinton rapidly arrives at the conclusion that neatly polished, cerebral answers are not just pastorally insensitive for failing to take individual experience into consideration, but ultimately "evil," in so far as they "fit such obscene forms of cruelty and evil into a framework that justifies it and draws it within the boundaries of the love and righteousness of God."[35]

His example is similar to one demonstrated vividly in Fyodor Dostoyevsky's novel *The Brothers Karamazov*. Ivan, one of the central characters, is described by philosopher Nick Trakakis as an "anti-theodicist."[36] Indeed, Ivan challenges the legitimacy of theodicy by pointing to a number of cases of extreme and excessive cruelty in the world. He presents a hypothetical case regarding the suffering of innocent children to state his point:

> Imagine a trembling mother with her baby in her arms, a circle of invading Turks around her. They've planned a diversion: they pet the baby, laugh to make it laugh. They succeed, the baby laughs. At that moment, a Turk points a pistol four inches from the baby's face. The baby laughs with glee, holds out its little hands to the pistol, and he pulls the trigger in the baby's face and blows out its brains. Artistic, isn't it?[37]

Ivan uses this example to highlight the senseless nature of suffering, and the extent of evil which humans are capable of. For Ivan, theodicy is an attempt to point towards an eschatological harmony in creation; the idea that suffering is only temporal, and that it will not last forever. Indeed, Augustine's soteriological view of evil, Aquinas's eschatological leanings, in addition to John Hick's perspective on suffering as "soul-making," would all fit within Ivan's impression of Christian theodicies. Yet, to Ivan, the eschatological goal of human process does not excuse, explain, or account for the realities of evil. There is too much evil in the world which theodicy cannot explain away. Alexander Boyce Gibson sees Ivan's challenge for theodicy as one which is particularly devastating and cannot be ignored. He writes that: "Henceforward, no justification of evil, by its outcome or its context, has been possible; Ivan Karamazov has seen to that."[38]

Theodicy is inapplicable

In *Darkness Is My Only Companion: A Christian Response to Mental Illness*, theologian Kathryn Greene-McCreight provides a grounded example of the way in which detached theorisations about suffering translate poorly into real experience, to the extent that they are largely inapplicable. In the text, Greene-McCreight chronicles and reflects theologically on her personal battles with bipolar and suicidal depression. In doing so, she discusses the potential for theodicy to be both ineffective and damaging:

> Theodicy as a philosophical question dwells at the level of theory. There is nothing wrong per se with theories about God's relation to human suffering, unless you are in the midst of suffering, in which case theories are the last thing you need. Don't try to give a theory to someone at the window ledge ready to jump.[39]

Greene-McCreight's example points to the way in which intellectual theodicy is rendered redundant and inessential in situations of radical suffering. A similar point is made by Rowan Williams, in his *Telegraph* article written days after the 2004 Indian Ocean earthquake and tsunami. Williams contemplates the way in which those closest to disaster are the least likely to engage in any kind of philosophical or theological debate regarding their predicament:

> The odd thing is that those who are most deeply involved—both as sufferers and as helpers—are so often the ones who spend least energy in raging over the lack of explanation. They are likely to shrug off, awkwardly and not very articulately, the great philosophical or religious questions we might want to press.[40]

Williams considers how responses to tragic events can have unintended yet damaging consequences for those positioned at the centre of tragic events. He refers to the "vacuous words" that so often manifest in the aftermath of atrocities, pulling on the nature of divine power or control or citing the afterlife as a kind of second-rate consolation prize. Central to his argument is an emphasis on the voices of the victims in any given situation:

> "Making sense" of a great disaster will always be a challenge simply because those who are closest to the cost are the ones least likely to accept some sort of intellectual explanation, however polished. Why should they?[41]

Williams argues that "what can be said with authority about these terrible matters can finally be said only by those closest to the cost."[42] In other words, it is imperative that the voices of those who have suffered are not silenced, or sacrificed in pursuit of producing tidily constructed answers or defences of God. Only those who have lived and experienced the particularities of suffering have the first authority to speak. Any other intellectual renderings of theodicy are bound to be inapplicable. As Wendy Farley surmises, ultimately, "suffering yearns more for experiences of presence than for logical arguments."[43]

Alvin Plantinga, whose work falls within the Augustinian tradition, addresses the separation between "intellectual" and "practical" theodicy:

> Neither a free-will defence nor a free will theodicy is designed to be of much help or comfort to one suffering . . . a storm of the soul. . . . Neither is thought of first of all as a means to pastoral counselling . . . neither will enable someone to find peace within and with God in the face of the evil the world contains. But then, of course, neither is intended for that practice.[44]

Here, Plantinga admits the limitations of intellectual theodicy, but in doing so, reframes the argument; his philosophical explanations for the problem of evil are not *intended* to be used in pastoral situations. This assertion is echoed by David O'Connor:

> [Theoretical theodicy] is not, and to my knowledge, never has been offered as, a response to in the quite different sense of being an address to the victims, of being an attempt to minister to the afflicted, or as a substitute for such a response.[45]

It may well be the case that Plantinga and O'Connor have never offered their renderings of intellectual theodicy to someone suffering the loss of a loved one, or the destruction of their home by an earthquake. From a practical theological perspective, however, it is prudent to question why such theoretical explanations of the problem of evil are required, if they are not intended to encounter the grief and trauma of real people.

Furthermore, while both Plantinga and O'Connor are convinced that their theodicies can be kept out of reach of the average Christian, they underestimate the influence of such theories on the behaviour and actions of people at Church level. Swinton points to a particularly poignant illustration, put forth by Richard Zaner. Zaner tells the story of a young boy, who is born with short-gut syndrome; a bowel condition, which can result in gradual dehydration, malnutrition, and ultimately, death. He notes that the boy's parents were "fundamentalist" Christians, who had had their son out of wedlock. When their religious community discovered that the boy had this illness, they informed the couple that their son's illness was a punishment from God for their sins. In response to this theodicy, the parents became more and more "withdrawn" from their son and stopped visiting and caring for him.[46] In their case, theodicy caused tangible harm, intensifying the suffering of the parents and impacting upon their ability to care for their son.

While Plantinga and O'Connor can argue that *they* would never propose such theodicy in a pastoral situation, they cannot prevent others from construing the problem of evil in this way, and from using different configurations of the "free will defence" to blame those whose lives are touched by trauma. Further, the explanations given by the particular church in Zaner's narrative may not have stemmed directly from the writings of an intellectual justification for the problem of evil. Nevertheless, Zaner's story illustrates the way in which Church doctrine, and therefore the actions or ordinary Christians, *can* be influenced by renderings of theodicy, in damaging and dangerous ways.

Theodicy is too universal in scope

Another issue with theodicy is identified by Swinton in his response to the problem of evil. Swinton describes how the use of theodicy can have "devastating" pastoral consequences.[47] He is particularly critical of certain forms of theodicy for "seeking to apply general and universal explanations of suffering and evil to situations that are profoundly unique and particular."[48] Besides being divorced from grounded consideration of the realities of pain and evil, theodicy can also stifle the particularities of individual experiences with wide-ranging, poorly fitting explanations.

One such universal explanation is put forward by the aforementioned John Hick. In Hick's philosophical framework, the course of life is "soul making." Suffering emerges as an essential component of God's ultimate purpose.[49] It has a teleological role and is counted first and foremost as a learning experience. Hick goes as far as to suggest that innocent suffering can be justified on the grounds that those who suffer innocently display compassionate love and self-giving for others.[50] For Hick, human life is enhanced by challenges, and suffering is ultimately a character-building exercise that brings us into closer communion with God.[51]

As McGrath brings to light, Hick's perspective has the potential to resonate with "many Christians, who have found that God's grace and love are experienced most profoundly in situations of distress or suffering."[52] Greene-McCreight, in her account of her mental illness, explains that she found God to be present in her experiences of depression. Suffering was, ultimately, "redemptive" for her. Nonetheless, she makes the point that:

> [T]his is a witness to the working of the triune God in the pain of one mentally ill Christian. I write . . . of my own experience.[53]

Greene-McCreight's work leaves room for other experiences of mental illness to speak and acknowledges that not all cases will be like hers. By contrast, Hick's model of classical theodicy has attracted criticism for being too general and far-reaching, and, in turn, for failing to notice the particularities of the human pain. For example, Frances Young is concerned that Hick's link between sin and suffering might oppress sufferers rather than help them to better understand their situation.[54] She suggests that his theology could have "damaging repercussions," especially when applied to individual situations.[55] Hick neglects to confront the actualities of suffering, ignoring the possibility that suffering might not result in a more developed character, but in a loss of meaning and hope.

Theodicy perpetuates blame culture

Not all theodicy is intellectual, and yet that which falls outwith the classical traditions of orthodox theology can still be problematic. Because questions of suffering and God's place within it are so readily raised in the public sphere ("Why is there suffering in the world?" "Why does evil exist?"), answers to them are not limited to the confines of the academy. Indeed, Brittain posits that:

> some people respond to the emotional anger and confusion that human tragedies cause by projecting their inner turmoil outwards to some scapegoat they can target and blame.[56]

Zaner's illustration of the couple blamed by their church community for their son's short-gut syndrome is one such example of this. On a larger scale, in the wake of the attacks of 9–11, Pat Robertson and Jerry Falwell, two prominent figures within the American Baptist tradition, presented a particular theodicy for the suffering of the American people. Falwell, a Southern Baptist pastor and televangelist, joined Robertson, of the Christian Broadcasting Network, on his programme *The 700 Club* two days after the attacks in New York had taken place. In a transcript of the interview printed in Bruce Lincoln's text *Holy Terrors*, their conversation turns immediately to possible "theological" explanations for the event.

Robertson begins by suggesting that 9–11 was an act of divine retribution for secularism, pornography, abortion, and the removal of religious observance from schools and government.[57] Falwell advocates a "time of prayer and fasting" by way of response, supporting Robertson's explanation that the violence occurred as a result of diminished divine protection of America.[58] He reiterates that 9–11 is a direct result of God's anger at:

> The pagans and the abortionists and the feminists, and the gays and the lesbians who are actively trying to make that an alternative lifestyle, the ACLU [American Civil Liberties Union], People for the American Way, all of them who tried to secularise America. I point the finger in their face and say: "You helped this happen."[59]

Here, Robertson draws on numerous social groups, blaming their perceived "sin" as the causal factor in God's wrath. This is not the only instance in which Robertson has deployed theodicies of blame. After the 2010 earthquake in Haiti, which killed between 220,000–316,000 people, Robertson blamed the Haitian people, suggesting that they had sworn a "sinful pact with Satan" in exchange for delivering them from French colonial rule in 1804. He conceptualised the earthquake as divine retribution for their bargain.[60]

It should be noted that Robertson's theodicy is not soul-deciding, in that he proposes no eschatological reconciliation or healing. Neither is it "soul-making"; he does not necessarily point to any improvements in human nature as a result. The latter point is important; Robertson's theodicy is particularly damaging because it offers no grace, and no divine forgiveness. Rather than seeking to bring healing and peace, he uses this catastrophe to press the agenda of his own church, turning his face from the suffering of the American people, and instead calling for a "religious revival."

The fate of theodicy: what now?

What, then, is to be done about theodicy? Some theologians mentioned in this chapter, such as Swinton, advocate an end to the practice. Theologian Todd Billings, who himself has been shaped by personal experiences of chronic suffering, having been diagnosed with blood cancer, deems theodicy to be a "destructive practice."[61] In a similar vein, Nick Trakakis observes that "theodical discourse can only add to the word's evils, not remove or illuminate them."[62]

Others have suggested that theodicy should be replaced with theological reflection on tragedy. In particular, Wendy Farley, who describes theodicy as a set of "cool justifications of evil,"[63] advocates for a Christian response which entails righteous anger towards suffering, and a "desire for justice" in the aftermath of "ground zero" events.[64] Similarly, Jewish theologian Sarah Pinnock, in her study of post-Holocaust anti-theodicy, proposes that theodicy can and should be retained where it is not abstract, but grounded, and allows people to ponder divine providence from a practical faith perspective.[65] Nonetheless, having explored in detail the problems of theodicy on a pastoral level in the latter half of this chapter, it is difficult to imagine that the retention of it, even in the "practical" forms suggested by Farley and Pinnock, would be without complication or issue. As such, I agree with Swinton and others that the practice of theodicy must give way to practical Christian approaches. I argue that the Church and theological community must be equipped with creative and grounded approaches to suffering, which do not seek to account for evil, but to bring healing.

Conclusion

How might this be done? This is the question to which I dedicate this book. In light of the particular intersection of less religiously inclined societies, greater access than ever before to news of suffering and the undoing of theodicy as a practice, the Church and theology requires a new dialogue about suffering. Approaches to these questions from a practical perspective may draw from existing traditions or create new ways of relating and responding to those who are experiencing pain and distress. In viewing the way in which theodicy may (or may not) take place outwith the Church, in a non-religious space, I intend to gather information about how responses to suffering are constructed in twenty-first-century communities, and whether or not these are influenced by Church practices or are entirely new. Using the Sunday Assembly as a lens of critical interpretation for such questions, I reflect theologically on what might be done to respond to suffering more effectively in modern day Church congregations.

Notes

1 Rebecca S. Chopp, *The Praxis of Suffering: An Interpretation of Liberation and Political Theologies* (Eugene: Wipf & Stock, 2007), 1.
2 In this work, the terminology of "ground zero" events is used to refer to "far-reaching," catastrophic events of suffering. This term is utilised by Brittain in his text *Religion at Ground Zero*. Speaking metaphorically, Brittain explains that the "ground zeroes" of human history are locations wherein the capacity of some tragedies to inflict destruction, trauma, and suffering surpassed the immediate physical damage they caused, so that they shocked and wounded entire societies and cultures. He gives several examples of such events, including the 9–11 attacks, the Holocaust, and the 2004 Indian Ocean earthquake and tsunami. See: Christopher Craig Brittain, *Religion at Ground Zero: Theological Responses to Times of Crisis* (London: Continuum, 2011), 14–15.
3 John Swinton, *Raging with Compassion: Pastoral Responses to the Problem of Evil* (Grand Rapids, MI: Wm. B. Eerdmans, 2007), 12.
4 Alister McGrath, *Christian Theology: An Introduction* (Oxford: Blackwell, 2007), 232.
5 G. R. Evans, "Augustine," in G. R. Evans (ed.) *The First Christian Theologians* (Oxford: Blackwell, 2004), 238.
6 R. Douglas Geivett, *Evil and the Evidence for God: The Challenge of John Hick's Theodicy* (Philadelphia: Temple University Press, 1993), 17.
7 Ibid. 18.
8 Eleonore Stump, *Wandering in Darkness: Narrative and the Problem of Suffering* (Oxford: Oxford University Press, 2013), 389.
9 Etymologically considered, the word "theodicy" comes from Leibniz's French *théodicée*, which is an amalgamation of two Ancient Greek words: θεός (theós, "God") and δίκέ (díkē, "justice").
10 Kristen Irwin, "Which 'Reason?' Bayle on the Intractability of Evil," in Larry M. Jorgensen and Samuel Newlands (eds.) *New Essays on Leibniz's Theodicy* (Oxford: Oxford University Press, 2014), 43.
11 Ibid. 43.
12 Gottfried Willheld Leibniz, *Theodicy: Essays on the Goodness of God, the Freedom of Man, and the Origin of Evil* (Lasalle: Open Court, 1985), 127–128.
13 McGrath, 233.
14 Alvin Plantinga, *God, Freedom and Evil* (Grand Rapids: Wm. B. Eerdmans, 1974), 30.
15 Ibid.
16 Ibid.
17 Ibid.
18 Ibid.
19 Richard Swinburne, *Is There a God?* (Oxford: Oxford University Press, 2010), 86.

20 Richard Swinburne, *The Existence of God* (Oxford: Clarendon Press, 1991), 200.
21 Nevertheless, this position allows for the possibility that God might be *indirectly* responsible for the existence of evil, since the power to intervene or not intervene in human life still implies choice.
22 John Hick, *Evil and the God of Love* (London: Macmillan, 1966), 207, 43.
23 Irenaeus of Lyons in McGrath, *Christian Theology*, 203.
24 Alister McGrath, *Theology: The Basics* (Oxford: Blackwell, 2008), 14.
25 Friedrich Schleiermacher, *The Christian Faith*, trans. H. R. Mackintosh (Edinburgh: T&T Clark, 1989), 75.
26 John Hick, *Evil and the God of Love* (London: Harper and Row, 1973), 291.
27 Ibid. 292.
28 Mark S. M. Scott, "Theodicy at the Margins: New Trajectories for the Problem of Evil," *Theology Today*, (68), July 2011, 149.
29 Ibid. 150.
30 Mark Scott, *Pathways in Theodicy: An Introduction to the Problem of Evil* (Minneapolis: Fortress Press, 2015), 151.
31 Ibid. 156.
32 Swinton, *Raging with Compassion*, 14.
33 Ibid. 15.
34 Ibid. 13.
35 Ibid.
36 Nick Trakakis, "Theodicy: The Solution to the Problem of Evil, or Part of the Problem?," *Sophia*, 47, 2008, 161.
37 Fyodor Dostoevsky, *The Brothers Karamazov* (London: J. M. Dent & Sons Ltd., 1942), 243.
38 A. Boyce Gibson, *The Religion of Dostoevsky* (London: SCM, 1973), 176.
39 Kathryn Greene-McCreight, *Darkness Is My Only Companion: A Christian Response to Mental Illness* (Grand Rapids: Brazos Press, 2015), 173.
40 Rowan Williams, "Of Course This Makes Us Doubt God's Existence," *The Telegraph*, 2nd January 2005: www.telegraph.co.uk/comment/personal-view/3613928/Of-course-this-makes-us-doubt-Gods-existence.html (accessed 7th January 2020).
41 Ibid.
42 Ibid.
43 Wendy Farley, "The Practice of Theodicy," in Margaret Mohrmann and Mark Hanson (eds.) *Pain Seeking Understanding: Suffering, Medicine and Faith* (Cleveland: The Pilgrim Press, 1999), 103.
44 Plantinga, *God, Freedom and Evil*, 28–29.
45 David O'Connor, "In Defence of Theoretical Theodicy," *Modern Theology* (1), 1988, 64.
46 Richard Zaner, *Troubled Voices: Stories of Ethics and Illness* (Cleveland: Pilgrim Press, 1993), 43.
47 Swinton, *Raging with Compassion*, 4.
48 Ibid.
49 C. Robert Mesle, *John Hick's Theodicy: A Process Humanist Critique* (London: Macmillan, 1991), xxi.
50 Hick, 334.
51 Ibid. 335.
52 McGrath, *Christian Theology*, 232.
53 Greene-McCreight, xxiii.
54 Frances Young, "Suffering," in A. Hastings, A. Mason, and H. Pyper (eds.) *The Oxford Companion to Christian Thought* (Oxford: Oxford University Press, 2000), 688.

55 Ibid.
56 Brittain, 8.
57 Pat Robertson and Jerry Falwell, "Transcript of Pat Robertson's Interview with Jerry Falwell, Broadcast on the 700 Club, September 13th 2001," in Bruce Lincoln (ed.) *Holy Terrors: Thinking about Religion after September 11th* (Chicago: University of Chicago Press, 2010), 104.
58 Ibid. 105.
59 Ibid. 106.
60 Irene Monroe, "Pat Robertson's Haitian Theodicy," *The Huffington Post*, 26th March 2010: www.huffingtonpost.com/irene-monroe/pat-robertsons-haitian-th_b_434534.html (accessed 7th January 2020).
61 Todd Billings, "Theodicy as a 'Lived Question': Moving Beyond a Theoretical Approach to Theodicy," *Journal for Christian Theological Research*, 5 (2), 2000, 27.
62 Trakakis, "Theodicy: The Solution to the Problem of Evil, or Part of the Problem?," 161.
63 Wendy Farley, *Tragic Vision and Divine Compassion: A Contemporary Theodicy* (Louisville: Westminster John Knox Press, 1990), 154.
64 Ibid. 13, 47, 108.
65 Sarah K. Pinnock, *Beyond Theodicy: Jewish and Christian Continental Thinkers Respond to the Holocaust* (New York: SUNY Press, 2002), 144.

References

Billings, Todd. "Theodicy as a 'Lived Question': Moving beyond a Theoretical Approach to Theodicy." *Journal for Christian Theological Research*. 5 (2), 2000: 1–9.

Brittain, Christopher Craig. *Religion at Ground Zero: Theological Responses to Times of Crisis*. London: Continuum, 2011.

Chopp, Rebecca S. *The Praxis of Suffering: An Interpretation of Liberation and Political Theologies*. Eugene: Wipf & Stock, 2007.

Dostoevsky, Fyodor. *The Brothers Karamazov*. London: J. M. Dent & Sons Ltd., 1942.

Evans, G. R. "Augustine." In *The First Christian Theologians*, edited by G. R. Evans, 238–242. Oxford: Blackwell, 2004.

Farley, Wendy. "The Practice of Theodicy." In *Pain Seeking Understanding: Suffering, Medicine and Faith*, edited by Margaret Mohrmann and Mark Hanson, 103–114. Cleveland: The Pilgrim Press, 1999.

———. *Tragic Vision and Divine Compassion: A Contemporary Theodicy*. Louisville: Westminster John Knox Press, 1990.

Geivett, Douglas R. *Evil and the Evidence for God: The Challenge of John Hick's Theodicy*. Philadelphia: Temple University Press, 1993.

Gibson, Alexander Boyce. *The Religion of Dostoevsky*. London: SCM, 1973.

Greene-McCreight, Kathryn. *Darkness Is My Only Companion: A Christian Response to Mental Illness*. Grand Rapids: Brazos Press, 2015.

Hick, John. *Evil and the God of Love*. London: Harper and Row, 1973.

Irwin, Kristen. "Which 'Reason?' Bayle on the Intractability of Evil." In *New Essays on Leibniz's Theodicy*, edited by Larry M. Jorgensen and Samuel Newland, 43–54. Oxford: Oxford University Press, 2014.

Leibniz, Gottfried Willheld. *Theodicy: Essays on the Goodness of God, the Freedom of Man, and the Origin of Evil*. Translated by E. M. Huggard. Lasalle: Open Court, 1985.

McGrath, Alister. *Christian Theology: An Introduction*. Oxford: Blackwell, 2007.

———. *Theology: The Basics*. Oxford: Blackwell, 2008.

Mesle, C. Robert. *John Hick's Theodicy: A Process Humanist Critique*. London: Macmillan, 1991.

Monroe, Irene. "Pat Robertson's Haitian Theodicy." *The Huffington Post*. 26th March 2010. www.huffingtonpost.com/irene-monroe/pat-robertsons-haitian-th_b_434534.html

O'Connor, David. "In Defence of Theoretical Theodicy." *Modern Theology*. (1), 1988: 61–74.

Pinnock, Sarah K. *Beyond Theodicy: Jewish and Christian Continental Thinkers Respond to the Holocaust*. New York: SUNY Press, 2002.

Plantinga, Alvin. *God, Freedom and Evil*. Grand Rapids: Wm. B. Eerdmans, 1974.

Robertson, Pat, and Falwell, Jerry. "Transcript of Pat Robertson's Interview with Jerry Falwell, Broadcast on the 700 Club, September 13th 2001." In *Holy Terrors: Thinking about Religion after September 11th*, edited by Bruce Lincoln, 108–112. Chicago: University of Chicago Press, 2010.

Scott, Mark S. M. "Theodicy at the Margins: New Trajectories for the Problem of Evil." *Theology Today*. 68 (2), 2011: 149–152.

Stump, Eleonore. *Wandering in Darkness: Narrative and the Problem of Suffering*. Oxford: Oxford University Press, 2013.

Swinburne, Richard. *The Existence of God*. Oxford: Clarendon Press, 1991.

———. *Is There a God?* Oxford: Oxford University Press, 2010.

Swinton, John. *Raging with Compassion: Pastoral Responses to the Problem of Evil*. Grand Rapids, MI: Wm. B. Eerdmans, 2007.

Trakakis, Nick. "Theodicy: The Solution to the Problem of Evil, or Part of the Problem?" *Sophia*. 47, 2008: 161–191.

Williams, Rowan. "Of Course This Makes Us Doubt God's Existence." *The Telegraph*. 2nd January 2005. www.telegraph.co.uk/comment/personal-view/3613928/Of-course-this-makes-us-doubt-Gods-existence.html

Young, Frances. "Suffering." In *The Oxford Companion to Christian Thought*, edited by Adrian Hastings, Alistair Mason, and Hugh Pyper, 687–688. Oxford: Oxford University Press, 2000.

Zaner, Richard. *Troubled Voices: Stories of Ethics and Illness*. Cleveland: Pilgrim Press, 1993.

2 Temperate atheism

The philosophical basis of the Sunday Assembly

In February 2015, British comedian and actor Stephen Fry appeared on *The Meaning of Life*, an Irish religious affairs programme. Presenter Gay Byrne asked Fry, a self-identifying atheist, what he would say to God if confronted with irrefutable evidence of divine existence. Fry replied:

> I'd say, "bone cancer in children? What's that about? How dare you? How dare you create a world to which there is such misery that is not our fault. It's not right, it's utterly, utterly evil. Why should I respect a capricious, mean-minded, stupid God who creates a world which is so full of injustice and pain?" Because the God who created this universe, if it was created by God, is quite clearly a maniac, utter maniac. Totally selfish.[1]

Fry's disquisition on Irish television attracted a great deal of media attention, and even a legal prosecution on the grounds of blasphemy, which was later dropped.[2] His words constitute a vivid presentation of the problem of evil as fodder for the argument against religious belief. In a similar vein, British sociologist Annie Besant's influential text, *Why I Do Not Believe in God*, outlines her reasoning for her atheism as being linked with "Almighty Indifference to the pain of sentient beings."[3] She rails against the idea of a God who, having created the world, then abandons it to pain and suffering. Catholic theologian Hans Küng suggests that the existence of human suffering is "the rock of atheism," and that the entirety of atheist belief could be built upon it.[4]

Indeed, the problem of evil provides a robust challenge, not only to divine goodness, but to the very existence of God. As Ross Douthat explains, this particular conundrum can have the effect of "sharpening one of the best arrows of in the anti-theist's quiver."[5] The events of 9–11 were, according to Alister McGrath, directly influential in the creation a movement that came to be known as New Atheism. He writes that "9–11 turned out to be the intellectual and moral launch pad for New Atheism."[6] Arguments about the danger and irrationality of religion by atheists such as Richard Dawkins had previously failed to capture public support. But 9–11 left enough residual public fear and anxiety about religious fanaticism to make atheist arguments seem both appealing and culturally persuasive. Blind outrage demanded answers; who was to be blamed? Islamic religious fanaticism seemed one obvious possibility. Thereafter, this became reduced and simplified to "religious fanaticism" and, later, simply "religion." The "Four Horsemen" of New Atheism—Richard Dawkins, Christopher Hitchens, Sam Harris, and Daniel Dennett—capitalised on the resulting climate of anger and suspicion. For each of these thinkers, the events of 9–11 served as definitive proof that religion could no longer be reasoned with. New Atheists set out to prevent religious ideas from corrupting society, producing more forceful arguments than their historical equivalents.

Yet while New Atheism dominated popular public discourse for several years in the early 2000s, the landscape of non-religious thought has undergone a slow but significant diversification. Militant atheists continue to criticise religion, but now do so in the presence of a new, less antagonistic form of unbelief. Alain De Botton, Philip Kitcher, and Geoff Crocker (amongst others) retain that there is no God, yet are set apart from their more polemic New Atheist counterparts by their syntheses of the sacred and the secular. These writers encourage greater respect for religion, particularly its rituals and ethics. They are intent on preserving what they perceive to be the most valuable human and social qualities of religion for use in an increasingly non-religious society. Because these writers share similar characteristics and desires, I suggest that they might be grouped together and termed "temperate atheists." Some brief consideration of their ideas is important, as it is the work of these "temperate atheists" which has, in many ways, laid philosophical ground for the Sunday Assembly to emerge.

A "new" New Atheism? The temperate atheists

In an article published in May 2007, Christopher Orlet of *The American Spectator* draws attention to a division in the ranks of unbelievers. Using the terminology of "soft atheism," he describes a new, emerging outlook, founded on concerns that the New Atheists "are becoming too outspoken, too uppity, indeed that they are giving unbelievers a bad name."[7] He refers primarily to Greg Epstein, a humanist chaplain at Harvard University. Epstein feels that Humanism is on the verge of explosive growth, but that it is at risk of being dragged down by the militant tendencies of the New Atheists, which publicly reflect poorly on all atheists. Epstein's work, *Good Without God*, focuses on human potential for goodness, purpose, and compassion. By way of response to the New Atheist movement, Epstein draws on the comfort and hope that can be found in Humanism. He illustrates a positive arrangement of atheism, as opposed to mounting further attack against religious believers.

Epstein's thoughts are characteristic of a wider, emerging movement. In the first instance, this group of thinkers would refer to themselves as humanists, or secular humanists. De Botton and Kitcher have also used the terms "gentle atheism" and "soft atheism" to describe their respective outlooks. In a companion piece to his TED Talk entitled "Atheism 2.0," De Botton explained: "I am an atheist, but a gentle one. I don't feel the need to mock anyone who believes." He also expressed opposition to the literature and rhetoric of New Atheism:

> I really disagree with the hard tone of some atheists who approach religion like a silly fairy tale. I am deeply respectful of religion, but I believe in none of its supernatural aspects. . . . I am at once very respectful and completely impious.[8]

In like manner, Kitcher told Gary Gutting of the *New York Times*: "Because I'm more sympathetic to religion than the prominent new atheists, I label my position "soft atheism.""[9]

While such terminology is useful to an extent, its connotations of passiveness are problematic, suggesting that proponents of this particular type of atheism are not actively promoting their views. It will become clear that this is not the case; "soft" atheists continue to define their work as godless and promote a humanist lifestyle in a positive way. "Gentle" or "soft" might also suggest that their work is closer to agnosticism; again, it will become apparent that this is untrue. I suggest, therefore, that the term "temperate atheism" provides a more accurate description of this movement, which, it bears noting, has not yet been conflated or described in any great detail in academic writing.

The phrase "temperate atheism" implies the self-restraint of its thinkers, particularly with regard to the criticism of religion, while also pointing to the fact that their work is more agreeable to dialogical engagement with theologians and religious groups. Practically speaking, this could have broader social and political implications.[10] At the same time, the potential for such engagement remains largely unrealised. This recent diversification of atheistic thought has not been referred to more than passingly in the field of theology, and neither sociologists nor secular theorists have yet moved to explore its practical out workings. Perhaps this can be explained. "Temperate atheism" remains a live issue; it is unresolved, insofar as it is unfolding. It should be cautioned that the long-term significance of this body of work is unknown, and it may yet turn out to be a short-lived cultural phenomenon.

"Temperate atheism" in practice

What does "temperate atheism" mean to its proponents? Central to the cause is a critique of modern atheism for failing to provide an alternative to the social structures and community aspects of Church. Out of this comes a positive emphasis on Humanism, and its uses for non-believers. Philip Kitcher criticises New Atheists for being "blind to the apparently irreplaceable roles religion and religious community play in millions, if not billions, of lives."[11] The central purpose of his work, *Life After Faith*, is to illustrate how a "secular perspective" can fulfil some of the same important functions that religion has historically carried out. For Kitcher, the atheist movement has been too insistent that doctrines and beliefs form the bedrock of religion. He works to disentangle religion from doctrine, showing how it has articulated strong values and emphasised community. Indeed, he suggests that these are facets which can still be extracted from religion in a positive way.

Similarly, in *Religion for Atheists*, De Botton argues that the many benefits of religion simply cannot be replicated within a godless society. Although an atheist, he respects the way in which religion sees humans not simply as rational minds, but as emotional and physical creatures too. Working along comparable lines to Kitcher, De Botton goes a little further, challenging the idea that non-believers face a stark choice between "swallowing doctrine" or doing away with lots of "consoling and beautiful" ideas and concepts.[12] Accordingly, atheists can use religions as rich sources of insight, particularly for community building, maintaining relationships, overcoming envy and inadequacy, and getting more out of art, architecture and music. The fundamental problem of New Atheism, according to De Botton, is its disregard for the powerful social ideas contained within religious texts and traditions. Rather than mocking religion, atheists should be shrewd, and steal from them ideas about how to live in social harmony. In a similar vein, Julian Baggini has observed that gratitude is widely lacking as a concept within non-religious culture. He suggests that humanists might draw on religious practices such as fasting in order to rectify this, explaining that "eating at certain times is a way of countering our tendency to slavishly follow our desire."[13]

A refusal to attack religious groups is also a characteristic of these writings. In an interview for *Religion News Service*, Kitcher was asked why he sought to "resist the now dominant atheist idea that religion is noxious rubbish to be buried as deeply, as thoroughly, as possible."[14] By way of reply, he explained that his aim is to "be more sympathetic to religion at its best, and strive towards finding a positive position that could replace religion."[15] In *The Book of Atheist Spirituality*, French philosopher Andre Comte-Sponville acknowledges religion as an important part of human history, arguing that it is entirely possible to retain an atheistic standpoint without engaging in malicious, anti-religious rhetoric:

> There is no reason to take faith away from those who need it-or even those who simply live better because they have it. . . . Their faith in no way offends me. Why should I combat it? My intention is not to convert people to atheism. It is merely to explain my position and the arguments in its favour, motivated more by the love of philosophy than by the hatred of religion.[16]

Contrary to New Atheist theory, Comte-Sponville suggests that the universal eradication of religion may not, in fact, be a good thing. In his opinion, believers are not innately evil. He suggests that "some believers are admirable . . . most are worthy of respect."[17] *The New Humanist* magazine has echoed these sentiments. In particular, its new editor Daniel Trilling began his tenure with an article entitled "Beyond Dawkins," in which he stated that atheists should be made aware that "some 'criticism' of religion is racist," that "religious believers are no less intelligent than non-believers," and that "secularism does not mean excluding religious believers from society."[18] His words were intended as both a critique of New Atheist thought and an illustration of Humanism's capacity for more nuanced debate and discussion with religious believers.

The Sunday Assembly: a church of "temperate atheists"?

Pressing for the work at hand is the question: how has the philosophy of "temperate atheists" like De Botton influenced the formation and expansion of the Sunday Assembly?

The Sunday Assembly's godless gatherings, which are mimetic of (some) traditional Christian Church services, bring to mind De Botton's ideas about the atheistic adoption of religious rituals. In addition to his book, De Botton founded the School of Life centre in London in 2008. The School titles its courses according to major life issues, such as "careers, relationships, politics, travels, families." It also holds communal gatherings, such as meals, on a regular basis. In the early days of the Sunday Assembly, De Botton suggested that both his organisation and *Religion for Atheists* had contained the idea of an "atheist church" for many years previously. As such, he argued that the Sunday Assembly "shouldn't therefore claim the idea as their own." He later referred to the Assembly as "a blatant rip-off of what we do," presumably referring to his Sunday sermon at the School of Life.[19]

By way of a response, the founders of the Sunday Assembly claimed not to be familiar with De Botton's work, or his Sunday Sermon. Assembly co-founder Sanderson Jones stated: "Neither Pippa [Evans, the other co-founder of the Sunday Assembly] nor I have ever been to the Sunday Sermon, so it would be tricky to rip him off."[20] Jones also suggested that De Botton's ideas about an "atheist church" were centred around space and architecture rather than community and congregation. Towards the end of *Religion for Atheists*, De Botton writes about religious architecture and how it can "perform a critical function in relation to egotism."[21] He discusses his plans for a "Temple to Perspective," intended to make human beings feel small by something "mighty, noble, accomplished and intelligent."[22] "These are churches," he writes, "that can induce us to surrender our egoism without in any way humiliating us."[23] For Jones, the Sunday Assembly is "more focussed on people, celebration and life." In response to De Botton's comments, Jones said: "I think it is probably reflective of our different approaches that when Alain De Botton wanted to create the first temple to atheism he wanted to create a building, not a congregation."

While Jones may not see a direct correlation between his organisation and the work of Alain De Botton, it is clear that "temperate atheism," for all that it is still shifting and unfolding, has created a philosophical space for alternative expressions of atheism in the early years of the twenty-first century. Previously, that landscape of thought was dominated by the books, debates, and journalism of New Atheists. Proponents of "temperate atheism" have challenged the approach of New Atheists, deconstructing their arguments about the danger and incompetence of religion. They have argued instead that religion can be drawn on in myriad ways by those who consider themselves to be non-religious. Baggini and De Botton in particular have provided concrete examples of how atheists might draw on varying religious traditions, extracting various practices for their "universal wisdom" and scope. Whether or not the Sunday Assembly is a direct result of these writings is unclear; its creators attest that it is not. Regardless, the work of "temperate atheists" has provided an alternative to New Atheism in wider public discourse. At the least, this has provided an indication that other approaches to atheism have momentum, and it has created a philosophical space in which atheists and agnostics might draw on the practices of the Christian church in one form or another.

Conclusion

It is interesting to note how rapidly the landscape of modern atheism has shifted in recent years. Arguably, the growth of these movements has been historically unprecedented, at least with regards to the method by which their ideas have been disseminated. Wide social changes at the turn of the century, coupled with the intensely public real-time disaster of 9–11, propelled questions about the existence of God and the moral and ethical approaches of religion, into the arena of worldwide social debate. It was in these conditions that the two movements focused on here rose to prominence. While their immediate impact on the Sunday Assembly may seem minimal, this is open to interpretation, particularly as this study shifts towards a more detailed examination of the opinions and remarks of those who have the greatest knowledge of the workings and activities of the Sunday Assembly: the attendees themselves.

Notes

1 Stephen Fry as quoted by Pádraig Collins, "Stephen Fry Investigated by Irish Police for Alleged Blasphemy," *The Guardian*, 7th May 2017: www.theguardian. com/culture/2017/may/07/stephen-fry-investigated-by-irish-police-for-alleged-blasphemy (accessed 7th January 2020).

2 Ibid.
3 Annie Besant in Alister McGrath, *Theology: The Basics* (Oxford: Blackwell, 2008), 16.
4 Hans Küng in Michael Palmer, *The Atheist's Primer* (Cambridge: Lutterworth Press, 2012), 55.
5 Ross Douthat, "The Implications of Christmas," *The Atlantic*, 25th December 2008: www.theatlantic.com/personal/archive/2008/12/the-implications-of-christmas/55868/ (accessed 7th January 2020).
6 Alister McGrath, *Why God Won't Go Away: Engaging with the New Atheism* (London: SPCK, 2011), viii.
7 Christopher Orlet, "Fundamentalist Atheists," *The American Spectator*, 26th April 2007: http://spectator.org/articles/45469/fundamentalist-atheists (accessed 7th January 2020).
8 Alain De Botton, "I am an Atheist, But a Gentle One: Alain De Botton on Religion for Atheists," *TED Blogs*, 17th January 2012: http://blog.ted.com/faq-with-alain-de-botton-on-religion-for-atheists/ (accessed 7th January 2020).
9 Philip Kitcher in Gary Gutting, "The Case for Soft Atheism," *The New York Times*, 15th May 2014: http://opinionator.blogs.nytimes.com/2014/05/15/the-case-for-soft-atheism/?_php=true&_type=blogs&_r=1 (accessed 7th January 2020).
10 The work of political scientist Phil Ryan seeks to foster and encourage the identification of shared ethics for a "secular society" through dialogue between believers and unbelievers. His sets aside the question of whether or not belief in God is reasonable, in order to examine whether atheists and theists can find a common ground upon which to speak about social norms and ethical matters in a productive way: "The existence and nature of God is a matter on which the respectful coexistence of many perspectives is entirely possible, as we find in most developed societies today" (Ryan, 7). Ryan's key argument hinges on the need to move beyond accusatory debate to space where respectful discussion and "ethical dialogue" can take place. His work identifies unhelpful stereotypes, which may prevent such dialogue from taking place. However, Ryan's perspective does involve the "setting aside" of "moral foundations," such as holy texts. It is worth briefly noting that this particular aspect of his work may be problematic from a practical theological perspective, which is grounded in questions regarding the Christian faith. See Phil Ryan, *After the New Atheist Debate* (Toronto: University of Toronto Press, 2014).
11 Philip Kitcher, *Life after Faith: The Case for Secular Humanism* (New Haven, CT: Yale University Press, 2014), xiii.
12 Alain De Botton, "Religion for Atheists": http://alaindebotton.com/religion/ (accessed 7th January 2020).
13 Baggini himself underwent a ten-day fast, based on the Hindu festival of Navrati, in 2012. See Julian Baggini, "Navrati and the Lessons of Fasting for Atheists," *The Guardian*, 22nd October 2012: www.theguardian.com/commentisfree/belief/2012/oct/22/navratri-lessons-fasting-atheists (accessed 7th January 2020).
14 Chris Stedman, "Philip Kitcher: 'New Atheism' Hasn't Supplied Anything New to Replace Religion," *Religion News Service*, 1st December 2014: https://religionnews.com/2014/12/01/philip-kitcher-new-atheism/ (accessed 7th January 2020).
15 Ibid.
16 Andre Comte-Sponville, *The Book of Atheist Spirituality* (London: Bantam, 2009), 10–11.
17 Ibid. 11.

18 Daniel Trilling, "Beyond Dawkins," *New Humanist Magazine*, 16th August 2013: https://newhumanist.org.uk/articles/4271/beyond-dawkins (accessed 7th January 2020).
19 Alain De Botton in Andrjez Lukowski, "Sunday Assembly: Move Over, Jehova," *Time Out: London*, 23rd September 2013: www.timeout.com/london/things-to-do/sunday-assembly-move-over-jehova (accessed 7th January 2020).
20 Sanderson Jones in Olivia Solon, "Atheist Church Seeks £500,000 in Crowd Funding to Build Online Platform," *Wired*, 20th October 2013: www.wired.co.uk/news/archive/2013-10/20/sunday-assembly-expansion (accessed 7th January 2020).
21 Alain De Botton, *Religion for Atheists: A Non-Believer's Guide to the Uses of Religion* (London: Penguin Books, 2012), 259.
22 Ibid
23 Ibid. 261.

References

Baggini, Julian. "Navratri and the Lessons of Fasting for Atheists." *The Guardian*. 22nd October 2012. www.theguardian.com/commentisfree/belief/2012/oct/22/navratri-lessons-fasting-atheists

Collins, Pádraig. "Stephen Fry Investigated by Irish Police for Alleged Blasphemy." *The Guardian*. 7th May 2017. www.theguardian.com/culture/2017/may/07/stephen-fry-investigated-by-irish-police-for-alleged-blasphemy

Comte-Sponville, Andre. *The Book of Atheist Spirituality*. London: Bantam, 2009.

De Botton, Alain. "I am an Atheist, But a Gentle One: Alain De Botton on Religion for Atheists." *TED Blogs*. 17th January 2012. http://blog.ted.com/faq-with-alain-de-botton-on-religion-for-atheists/

———. "Religion for Atheists." http://alaindebotton.com/religion/

———. *Religion for Atheists: A Non-Believer's Guide to the Uses of Religion*. London: Penguin Books, 2012.

Douthat, Ross. "The Implications of Christmas." *The Atlantic*. 25th December 2008. www.theatlantic.com/personal/archive/2008/12/the-implications-of-christmas/55868/

Gutting, Gary. "The Case for Soft Atheism." *The New York Times*. 15th May 2014. https://opinionator.blogs.nytimes.com/2014/05/15/the-case-for-soft-atheism/

Kitcher, Philip. *Life after Faith: The Case for Secular Humanism*. New Haven: Yale University Press, 2014.

Lukowski, Andrjez. "Sunday Assembly: Move Over, Jehova." *Time Out: London*. 23rd September 2013. www.timeout.com/london/things-to-do/sunday-assembly-move-over-jehova

McGrath, Alister. *Theology: The Basics*. Oxford: Blackwell, 2008.

———. *Why God Won't Go Away: Engaging with the New Atheism*. London: SPCK, 2011.

Orlet, Christopher. "Fundamentalist Atheists." *The American Spectator*. 26th April 2007. http://spectator.org/articles/45469/fundamentalist-atheists

Palmer, Michael. *The Atheist's Primer*. Cambridge: Lutterworth Press, 2012.

Ryan, Phil. *After the New Atheist Debate*. Toronto: University of Toronto Press, 2014.

Solon, Olivia. "Atheist Church Seeks £500,000 in Crowd Funding to Build Online Platform." *Wired*. 20th October 2013. www.wired.co.uk/news/archive/2013-10/20/sunday-assembly-expansion

Stedman, Chris. "Philip Kitcher: 'New Atheism' Hasn't Supplied Anything New to Replace Religion." *Religion News Service*. 1st December 2014. http://chrisstedman.religionnews.com/2014/12/01/philip-kitcher-new-atheism/

Trilling, Daniel. "Beyond Dawkins." *New Humanist Magazine*. 16th August 2013. https://newhumanist.org.uk/articles/4271/beyond-dawkins

3 "Live better, help often, wonder more"
The Sunday Assembly

Having explained the theological roots of this work and charted the philosophical space in which the Sunday Assembly exists, I now move to describe and explain the many facets of this community in detail. In doing so, I explore the history and objectives of this movement, and its position as a "church without God."

A short history of the Sunday Assembly

The Sunday Assembly was created by comedians Sanderson Jones and Pippa Evans, who admired the collective inspiration and congregational structure of British churches and desired a space in which to encounter these elements without the inclusion of religion or dogma.[1] Both formerly attended Church. Jones enjoyed the "songs, community and structures" but held no belief in God.[2] Evans was a committed churchgoer, first attending the Church of England, and then becoming involved in a more evangelical movement. She described her experiences to journalist Stephen Tomkins in the following way:

> I went to church till I was 17. What I call "classic church" when I was a kid—with a proper old-school vicar with a white dress. Then I had a friend at school who went to a happy-clappy church, so I started going to the youth group, and from the age of 11 to 17 I was proper into church, got baptised, preached on Haven Green, ran the Sunday school. Then I started questioning, and I just stopped believing in God. And when I left I realised it wasn't God that I missed or Jesus, it was church. I really missed church.[3]

When Evans stopped attending, she yearned for the congregational "culture" of Church, which, in her words, involved "helping people, sharing experiences and thinking about life."[4] Jones shared her desires for a new movement, incorporating, in his words, "the best of church, without God."[5] To that end, services were designed to incorporate elements which Jones and Evans both "missed." In particular, an emphasis was placed on gathering in community after services, and on communal singing.

The movement held its inaugural event in January 2013 in "The Nave," a deconsecrated Church building in North London.[6] Advertised as a "church for atheists," the first service drew almost 200 attendees.[7] Meetings were moved thereafter due to health and safety concerns regarding capacity, although Jones claims that the Church of England raised concerns about the appropriateness of a "godless congregation" gathering in an ecumenical building (the Diocese of London would not comment on these claims).[8] The Sunday Assembly's flagship congregation found a new and permeant base at Conway Hall, which houses the Conway Hall Ethical Society, a secular humanist organisation dating back to the late eighteenth century.[9] They have met here ever since on a fortnightly basis.

In October 2013, in response to sustained media attention and a world-wide demand for expansion, the Assembly began a major crowd-funding campaign. They intended that their goal of £500,000 would be used to launch more local Assemblies.[10] Concurrently, Jones and Evans embarked on a comedy tour of the US and Australia, called "40 Days and 40 Nights," to raise the profile of their fledgling organisation and advertise their financial campaign. Fundraising efforts were largely unsuccessful. By December, £33,668, or just over 7% of the target amount, had been raised. Jones addressed this in a blog post, in which he referred to the initial target as an "outrageously ambitious goal" yet noted that plans for expansion would still go ahead.[11]

By August 2014, there were 28 registered local Assemblies in existence. One month later, on 28th September, the Assembly held a global launch event, titled "Assemble Everywhere." The introduction of 35 new assemblies was planned.[12] The year 2014 also saw the Assembly adopt a system of church-like management, when its first "Synod" took place.[13] The movement continued to expand its reach. In an article for *The Guardian*, Jones described the influx of global enquiries about his new organisation:

> If I open my email box the first email is in Hungarian, discussing Sunday Assembly Budapest, after there is something from Kenya, then the Western Cape, then Richmond, Virginia, then Cincinnati, then Boston . . .[14]

Indeed, something of the format of a Church without God appears to have been culturally transcendent, to the extent that it merited such sustained worldwide interest. At its high point (2014–2016), the Sunday Assembly estimated a presence in more than 70 cities worldwide, with the majority of congregation situated in Europe, the United States, and Australia.[15] It continues to hold a yearly international conference, during which it continues to conduct General Synod meetings for its accredited members.[16] Most Assemblies plan social events and external interest groups, which take place outwith the context of Sunday "services." Additionally, the flagship congregation in London has developed and run a number of self-improvement courses for its members (more on this later). The organisation has also been commissioned by a housing association in London and Manchester to build Sunday Assembly communities.[17] Further, it is mentioned in the GCSE Religion Education Syllabus as a "case study" on non-religious communities.[18]

The "doctrine" of the Sunday Assembly

The Assembly claims not to have any particular doctrinal leanings; indeed, the second article of its Public Charter declares that the movement has "no doctrine."[19] Nevertheless, it does ascribe to three founding principles, which are contained within its motto: "Live Better, Help Often, and Wonder More." In addition to facilitating self-growth for attendees, the Assembly has drawn particular attention to its policy of "radical inclusivity" and frequently uses the term "celebration of life" to describe its ethos. Whether or not the Sunday Assembly has any doctrine in practice will be uncovered by the qualitative component of the research undertaken in this study. At this point, however, it is prudent to note some of the key features of its ethos, as presented in publicly accessible literature, which might be construed as "doctrinal" in character, given that they appear to constitute a set of beliefs and "truth claims."[20]

"Live better"

The first section of the Sunday Assembly's three-part motto is "live better." According to Assembly literature, the organisation: "aim[s] to provide inspiring, thought-provoking and practical ideas that help people to live the lives they want to lead and be the people they want to be."[21] In other words, the movement places particular emphasis on self-improvement. In 2014, the first "Live Better groups" were established in London. Described by a Sunday Assembly source as "peer support groups, where people come together to help each other achieve their goals [and] fulfil their ambitions," these were small collectives of four to eight members who met for up to eight weeks in the first instance. The same source, who I later interviewed as part of this project, was careful to stress that these meetings "are not intended as counselling," and that attendees might not be able to deal with multiple aims or goals in the sessions, given their limited run.

In addition to these groups, which were run only at the flagship congregation in London, the Assembly piloted a "Life Course" in 2016, which it described as a "way of helping people through the big (and small) questions."[22] It was (and remains) unclear as to whether this model was intended as an eventual replacement of the "Live Better groups," but the two are broadly similar. The content of the "Life Course" is based on the work of Martin Seligman and makes use of his PERMA model of positive psychology, which draws on positive emotions "to help individuals . . . find lives of happiness, fulfilment, and meaning."[23] Structurally, it draws on the format of the Alpha Course, a series of interactive sessions exploring the Christian faith, developed by Holy Trinity Brompton Church.[24] From Alpha, the "Life Course" has adopted the structure of a shared meal, a short talk, and a time of discussion. In 2017, the Assembly advertised a new programme, entitled "Retreat to the Future," which it described as incorporating some of the elements piloted in the "Life Course." Rather than taking place across a series of weeks, however, this is a two-day retreat, designed to give help attendees the tools they require to "live life as fully as possible." The "Retreat to the Future" includes a series of activities, such as mindfulness, music, and talks. Like the "Live Better groups" and the "Life Course," this event is one of a number which promotes and encourages self-improvement, emphasising the "live better" part of the movement's motto. This mandate is not a prescriptive one, however; attendees at the mentioned events are encouraged to decide what "living better" might look like within their own situation, and what implications it might hold for them on a personal level.

Sanderson Jones has since expanded these ideas further, coining the term "Lifefullness" to encapsulate "the practice of building secular and inclusive communities, to create a world rich in meaning and belonging."[25]

"Help often"

"Assemblies are communities of action building lives of purpose, encouraging us all to help anyone who needs it to support each other," claims Jones.[26] To that end, the Sunday Assembly has committed itself to volunteering in local communities and causes wherever possible. Globally, this has involved a wide range of volunteering projects and opportunities, including a litter picking event in Hamburg, packing care kits for the homeless in LA, helping at a foodbank in Portland and working with the charity Open Age in London.[27] Local assemblies are tasked with locating and organising their own volunteering opportunities.

In addition, the Assembly is a largely volunteer-run organisation. In London, a large number of "helping" opportunities related to the operation of Sunday services are listed. These include (but are not limited to): helping to prepare, serve, and wash up tea and coffee, welcoming assemblers, answering queries for first time visitors, playing an instrument in the band or singing in the choir, and assisting with the technical team. Other administrative responsibilities are advertised, also on a volunteer basis, such as filtering and trafficking emails, updating the website, and assisting with data entry of sign-up lists.[28]

"Wonder more"

The third aspect of Assembly's motto relates to the concept of wonder. Indeed, the Assembly has described itself as "a global movement for wonder and good."[29] Jones explains that: "hearing talks, singing as one, listening to readings and even playing games helps us to connect with each other and the . . . world we live in."[30] For sociologist Jacqui Frost, who undertook ethnographic research on the Sunday Assembly in Atlanta, Georgia, this sense of "wonderment" is primarily achieved by listening to invited speakers, "who impart knowledge," and by having attendees "reflect on the things they have learned and how they might apply them to their lives going forward."[31]

The concept of wonder also appears to be related to an understanding of life as fleeting and fragile. Indeed, the Assembly's Public Charter places emphasis on recognition of "the one life we know we have."[32] Brian Wheeler of *BBC News Magazine* attended one of the first assemblies to take place in London in 2013. Wheeler describes the service, which was on the theme of "wonder":

> There [was] a reading from Alice in Wonderland and a power-point presentation from a particle physicist, Dr Harry Cliff, who explain[ed] the origins of antimatter theory. . . . But there [were] more serious moments . . . we [bowed] our heads for two minutes of contemplation about the miracle of life and, in his closing sermon, Jones [spoke] about how the death of his mother influenced his own spiritual journey and determination to get the most out of every second, aware that life is all too brief and nothing comes after it.[33]

In fact, at the first Assembly I attended for research relating to this project, Jones spoke of his mother, her death, and his desire to "live life fully" and "recognise the wonder of the world," since life is so short. In this respect, the Assembly's appeal for attendees to "wonder more" is closely related to its ethos of "celebrating life."

"Radical inclusivity"

The notion of "radical inclusivity" has been prevalent within Sunday Assembly literature and rhetoric since 2014. The fourth article of the movement's public charter proclaims that the Assembly is that "everyone is welcome, regardless of their beliefs—this is a place of love that is open and accepting."[34] The terminology of "radical inclusivity" was adopted by Jones from Glide Memorial Methodist Church in San Francisco, a congregation whose philosophy is founded in the "love and justice" of the gospels.[35] At Glide Church, the core principle of "radical inclusion" involves "valuing difference."[36] Sandhya Rani Jha explains that a visitor to Glide would be likely to "worship between someone off the street and a truly fabulous drag queen on a Sunday morning," and that attendees are expected to participate in outreach projects, such as serving meals to the homeless.[37]

What does this concept, plucked from its gospel roots, look like for the Sunday Assembly? The Assembly emphasises their inclusion of all who wish to attend, regardless of atheistic leanings or religious beliefs. On its website, the organisation claims that it is "absolutely not" exclusively for atheists, and invites people to attend and "celebrate life together, regardless of what [they] believe in."[38] Below this is written: "We have people from all walks of life as part of our community—whatever your background, race, faith or age you are welcome."[39] Jones admits that he "stole" the wording of "radical inclusivity" from Glide Church because it summarised his objectives for his movement. Thereafter, in 2015, he commissioned Sam Brown,[40] a philosopher and member of the late Sunday Assembly Oxford, to conceptualise the terminology for Assembly use. I spoke briefly with Sam about this project, and he explained the meaning of "radical inclusivity" for the organisation:

> "Inclusivity" transcends "us-and-them" thinking by dissolving classical boundaries and binary oppositions; "radical" means the difference is fundamental to the approach. Unlike diversity, "radical inclusivity" doesn't specify types or invoke inclusion criteria. It undermines classical methods of categorisation. There are simplistic ways of recasting it in classical terms, but they tend to entail logical paradoxes. It certainly doesn't imply (as some people have suggested) accepting every conceivable worldview, embracing radical ideologies, or avoiding a core set of beliefs. Nor does it involve appealing to everyone regardless of their preconceptions. It has more in common with progressive paradigms in politics, philosophy and pop culture—such as anti-racism, feminism, deconstructionism, and embodiment. It needs to be placed in that context to be understood properly.[41]

Brown's description contains some salient points; in particular, he is clear that the Assembly's adoption of "radical inclusivity" does not mean "avoiding a core set of beliefs." Furthermore, he explains that the Sunday Assembly will not accept "every conceivable worldview." This would appear to support my earlier suggestion that the Assembly does not completely evade doctrine and that it is operating under a particular system of belief. In later chapters, the concept of "radical inclusivity" in practice will be discussed in dialogue with the qualitative research findings of this study.

"Celebration of life"

The Sunday Assembly constitutes a "celebration of life"; something which is communicated at the start of every service in London. By way of introduction, Jones asks the congregation if they are "in the mood to celebrate being alive"; a rhetorical question, which is routinely received positively with cheers and clapping from gathered attendees.

As noted, the concept of "celebrating life" is closely tied to a sense of "wonder" and to the finite nature of human life. In an early interview which I conducted with Jones for this project, he explained that his mother's death was a "launch pad" for reminding him of how "amazing and celebration-worthy" life is. Because life is so fragile within his non-religious worldview, which contains no clear eschatological leanings, the celebration of it appears to be imperative.

Jones has spoken extensively, both with the media and with his congregation in London, about his desire to celebrate life originating with his mother's death, when he was aged ten. Jones recognised that he was "privileged" to have known his mother. At the first Assembly event I attended, he acknowledged that her death was the catalyst for his determination to celebrate life. Indeed, as my opening description of the Sunday Assembly in the introduction to this book illustrates, Jones is, on a personal level, almost strenuously excitable, both when presenting the Assembly and speaking about it. The language of "celebration" is not reserved for Sundays; it peppers his everyday speech and rhetoric. It is clearly a central part of both Assembly doctrine, and his own ethos and outlook.

Jones provides a more descriptive explanation of the concept of "celebrating life" in an interview with Kevin Primrose of *The Examined Life*:[42]

> For me, I think "celebrating life", or looking at the naturalistic worldview of being an evolved human being—out of the nothingness of matter, then going to nothingness afterwards, and for a moment existing—that cosmic view can inform an ethos of behaviour in everyday life. That feeling of how lucky it is, gives us that compulsion to go and ask yourself the question—if this life is a blessing, then how am I spending it? It's a kick up the arse really. To really ask yourself that question from that perspective, is like realising you're sitting on a cheque for a million dollars—you know, let's go and make the most of it![43]

From Jones's description, it might be deduced that the "celebration of life" is tied to the concept of wonder (explored previously in this chapter), which, in turn, is founded on the notion that this life is the only one we have. Jones uses terms such as "blessed" and "lucky" to describe the situation of human life. One might question how all-encompassing, and indeed "radically inclusive," his particular vision of celebration, as outlined earlier, is in practice. Later in this book, data collected at the Sunday Assembly in London and Edinburgh will be used to explore such questions.

Ebbing away? The Sunday Assembly in recent years

In recent years, the Sunday Assembly has experienced something of a downturn. The organisation has reported a significant loss in its total number of attendees. Globally, numbers have fallen from around 5,000 monthly attendees in 2016 to 3,500 in 2018. Similarly, the number of chapters has reduced from 70 in 2016 to around 40 in 2019.[44] In an article about the Sunday Assembly for *The Atlantic*, published in 2019, Faith Hill writes that:

even as the growth of "none's" has revved up . . . the growth of secular congregations hasn't kept pace. After a promising start, attendance declined, and nearly half the chapters have fizzled out. Building a durable community of nonbelievers, it turns out, is more complicated than just excising God.[45]

Hill's observation is one with which I concur. I would suggest that the Sunday Assembly peaked during the time frame in which the majority of the research for this book was conducted (2014–2017). As far back as 2016, rumours of closed Assemblies had already begun to spread. At the Assembly's international meeting in Utrecht that year, I made the following note in my field journal:

> Even just a couple of hours into the conference, we had heard repeatedly from folk about assemblies shutting down. A woman from Berlin told us that the assembly there was on its last legs, and had not met since November 2015. We had heard that assemblies in Paris and Brussels had shut, and I mentioned Glasgow (which seems to have disappeared too). Members of the Utrecht team were being recruited to help re-launch the Amsterdam chapter, which was also "on a hiatus." The same was true of Rotterdam.

Why were these chapters beginning to close down? According to further notes made in my field journal, the lack of "people power" needed to organise, set up, and run Assembly events had become prohibitive to the movement's growth. In reference to the New York chapter, Hill writes that:

> There just weren't enough people. Making a congregation happen basically meant putting on a big show on a regular basis. Somebody needed to book bands, find speakers, set up chairs, pick up snacks. Anne Klaeysen, who was a board member for the New York chapter at the time, told me the same thing. "The core group worked their hearts out, but it wasn't sustainable."

Hill adds that varied perspectives on atheism and the movement's priorities led to internal conflict at some Assemblies. Indeed, the New York chapter experienced something of a "schism" in 2014 over disagreements about how prominent non-religion should be at the Sunday Assembly. While some members felt that the Assembly should promote atheism, others simply wanted to gather in community and "celebrate life." Hill also mentions that the Assembly has had to compete with other Sunday commitments, such as "boot camps, SoulCycle and brunch."[46] This points to a deeper issue concerning the lack of incentive that members have to attend. This, along with some further reasoning for the movement's loss of members, will be detailed further in due course.

Conclusion

In this chapter, I have presented and described the history and outlook of the Sunday Assembly, a fledgling organisation of self-titled "secular congregations," which initially expanded rapidly across the UK and US. I have drawn attention to some of the Assembly's core beliefs, deduced from public sources of information, such as interviews with its founders, and discussions with the British and American media. This has formed only a brief sketch of what Sunday Assembly doctrine might entail, and has not yet addressed the central, theological query of this book. What might be learnt about suffering and meaning making in the twenty-first century by observing a non-religious community at work?

Notes

1 The Sunday Assembly, "About Sunday Assembly": https://sundayassembly.online/about-sunday-assembly/ (accessed 7th January 2020).
2 Stephen Tomkins, "Pippa Evans & Sanderson Jones interview: How Great Thou Aren't," *Reform Magazine*, March 2013: www.reform-magazine.co.uk/2013/10/pippa-evans-sanderson-jones-interview-how-great-thou-arent/ (accessed 7th January 2020).
3 Ibid.
4 Robert Pigott, "Doing Church without God," *BBC News*, 1st November 2013: www.bbc.co.uk/news/uk-24766314 (accessed 7th January 2020).
5 Ibid.
6 Esther Addley, ""Not Believing in God Makes Life More Precious:" Meet the Atheist Churchgoers," *The Guardian*, 2nd February 2013: www.theguardian.com/world/2013/feb/03/atheist-church-sunday-assembly-islington (accessed 7th January 2020).
7 The Sunday Assembly, "About Sunday Assembly."
8 Mark Blunden, "Atheists Banned from Church Land," *The Evening Standard*, 29th April 2013: www.standard.co.uk/news/london/atheists-banned-from-church-land-8594364.html (accessed 7th January 2020).
9 Emma Jacobs, "'Church without God' Looks for New Ways of Funding Mission," *Financial Times*, 18th October 2013: www.ft.com/content/6f6fee48-3737-11e3-9603-00144feab7de?mhq5j=e6 (accessed 7th January 2020).
10 Ibid.
11 The Sunday Assembly, "We're Not Going to Hit Our Crowdfunding Target, and That's OK": www.sundayassembly.com/blog/were-not-going-to-hit-our-crowd-funding-target-and-thats-ok (accessed 7th January 2020).
12 It is difficult to tell how many of the planned new congregations launched on 28th September 2014. As will become apparent, the Assembly's central office has been unable to estimate an exact number of operational outposts at any given time, since it relies solely on information being communicated by organisers in each location. For example, Yutaka Osakabe and Isaac Gagné, writing for the Non-Religion and Secularity Network, noted that a launch event was planned in Tokyo and never took place. See "Non-Event Report: Why the Sunday Assembly Event Did Not Launch in Japan," *Non-Religion and Secularity Network* (blog): https://blog.nsrn.net/2015/04/17/non-event-report-why-the-sunday-assembly-event-did-not-launch-in-japan/ (accessed 7th January 2020).
13 Esther Addley, "Atheist Sunday Assembly Prepares for First 'Synod' as Expansion Continues," *The Guardian*, 29th April 2014: www.theguardian.com/

world/2014/apr/29/atheist-sunday-assembly-first-synod (accessed 7th January 2020).

14 Ibid.

15 As explained earlier, it is difficult for the organisation to give an accurate figure of how many Assemblies are running regularly. In later chapters, some examples of this, and the reasoning behind it, will be discussed more fully.

16 New Assemblies require an organising team, a venue, and some local press, and must accept the movement's terms and conditions. Initially, there was no requirement for quality control. However, in recent years, the organisation has introduced some formal barriers to accredited membership. New Assemblies should seek accreditation between six months and two years of starting. This requires video documentation of at least three services, as well as information regarding the organising team, social media accounts, and insurance. Thereafter, two accreditors from within the organisation attend a service and meet with the organising team. Full accreditation may be awarded thereafter. At the time in which I conducted this study, only seven congregations (not including the founding congregation in London) within the movement had fulfilled all of the tasks necessary for full accreditation. These were Bristol, Los Angeles, San Diego, Nashville, Silicon Valley, Portland, and Brighton. See: The Sunday Assembly, "Accreditation": www.sundayassembly.com/accreditation (accessed 7th January 2020).

17 The Sunday Assembly, "An Open Letter to Housing Association Residents": www.sundayassembly.com/an-open-letter-to-housing-association-residents/ (accessed 7th January 2020).

18 GCSE (9–1) "Specification- Religious Studies (Short Course)": www.ocr.org. uk/Images/240624-specification-accredited-gcse-religious-studies-short-course-j125.pdf (accessed 7th January 2020).

19 The Sunday Assembly, "Public Charter for the Sunday Assembly": www.sun dayassembly.com/blog/public-charter-for-sunday-assembly (accessed 7th January 2020).

20 Alister McGrath describes doctrine as a "set of truth-claims" about something. Though he is referring to Christianity in particular, the language of doctrine can encompass other groups, such as political parties. See McGrath, *Studies in Doctrine* (Grand Rapids: Zondervan, 1997), 244.

21 The Sunday Assembly, "About Sunday Assembly."

22 This definition was obtained during the fieldwork component of the research. In particular, it was communicated by Sunday Assembly leadership, including Sanderson Jones, at a "Life Course" pilot session, which took place during the Assembly's international conference in Utrecht in May 2016.

23 Stuart J. Slavin, Debra Schindler, John T. Chibnall, Ginny Fendell, and Mindy Schloss, "PERMA: A Model for Institutional Leadership and Culture Change," *Academic Medicine*, 87 (11), 2012, 1481.

24 Alpha Course, "What Is Alpha?": https://alpha.org/about/ (accessed 7th January 2020).

25 See Sanderson Jones, "About Sanderson Jones": http://sandersonjones.co/about-1 (accessed 7th January 2020).

26 The Sunday Assembly, "About Sunday Assembly."

27 The Sunday Assembly, "Litter Picking or Counting Penguins? #HelpOften Day 2016": www.sundayassembly.com/litter-picking-or-counting-penguins-helpoften-day-2016/ (accessed 7th January 2020).

28 The Sunday Assembly London, "Volunteer": www.sundayassemblylondon.com/volunteer/ (accessed 7th January 2020).

29 The Sunday Assembly, "About Sunday Assembly."

30 Ibid.

31 Jacqui Frost, "Rejecting Rejection Identities: Negotiating Positive Non-Religiosity at the Sunday Assembly," in Ryan Cragun, Lori Fazzino, and Christel Manning (eds.) *Organized Secularism in the United States: New Directions in Research* (Boston: De Gruyer, 2017), 174.
32 The Sunday Assembly, "Public Charter for the Sunday Assembly."
33 Brian Wheeler, "What Happens at an Atheist Church?," *BBC News Magazine*, 4th February 2013: www.bbc.co.uk/news/magazine-21319945 (accessed 7th January 2020).
34 The Sunday Assembly, "Public Charter for the Sunday Assembly."
35 Glide Church, "Mission and Values": www.glide.org/about (accessed 7th January 2020).
36 Ibid.
37 Sandhya Rani Jha, *Pre-Post-Racial America: Spiritual Stories from the Front Lines* (St. Louis: Chalice Press, 2015), 150.
38 The Sunday Assembly, "Frequently Asked Questions": https://sundayassembly.online/faqs/ (accessed 7th January 2020).
39 The Sunday Assembly, "About Sunday Assembly."
40 Real name used, with permission.
41 Sam Brown, email message to the author, 3rd August 2015.
42 The Examined Life is a project which "seeks to elicit and explore questions from some of today's most interesting thinkers." Each contributor is asked to "distil their concerns, passions or preoccupations into a single question that we should be asking ourselves."
43 Sanderson Jones, "Am I Living Life to the Full?," *The Examined Life*: http://examined-life.com/interviews/sanderson-jones/ (accessed 7th January 2020).
44 Faith Hill, "They Tried to Start a Church Without God: For a While, It Worked," *The Atlantic*, 21st July 2019: www.theatlantic.com/ideas/archive/2019/07/secular-churches-rethink-their-sales-pitch/594109/ (accessed 7th January 2020).
45 Ibid.
46 Ibid.

References

Addley, Esther. "Atheist Sunday Assembly Prepares for First 'Synod' as Expansion Continues." *The Guardian*. 29th April 2014. www.theguardian.com/world/2014/apr/29/atheist-sunday-assembly-first-synod
———. "'Not Believing in God Makes Life More Precious:' Meet the Atheist Churchgoers." *The Guardian*. 2nd February 2013. www.theguardian.com/world/2013/feb/03/atheist-church-sunday-assembly-islington
The Alpha Course. "What Is Alpha?" https://alpha.org/about/
Blunden, Mark. "Atheists Banned from Church Land." *The Evening Standard*. 29th April 2013. www.standard.co.uk/news/london/atheists-banned-from-church-land-8594364.html
Frost, Jacqui. "Rejecting Rejection Identities: Negotiating Positive Non-Religiosity at the Sunday Assembly." In *Organized Secularism in the United States: New Directions in Research*, edited by Ryan Cragun, Lori Fazzino, and Christel Manning, 171–190. Boston: De Gruyer, 2017.
GCSE (9–1). "Specification-Religious Studies (Short Course)." www.ocr.org.uk/Images/240624-specification-accredited-gcse-religious-studies-short-course-j125.pdf
Glide Church. "Mission and Values." www.glide.org/mission

Hill, Faith. "They Tried to Start a Church without God: For a While, It Worked." *The Atlantic*. 21st July 2019. www.theatlantic.com/ideas/archive/2019/07/secular-churches-rethink-their-sales-pitch/594109/

Jacobs, Emma. "'Church without God' Looks for New Ways of Funding Mission." *Financial Times*. 18th October 2013. www.ft.com/content/6f6fee48-3737-11e3-9603-00144feab7de?mhq5j=e6

Jha, Sandhya Rani. *Pre-Post-Racial America: Spiritual Stories from the Front Lines*. St. Louis: Chalice Press, 2015.

Jones, Sanderson. "About Sanderson Jones." http://sandersonjones.co/about-1

———. "Am I Living Life to the Full?" *The Examined Life*. http://examined-life.com/interviews/sanderson-jones/

McGrath, Alister. *Studies in Doctrine*. Grand Rapids: Zondervan, 1997.

Osakabe, Yutaka and Gagné, Isaac. "Non-Event Report: Why the Sunday Assembly Event Did Not Launch in Japan." *Non-Religion and Secularity Network*. https://blog.nsrn.net/2015/04/17/non-event-report-why-the-sunday-assembly-event-did-not-launch-in-japan/

Slavin, Stuart J., Schindler, Debra, Chibnall, John T., Fendell, Ginny, and Schloss, Mindy. "PERMA: A Model for Institutional Leadership and Culture Change." *Academic Medicine*. 87 (11), 2012.

The Sunday Assembly. "About Sunday Assembly." https://sundayassembly.online/about-sunday-assembly/

———. "Accreditation." www.sundayassembly.com/accreditation

———. "Frequently Asked Questions." https://sundayassembly.online/faqs/

———. "Litter Picking or Counting Penguins? #HelpOften Day 2016." www.sundayassembly.com/litter-picking-or-counting-penguins-helpoften-day-2016/

———. "An Open Letter to Housing Association Residents." www.sundayassembly.com/an-open-letter-to-housing-association-residents/

———. "Public Charter for the Sunday Assembly." www.sundayassembly.com/blog/public-charter-for-sunday-assembly

———. "We're Not Going to Hit Our Crowdfunding Target, and That's OK." www.sundayassembly.com/blog/were-not-going-to-hit-our-crowdfunding-target-and-thats-ok

The Sunday Assembly London. "Volunteer." www.sundayassemblylondon.com/volunteer/

Tomkins, Stephen. "Pippa Evans & Sanderson Jones Interview: How Great Thou Aren't." *Reform Magazine*. November 2013. www.reform-magazine.co.uk/2013/10/pippa-evans-sanderson-jones-interview-how-great-thou-arent/

Wheeler, Brian. "What Happens at an Atheist Church?" *BBC News Magazine*. 4th February 2013. www.bbc.co.uk/news/magazine-21319945

4 "The theologian and the atheist church"

Fieldwork at the Sunday Assembly

In this chapter, I turn to my qualitative research on the Sunday Assembly. I begin by discussing my rationale for doing qualitative research to find answers to a theological question, before introducing some reflexive points concerning my identity as a researcher who is white, a woman, and a Christian. I then move to describe how I went about collecting information at the Sunday Assembly, detailing the various methods and steps that were part of the data collection that underpins this work.

Doing qualitative research as a theologian

Because practical theology seeks to make sense of theological questions by way of human experience, and to "complexify" and explore social situations at a deeper level, it is an area in which other tools can be used to gain further insight about social phenomena. For this particular project, qualitative research methods were an indispensable part of the information-gathering process. Since no literature yet existed on the Sunday Assembly, the need to create data from scratch was pertinent at an early stage of the study design process. John Creswell describes qualitative research as:

> an inquiry process of understanding based on distinct methodological tradition of inquiry that explore a social or human problem. The researcher builds a complex, holistic picture, analyses words, reports detailed views of informants, and conducts the study in a natural setting.[1]

In addition, Zina O'Leary's definition points to the reliance of a qualitative approach on "words, images, experiences and observations that are not quantified."[2] Nonetheless, she explains that the term "qualitative," while related to assumptions of "multiple, constructed, subjective truths," is a loaded term, and one which points to a set of belief systems and value judgements.[3] O'Leary reasons that there is "a divide in the research world between those who accept chaos, complexity, the unknown and multiple realities, and those who do not."[4] Certainly, Swinton and Mowat acknowledge "areas of tension and apparent contradiction" between the respective epistemologies of practical theology that assume that truth is accessible through divine revelation and qualitative research, which is sceptical about the possibility of obtaining any kind of objective truth.[5] While the use of social-scientific methods for theological enquiry is becoming more widespread, how can practical theology, if it is to comprise *theological* reflection, make use of qualitative research in a way that is faithful to its own enterprise?[6] Swinton calls on theologians to "explore the implicit and explicit politics of their research, and to reflect on the significance of their allegiances to both theology and the social sciences."[7] As such, in what follows, I will reflect on the aforementioned epistemological tensions between theology and the social sciences.

Pete Ward notes that theologians are becoming more interested in "practice, culture and the embodied social nature of doctrine and the church." Yet, ironically, they have tended to avoid fieldwork. As a result, empirical research has been discussed by theologians as a theoretical practice, divorced from churches and communities.[8] However, Ward views qualitative research as an "evolving and shifting dialogical approach," which places attention on "the lived and the local."[9] Because of this, qualitative research can have particular significance for the ways in which theologians reflect on the church, and so its methods lend themselves to the practical theological approaches of critical enquiry and reflection.

Nevertheless, there are, as mentioned, points of tension between practical theology and qualitative research which are important to unpack. The presence of God in the research is an area of particular contestation. Because practical theology constitutes theological reflection, and because its practitioners are, for the most part, Christian, the whereabouts of faith and the habitation of the divine within the research are necessary to consider. However, this is not taken for granted within the structures and methods of qualitative research. Swinton suggests that practical theologians could introduce their own ways of reflecting on faith in their research, through reflexive practice and the introduction of prayer before and during the research.[10] This is something which practical theologians already engage in, but rarely acknowledge within the methods section of a research report. Swinton recalls an encounter he had with a researcher who was delivering a paper at a conference for hospital chaplains. The researcher explained that she would pray prior to interviews but added that she did not mention this in her written research, in case she did not get published.[11] In her case, the qualitative research methods took precedent. Moreover, Swinton considers the idea that theology has to be invisible for the benefit of "secular journals" looking for "unbiased" work. The issue here, for Swinton at least, is whether practical theology is considered to be overt or covert.

How, then, might such issues be addressed? There are several ways in which practical theologians have sought to address the tensions between theology and social-scientific methods. One approach is "mutual critical correlation," which stems from a Tillician understanding of the world and theology.[12] At its core, mutual critical correlation operates under the assumption that the world can provide answers to theological questions. Swinton describes it as a method which:

> sees the practical theological task as bringing situations into dialectical conversation with insights from the Christian tradition and perspectives drawn from other sources of knowledge (primarily in the social sciences).[13]

In sum, mutual critical correlation seeks to bring two dialogue partners together. Taking this at face value, such an approach appears to describe the pursuits and intentions of my work. However, there are several issues with a mutual critical correlative approach, which must be considered. For one, Swinton questions how "mutual" these conversations really are in practice. Sociology has a broader appeal, and so there is a danger that one conversation partner may be privileged over the other within this model.[14] Rather than a two-way dialogue, there is a risk that theology could be collapsed into the social sciences. Moreover, such correlative approaches are, suggests Swinton, normally sought by theologians. Sociological language is at home in theology, yet theological language (such as that concerning divine providence and prayer, as mentioned earlier), often has no place in sociology.[15] While theologians employing mutual critical correlative methodologies seek to work in both directions, sociologists do not have the same level of investment in theological research.

Swinton is not trying to claim that critical conversations between theology and the social sciences should be rejected. Rather, he is suggesting that theologians employing qualitative research:

> should approach the issue as theologians. Qualitative research should be perceived as occurring *within* a theological context, rather than theology speaking into a context that is already defined by qualitative methodology.[16]

Ultimately, for Swinton correlation supposes two sides which bear mutual relation.[17] Since he argues that this cannot be achieved in practice, he instead turns to the possibility of "sanctification" and "hospitality." The former involves qualitative methods being "blessed and set aside for a specific purpose." For Swinton, a theological bias is already at play within a practical theological investigation that makes use of qualitative methods, and so it is "not unreasonable to assume that theology should be the primary frame of reference" for the research process.[18] Another metaphor, in which Swinton holds together the tension of the theological and the social-scientific, is that of hospitality. Hospitality is, fundamentally, about respect and integrity. It does not require that parties pretend to agree with one another, nor does it entail the simplification of beliefs in order to have a "meaningful" discourse. Hospitality is an important Christian practice, and one which was prevalent in the ministry of Jesus, who moved fluidly from role to role without ceasing to the incarnate Son of God. Similarly, theology must be open to developing such an approach to the social sciences. Hospitality is key for bringing the two together, without affording one or the other too much emphasis.

Within this new framework, Swinton and Mowat devise a revised approach to mutual critical correlation, which allows practical theologians to continue to hold on to the reality of God's revelation *and* critically engage with other dialogue partners in ways that might be transformative for both. The first step concerns exploring the nature of current praxis, articulating the present situation, and explaining "what appears to be going on."[19] This process allows the practical theologian to articulate initial observations and identify the topics that will be explored in the research process. In this work, a provisional historical and cultural exploration of the problems of theodicy and the landscape of contemporary discourse regarding unbelief was presented in Chapters 1 and 2. The second step requires an analysis of the context, deepening the initial observations and reflections. For this study, I turned to the Sunday Assembly to "complexify" and shed light upon the issues at play. The third stage of Swinton and Mowat's revised outline concerns a theological reflection on that which has been discovered through research.[20] Theology is introduced in a more formal manner, and the theological significance of the data is handled overtly. Chapters 6 and 7 of this book will draw out some of the implicit and explicitly theological findings of my investigation.[21] The final step is the formulation of revised forms of practice, in which the cultural analysis from the beginning of the study is held together with the theological reflection, in order that new and original reflections on the situation may be revealed.[22] I conclude my research with some suggestions for the church concerning the revision of practice, in light of my findings. As evidenced, I largely adhere to Swinton and Mowat's four-point structure for practical theological research using qualitative methods.

Reflexivity and the "who" of the research

Before I explain how I did my research at the Sunday Assembly, and what I found there, it's worth taking some time to unpack the "baggage" I took with me into the field. In particular, it's important to note my position as a white, cisgender woman with Christian religious leanings.

In the 1980s and 1990s, the practice of ethnography underwent what Karen O'Reilly calls a "reflexive turn."[23] Awareness and discussion of the positionality of the field researcher, particularly with regards to gender and culture, became, for Sanar Kanafani and Zina Sawaf, "increasingly salient as a precondition *of* and *for* the analysis of and theorising about social experience."[24] In other words, the reflexive "turn" demanded that researchers examine and admit to "any combination of the filters we believe to be colouring our impression of the world, and through which others see us as we see them."[25] Further, as O'Reilly states, reflexivity in qualitative fieldwork involves thinking not only about: "who has conducted and written ethnographic research, how, and under what conditions" but "what impact these might have on the ethnography produced."[26] In what follows, I explore three reflexive points of consideration, relating specifically to my place within the research as a person who is white, a woman, and a Christian.

The Sunday Assembly as "white space": the white "who"

Whether looking to the organising committee or to the fringes of the Sunday Assembly, I was continually struck by the lack of racial diversity within the organisation. In an article for *The Spectator*, Andrew Watts describes the demographic of the London Assembly, which he visited in its early days, as "mostly white."[27] As a white person, afforded all of the societal benefits of white privilege, the outward effects of this upon my place in the research were, at least functionally, minimal. Yet the implications of the Sunday Assembly as "white space" deserve some further attention and exploration here, particularly since the majority of established congregations exist within large, multi-cultural cities.

Sociologist Elijah Anderson explains that "For Black people in particular, white spaces vary in kind, but their most visible and distinctive feature is their overwhelming presence of white people and their absence of Black people."[28] What makes the Sunday Assembly a "white space"? In both London and Edinburgh, the majority of the organising committee and almost the entire congregations were white. This was particularly noticeable during the recruitment stage. All 30 of my interview participants were white. While my sample reflects something of the diversity of Sunday Assembly experience, including that of organisers, regular attendees, and those who exist on the fringes of the organisation, and while it is balanced in its inclusion with regards to gender, sexuality, and other protected categories (including disability), it does not reflect the experiences of any Black or minority attendees in London or Edinburgh.[29]

How might the racial homogeneity of the Sunday Assembly be accounted for, particularly in such a multi-cultural city as London? Anderson argues that, overwhelmingly, white neighbourhoods, schools, workplaces, restaurants, and other public spaces remain, and that these spaces are perceived by Black and other minority groups to be informally "off limits."[30] While his work concerns "American society and culture" first and foremost, his conclusions are applicable to other "white urbanities," including places such as London. It is possible that the Sunday Assembly may have been informally marked as "white space" by Black and minority ethnic groups, either on account of its speakers, subject matter, or images prevalent in the mainstream media, which show the Sunday Assembly's congregation to be primarily white.[31] However, as a white person entering a "white space," I am aware that I cannot account for this, since any trepidation I felt about attending the Sunday Assembly would not stem from racial "othering."

A further point for consideration is the fact that atheism and non-religion are philosophical spaces which are also primarily white. Pew Research Centre's 2014 Religious Landscape Study found that 78% of atheists in the US were Caucasian.[32] *Guardian* journalist Adam Lee points out that "major atheist and humanist organisations" have begun a concerted effort to reach out to Black, Asian, and Hispanic communities, taking active roles in Black Lives Matter and other civil rights protests.[33] Nevertheless, any shift towards greater inclusion appears to be stuck at student level and has not had a discernible impact upon larger organisations such as the Sunday Assembly.

All of this could account for the lack of diversity amongst participants within this study. However, it is possible that my own research methods may potentially have contributed to the homogeneous sample I gathered. In particular, my decision to employ "snowball" techniques of recruitment could have made it more difficult to reach non-white members. Pranee Liamputtong points out that such methods are limited since they tend to attract "individuals who resemble each other."[34] Having spoken with nine members of the Assembly in London and three in Edinburgh, all of whom were white, the decision to rely on them for assistance in further recruitment may have had the adverse effect of "limiting the diversity"[35] of participants. Ultimately, Liamputtong's suggestion is an important one. In reflexive terms, this could have had an impact on the study as a whole. More widely speaking, however, it could be said that diversity of participants would ultimately have been impossible to attain, simply due to a lack of racial diversity within the movement as a whole.

Fieldwork and the woman "who"

The practice of reflexive thinking in ethnographic research was, in part, historically emboldened by feminist and post-colonial strains of scholarship. In addition to its emphasis on reflexivity, Faye Harrison suggests that ethnography lends suitable criteria to a feminist lens and approach to research, including an emphasis on the experiential, a "contextual and interpersonal approach to knowledge" and attention to the concrete realm of everyday life and human agency.[36] Further, ethnography can be conducted with the "empathy, connectedness, dialogue, and mutual conscious-raising" central (but not exclusive) to a feminist approach.[37] But while the processes of ethnographic fieldwork are, theoretically, compatible with a feminist outlook, the field into which women enter is still located in a world which remains significantly hostile to womankind. As such, the women ethnographer may simultaneously experience both advantages and disadvantages relating to gender in the field of study. Indeed, with regards to this study, I found that my gender had a profound impact on the data collection process in both directions.

R. F. Ellen suggests that "the lone female worker is usually (but not always) better placed than the single male worker."[38] For Ellen, women can be seen as less of a threat to the host society, and can therefore obtain greater accessibility to "domains of discourse."[39] I found this to be true within my own research, wherein obtaining access to the social gatherings, informal meetups, and extra-curricular activities of the Sunday Assembly was particularly straightforward. In addition, at the organisation's International Conference, I found that I was afforded a great deal of personal information in ethnographic conversations and short interviews.[40] This was particularly pronounced while working alongside Josh, a male sociologist collecting information on the Sunday Assembly for his own PhD study. Adam and Frances, two members from San Diego, spoke with me at length about the way in which the untimely death of a young man on their organising team had impacted their community. I was trusted with Phil's harrowing story of drug abuse and recovery, and his subsequent involvement at the Sunday Assembly in Reading. I spoke face to face with Carmen, who shared her experiences of bereavement, family illness, health problems, and unemployment.

On our second night in Utrecht, I found myself alone with Josh, my fellow researcher, and Daniel, a member of one of the small satellite Assemblies near London. We proceeded to conduct a short and informal ethnographic conversation with Daniel. While Josh was afforded some glimpses into the structural makeup of the Assembly, and some supplementary factual information regarding demographics, I was able to speak to Daniel about his own personal experiences of the Assembly, and how he felt about the organisation as a whole. Using feminist methodologies of listening, empathy, and mutual conscious-raising, I was able to ask more sensitive questions, which yielded rich and insightful data about Daniel's own experiences of loneliness at the Sunday Assembly, as well as his perception of the power structures at play within the organisation. O'Reilly explains that feminist critical ethnographies are intended to "give voice to the voiceless."[41] In this particular situation, my gender and feminist approach created a space in which Daniel could speak honestly about his concerns. This was especially observable, given that I had the opportunity to watch Daniel being questioned by a male researcher immediately beforehand.

Nevertheless, my gender did afford some limitations to the ethnographic encounter. Mariana Rios Sandoval, who undertook a qualitative study of constructions of fatherhood and masculinity in Mexico City, explains the sense of trepidation she felt at the prospect of interviewing men alone:

> Early in the fieldwork, I thought of interviewing men who were total strangers to me. . . . I confess that safety was always at the back of my mind.

Fearing for her personal safety as a lone female, Sandoval elected to conduct all of her interviews in public. I harboured similar anxieties, and so would routinely suggest to participants that we met and conducted our interview in a public space. In the few cases that this was not possible, I made sure to communicate my whereabouts and intentions to a third party beforehand. During the recruitment process, I lost three potential male participants in London as a direct consequence of my request to meet in a public place. While this sacrifice did have the unfortunate effect of lengthening the recruitment process by a number of weeks, it was worthwhile to protect my safety as a lone female (especially after one respondent became aggressive and challenged my "right to insist" on a public location).

The issue of gender in qualitative research was exacerbated for Terry Arendell in her study on divorce. She describes how some respondents sought to "take charge" of the interview straightaway, seeking to "instruct" her on the reality of being a divorced father, "about which I, as a woman, was no doubt uninformed or misinformed."[42] Additionally, the topic created some points of interaction in which male respondents would speak forcefully of their betrayal by women to Arendell, the interviewer. While my particular focus didn't create any discernible points of contention, I described feeling "vulnerable," "disrespected," and even "patronised" during several of the interviews conducted with male participants in my field journal. When interviewing with Bill, a member of the organising team at Sunday Assembly London, I found that he attempted to "steer" the conversation on a number of occasions, raising and replying to his own, rhetorical questions, while refusing to engage with my research questions. When I raised my central query (regarding the Assembly's responses to suffering), Bill remarked: "That's not the kind of thing I thought a young woman like you would be interested in!" When I asked the question for a second time, Bill reiterated: "Come on, now. That's a bit dark, for a woman." Ultimately, he did not answer my question. Tony, who I interviewed in his own home, attempted to have me rephrase several of my research questions. When I asked him about his personal engagement with the Sunday Assembly's motto, Tony replied: "I'd rather talk about what we do at Sunday Assembly than what it all *means*." Further, Tony took exception to a question that I asked in relation to the Assembly's use of church-like structures, stating firmly: "It isn't a church," before engaging in a lengthy explanation of Church history in England. Despite being aware that he was speaking with a researcher well-versed in theology, Tony made several suggestions for further, basic reading in this area. Jack, another key figure in the London Assembly, routinely intervened before I had finished talking, spoke over me when I was asking questions, and ignored my attempts to prevent his tangential explanations. When I attempted to regain control of our interview and steer him back towards the questions, Jack remarked: "Ok, alright. I'm used to having women nag me like this!" In two of the previous interactions (Bill and Jack), gender dynamics in the interview setting are explicitly referred to. In the third (Tony), they are implied through patronising language.

While gender had the positive effect of allowing me to probe difficult questions with participants, and to gain rich, insightful data of a personal nature quickly and efficiently, my place as a woman in the research did impact upon the recruitment process, the organisation of interviews, and, to some extent, the dynamic within the interview setting.

A Christian in an "atheist church": the religious "who"

Another aspect of my identity as a researcher, concerns my position as a Christian in a non-religious setting. Having made a theological case for researching a non-religious community (outlined in previous chapters), I did not foresee any particular issues. Indeed, my decision not to hide my identity during the first batch of interviews and observation did not provoke any concerns amongst respondents in London.[43] Nonetheless, I noticed that my religious identity was more of an issue for research participants in Edinburgh, and for those that I met from international Assemblies.

As part of my first field visit to Edinburgh, I delivered a short talk on my research, touching on the challenges of doing a PhD and the phenomenon of "imposer syndrome" in academia. Afterwards, I was approached by Klaus, a member of the organising committee. Klaus began by telling me how much he had appreciated my talk, but the conversation quickly moved towards my position as a theologian and a Christian. He pressed me on my reasons for engaging with the Sunday Assembly and asked if I had chosen to talk about "imposter syndrome" because I was "an imposter in the Sunday Assembly." Klaus added that he was "suspicious" of my research and wary of my intentions. Despite my efforts to reassure him that my presence at the Assembly was not missional, that I had permission to be there, and that I only intended to gather information for my research, Klaus relayed his concerns to several other attendees that day. Later, while recruiting interview participants in Edinburgh, two potential respondents declined to take part in this study, citing Klaus's warnings as the source of their apprehension. In this respect, my decision to answer questions regarding my religious views honestly had some impact on the recruitment process.

In general, I maintained full transparency with participants, taking the opportunity to explain what exactly the study of theology entails, and, if asked directly, I would touch briefly (and purely factually) on my own Christian background. This was the case for all but one interviewee. I made the decision to withhold information regarding my religious affiliation from Robert, a long-term attendee of the Edinburgh Assembly. I connected with Robert through Agnes, and, over email, we arranged an interview. I noted that I would have the opportunity to meet Robert before our interview took place, as I would be attending the Edinburgh Assembly on a field visit the weekend before. Robert brought a note for me on the day of the Assembly, comprising two A4 sides of hand-written text, entitled "The death of religion is certain." He explained that he had written me some notes about why the Sunday Assembly was growing and added that he had some books to bring for me about "the decay of the church" next time. Robert told me that he was a "former clergyman" from an evangelical tradition, and that, since leaving the church two decades previously, he had become a strongly convicted atheist. Taking into consideration my apprehensions about interviewing as a lone female, as well as Robert's direct communication of his disdain for religion, I made the conscious decision to withhold information about my religious background from him. There were still reasons to interview Robert, however. I was interested in finding out more about his reasons for leaving the church, and about his place in the Assembly as a former minister. Before the interview, I asked Robert if he had read the study outline. He had and was unconcerned about the subject matter. When we got started, it became evident that he had not become aware of my background, particularly since he asked me repeatedly if I would be interested in setting up a Sunday Assembly congregation myself.

A short entry from my field journal regarding Klaus and Robert points to my concern that my position as a Christian may affect the data gathering exercise in Edinburgh:

> Klaus was very inquisitive, made me feel a bit uncomfortable. I was worried, too, about what Robert might say if he found out. Worried either of them could have "blown my cover." I don't want them finding out I've got a Christian background, not because I'm embarrassed or ashamed or feel like I couldn't talk about it, but because I can guess what their perception of that will be, and whether they'll still want to talk with me afterwards.

Ultimately, I was able to recruit and interview eight participants from Edinburgh without any great difficulty. Nonetheless, the "overt" approach I took to disclosing my identity in the field became ever more precarious at the Assembly's international conference, where international delegates, particularly from North America, proved to harbour a deep-set aversion to, and even hatred of, religion. During dinner on the first evening, I found myself at a restaurant with several members of the London Assembly, and some others from the international chapters. Amongst their number was Ari, from the US. Ari took every opportunity to steer the conversation towards religion, and in particular, her anger at the Bible, which she described as being "full of lies." Nick from London, seemingly emboldened by Ari's comments, intercepted with some stirring opinions about the future of Christianity in Britain, and his hope that church attendance and belief would "completely die."

The next morning, I attended a workshop about the Sunday Assembly brand, led by the organisation's Chief Community Creator. During the workshop, which was attended by a roughly even number of American and British delegates, a cultural divide between the US and the UK regarding attitudes towards religion became apparent. While British members acknowledged "the presence of people of faith" at their meetings, American attendees described the Assembly as a place for "atheists" and "sceptics." Nathan from Nashville explained that de-conversion experiences in the American context are a "part of people's narratives." His remark invited several more polemic comments from other delegates about the "dangers of religion" and their desires not to include anyone still practising religion at their Assemblies. The London organisers quickly stepped in to moderate these comments, stressing the organisation's commitment to "radical inclusivity" and pressing for a more nuanced and less polarised debate.

Later, I spoke with Nathan one on one. He explained that, in states such as Tennessee and Utah, the Sunday Assembly provides support for people "recovering from religion" with "life after faith" groups. For Nathan, the social polarisation of faith and unbelief in the US context could account for some of the forceful comments of his fellow American delegates. In his mind, it was a form of self-preservation. However, as I made to leave, Nathan added: "I wouldn't have a Christian—any kind of Christian—in my Assembly, ever, under any circumstances." Knowing that he was aware of my position, I asked Nathan if he would have allowed me access to his community for research purposes. "You're a Christian?" he asked, rhetorically. "Then, no."

While the attitudes of American delegates did not have any particular impact upon my recruitment, or upon the results of my study, the differences between assemblies on both sides of the Atlantic were clearly perceptible. What united international delegates was a shared emphasis on community. What divided them was *who* should be included in that community. While this difference in opinion may be accounted for by the differing sociological positions of religion in the US and Europe, it may also be symptomatic of the Assembly's evolution of rhetoric. As explained, the Assembly has undergone changes to its official language and branding as a result of rapid expansion. In 2013, it was introduced as an "atheist church." Later, in order to distance itself from more vocal and active strains of atheism, the Assembly re-branded itself a "godless congregation." In 2016, it modified this statement once more, moving from "godless" to "secular" congregation. The explanation given for this final change was simply the adoption of a policy of "radically inclusivity." In the Assembly's "Tone of Voice" document, there is a specific guideline which reads: "[We do] not speak specifically about atheism (or any religion) . . . in order to retain [the] important value of radical inclusivity."[44] Particularly in the UK, the Assembly is attempting to be sensitive to on-going social and cultural connections with religion, and as such, the term "godless" does not fit as well with their ethos. This might go some way to explaining why I did not encounter any issues regarding my religious identity in London. It does not, however, account for the attitudes of Klaus and Robert in Edinburgh, whose reactions were at odds with the wider views of that particular chapter.

The theologian at the atheist church: research at the Sunday Assembly

I now move to discuss how I gathered data at the Sunday Assembly in London, Edinburgh, and at an international meeting. For the most part, the story of my research will be presented here in chronological order. However, in order to explain and expound upon each step in the research process in detail, it will be necessary to move back and forth across the timeline of the research.

Initial contact

I made contact with the Sunday Assembly through Linda Woodhead, a British Sociologist of Religion, who acted as a third-party in the initial contact I made with the Sunday Assembly. I met Linda at a talk she gave at Greenbelt Festival in August 2014. Upon speaking with her after the talk, I mentioned my intention to study the Sunday Assembly as part of my doctoral work. Linda asked if I had already been in contact with the organisation, and when I told her I had not, she offered to put me in touch with Sanderson Jones, the co-founder of the Sunday Assembly. Linda had become acquainted with Sanderson after giving a talk on the theme of ritual at the London Assembly in 2013.

After being introduced by Linda via email, Sanderson and I made plans to speak over the phone about my study. In our initial exchange of emails, Sanderson asked me to send him my research proposal, and raised the possibility of:

> align[ing] some of [the] research objectives with [Sunday Assembly] research objectives—finding out about how Sunday Assembly changes people lives, finding out about impact we have etc.[45]

I did not commit to this but rather sent him a projected outline of my research interests. Upon reading that I was interested in the Sunday Assembly's responses to suffering, Sanderson replied affirmatively, writing that the study was: "something that we would love to be involved with." He added: "We are very much looking to help people with their issues and suffering and I hope your work would show that."[46] Sanderson circulated some information about the study via email to a chosen group of people that he described as "Sunday Assembly regulars." Seven replied, and I was able to set up some initial interviews via email. It's pertinent to note that the first round of recruitment in London was fairly controlled by the Assembly leadership. Sanderson was able to choose who to direct me to, and in doing so, could (technically) ensure that I spoke primarily to people who he understood to have vested interests in the preservation and promotion of the Sunday Assembly.

Having completed the first round of research interviews, I began to doubt the level of authenticity that data gathered exclusively from the London Assembly would provide. That which made the London Assembly an ideal place to begin an enquiry also contributes to its "position of privilege," in the words of Jack,[47] a long-term London attendee. The international reach of the central London congregation is unique; no other regional assemblies can claim such influence in the Sunday Assembly's global network. The presence of the movement's founders, while a useful starting point for my study, set London apart from other chapters, as well. Several interviewees remarked that Sanderson's particular qualities, including his "effervescent character" and "strong performance skills," were not just integral to the identity of the movement but key to the success of the London chapter. Unlike Sanderson, leaders at regional Assemblies do not have the benefit of working at their Assembly full-time. These factors influenced my decision to expand my study to include a regional congregation. My intention was to make sure that data gathered through interviews and observation was representative of the Sunday Assembly as a whole, and not just its London hub. In widening my study to include data from smaller, local Assemblies, I made the decision to look closer to my base of study in Aberdeen for a second research site. In Scotland, the only regularly running Assembly was in Edinburgh. Sanderson passed my contact details on to Agnes, who at the time was the chair of Sunday Assembly Edinburgh. Agnes in turn emailed me to invite me along to their next Sunday meeting.

Within this study, Sanderson and Agnes assumed the roles of "gatekeepers." In qualitative research terms, these are individuals "who have the power to influence, to grant or to refuse access to a field or research setting."[48] Gatekeepers control or limit researcher's access to participants.[49] In the event that the researcher comes from outwith the organisation or community that they intend to study, gatekeepers have the power to control how exactly who and what the researcher has admittance to. It's worth noting that Sanderson and Agnes had a significant degree of control over the distribution of my study information and therefore, over my initial recruitment processes. Because of this, initial interviewees were often members of organising committees in both London and Edinburgh. It was useful to speak with those who were intimately involved with the organisation and its inner sanctums, but having done so, I turned to new and less regular attendees through a process of "snowball sampling"[50] in order to ensure a variety of perspectives on the organisation.

Interviews

I interviewed 30[51] members of the Sunday Assembly congregations in London and Edinburgh. Interviews were semi-structured and, for the most part, lasted between 45 minutes and an hour. This particular format of interviewing is used within qualitative research projects to gather focused, qualitative textual data. One particular strength of the semi-structured format is that it allows the interviewer both the flexibility of an open-ended line of questioning, and the focus of a structured conversation, which can yield data closely relevant to the leading questions of the investigation. Depending on the particular study, questions and their sequencing may be strictly predetermined, or the interviewer may rely on her own "judgement and tact"[52] to decide how closely to adhere to her guide and how much to follow up the answers of interviewees in any direction that they may lead. For this study, I prepared an interview script in advance. Participants were asked questions such as: "How long have you been attending the Sunday Assembly for?" and "What were your first impressions of the Sunday Assembly?" When ordering questions, I chose to begin with simpler topics like these, moving towards more sensitive and complex issues later on.

Observation

In addition to research interviews, my decision to study a new and burgeoning social movement prompted the use of field observation. For this study, observation took place primarily at Sunday Assembly events in London and Edinburgh. In addition, I had the opportunity to attend a number of Sunday Assembly socials in both locations, as well as extra-curricular or interest groups, including the London Yoga Group, the South London Book Group, and rehearsals for the London Assembly band. I later attended the Assembly's international gathering in Utrecht in the Netherlands, where I had the opportunity to observe some more.

Through presence and participation in the field, the ethnographic researcher has the opportunity to observe, and to view "how meanings emerge through talk and collective action, how understandings and interpretations change over time, and how these changes shape subsequent actions."[53] Indeed, the researcher may choose to adopt a highly participatory role during data collection, performing activities that are central to the lives of those studied.[54] Nonetheless, even with this kind of intensive participation, Robert Emersen, Rachel Fretz, and Linda Shaw recognise that "the ethnographer never becomes a member in the same sense that those who are "naturally" in the setting are members."[55] As the ethnographer engages in the lives of those that she is studying, she does not escape her own worldview and bias. In other words, reflexive practice is crucial; the researcher must note where their actions, or circumstances outwith their control, may have impacted data collection. For Swinton and Mowat, a "careful record of the data collection process" can support this.[56]

I kept multiple field journals throughout my study, in which I would note what I had observed and experienced while working in the field. Written records of "the observations, jottings, full notes, intellectual ideas, and emotional reflections that are created during the fieldwork process" are widely referred to as "field notes."[57] Selectivity and inherent bias are to be expected in the practice of field note construction. The field researcher cannot become a completely detached and neutral observer, who is outwith and independent of the phenomena they are studying, and as such, field notes often "select and emphasise different features and actions while ignoring and marginalising others."[58] This was true of my own research. As a theologian, I was interested in, and especially alert to, any mentions of church, or former faith.

In some ways, this was to be expected; the research in this book is grounded in practical theology, and so information regarding comparisons with the Church were especially pertinent.

Field notes can help the researcher point to their place within the research in a reflexive manner. The field journal has an analytic function, alerting the researcher to feelings and emotions that participants in the field may share.[59] O'Reilly adds that the use of a research diary helps to "retain the perspective of the stranger, guarding against merging instead of immersion."[60] My field journal contained a number of jottings about my position as a practical theologian and a Christian studying a "godless" congregation. I found that these were fewer when visiting Assemblies in London and Edinburgh, given the emphasis at UK Assemblies on "not speaking specifically about atheism (or any religion) . . . in order to retain [the] important value of radical inclusivity."[61] Nonetheless, at the international conference, when exposed to a series of spontaneous negative remarks about religion, I used my field journal to process my position as an "outsider." Here is a short extract, in which I draw together my own feelings on the events of the day with a scriptural reference:

> In Utrecht, there are a lot of heavy-handed comments about religion and how pointless it all is. . . . Didn't think this would have much of an impact since I've been doing this a while, but it's been hard to listen to at times. After a really hard morning, I went for a walk on my own to the Domtoren (the Cathedral Tower). It's a really beautiful building, and you can see it from all across the city. Having it there as a kind of vantage point reminded me (loosely) of Psalm 121: "I lift my eyes to the hills; from where does help come? My help comes from the God, the maker of heaven and earth." More than once since, I've looked up towards the *Domtoren* and listened for the church bells. I suppose in a way it does make me feel less alone.

Conversations, webinars, and documents

In addition to research interviews and field notes from observational activities, I was afforded the opportunity to speak with a large number of Assembly attendees on a more informal basis. In doing so, I undertook a series of "ethnographic conversations," or what David Fetterman terms "informal interviews."[62] Fetterman explains that such conversations are intended to gather intelligence from members of the studied community, and not to confirm research hypotheses. During these exchanges, the ethnographer is not looking for specific information, but the outcome of these may inform the kind of topics that the researcher follows up or highlights in structured interviews later on. The researcher asks the informant questions, but is led by them, and doesn't ask leading or directive questions. Conversations can happen in the environment as and when they arise, and do not have to be pre-arranged or under any set time constrictions. They can be recorded, or notes can be taken afterwards. I engaged in approximately 50 or so ethnographic conversations in London, Edinburgh, and Utrecht, and these supplemented (and in some instances corroborated) information gathered in interviews and via observation.

In addition to these further conversations, I was invited by a member of the organising team in London to join the Sunday Assembly Everywhere (SAE) Network's monthly webinars. Webinars are seminars or other presentations conducted over the internet. The format allows participants in different locations to see and hear the presenter and ask questions. The SAE webinars were, for a time, publicly accessible but largely unheard of outwith an exclusive group of facilitators who have regular contact with the Sunday Assembly's head office in London. They were largely "attended" by the organisers of international Assemblies, and those looking to attain official accreditation for their Assemblies. In order to collect further data for this project, I signed up to attend the monthly webinars that ran between June and December of 2016. Each webinar lasted for one hour. The format varied, but most began with updates from Assemblies around the world. Thereafter, there would be training for network members, or a short talk or seminar by an invited "expert." For example, in June 2016, the speaker was Michael Price from Brunel University, who has conducted a longitudinal quantitative study of wellbeing in relation to Sunday Assembly attendance. During each webinar, I took notes just as I would during field observation.

In addition, I had access to a series of internal documents, provided by the London organising team. The Sunday Assembly Brand Strategy document (Draft, 2014) outlined the organisation's core brand elements and provided guidance for new assemblies regarding regional advertising and promotion. The Assembly also allowed me access to a copy of their "Tone of Voice" document. Described as "evolving," this was (at the time of study) being updated by members of the Assembly's primary organising team in London. The document instructed member assemblies on how to "speak" on behalf of the brand and included details regarding "How to describe the Sunday Assembly," as well as how to respond to official emails and correspondence. At the international conference, I was also able to access the Assembly's Annual Report Preview for 2015, the first report of its kind. The report highlighted major events from the global Sunday Assembly network which took place in 2015, including Wilderness Festival, Yule Rock (a winter celebration in London), and Global "Help Often" Day. It also included details of monthly global attendance, as well as Assembly accounts.[63]

These documents provided additional insight into the everyday life and workings of the organisation. At times, they were useful as reference guides to the official position of the Assembly, particularly where attendees were unsure about the official stance on a certain issue. However, these documents were limited by the Assembly's on-going change in strategy and the continuing developments of its aims and outlook. Since Assembly leaders did not plan for the organisation to grow so rapidly, the organising team has had to adapt quickly, writing policy and guidelines in an impromptu manner, as the Assembly continued to expand in "stature, ambition, and scale."[64] As the Assembly matured into an international movement, it had to modify its language and terminology, as well as the official accreditation processes for allowing new assemblies to join the network. It is, therefore, difficult to trace all aspects of the organisation's development and outlook through its internal literature. As of 2020, the link I was provided to the "Tone of Voice" document no longer works and other files are likely out of date.

Conclusion

In conclusion, this chapter has presented a description of the key methods used to collect data as part of this investigation. I have drawn attention to some reflexive claims, which should be seen to underpin the data set during analysis and later theological comment on them. I have also addressed some of the relevant aspects of my researcher identity, which impacted upon the data collection process, as well as underpinning my approach to, and place in, the research as whole. By introducing reflexive considerations, I have tried to illustrate my awareness of the effects of my identity on the research, as well as other factors which may have influenced the creation of data and findings. This concludes my discussion of research methodology, and I move now to explicate my findings on the Sunday Assembly in more detail.

Notes

1 John W. Creswell, *Qualitative Enquiry and Research Design: Choosing among Five Traditions* (London: SAGE, 1998), 15.
2 Zina O'Leary, *The Essential Guide to Doing Your Research Project*, Third Edition (London: SAGE, 2017), 8.
3 Ibid.
4 John Swinton and Harriet Mowat, *Practical Theology and Qualitative Research*, Second Edition (London: SCM Press, 2016), 9.
5 Ibid. 73.
6 Ibid. ix.
7 John Swinton, "'Where Is Your Church?' Moving toward a Hospitable and Sanctified Ethnography," in Pete Ward (ed.) *Perspectives on Ecclesiology and Ethnography* (Cambridge: W. B. Eerdmans, 2012), 74.
8 Pete Ward in Pete Ward (ed.) *Perspectives on Ecclesiology and Ethnography* (Cambridge: W. B. Eerdmans, 2012), 1.
9 Ward, 7, 9.
10 Swinton in Ward, 85.
11 Ibid.
12 Paul Tillich suggests a straight correlational methodology in which experience raises questions and theology provides answers. Methods of mutual critical correlation have their roots in Tillich's method of correlation. See Paul Tillich, *Systematic Theology*, Vol. 1 (London: SCM Press, 1951) and Daniel L. Migliore, *Faith Seeking Understanding: An Introduction to Christianity* (Grand Rapids: Wm B. Eerdmans, 2004), 17.

13 Swinton in Ward, 86.
14 Ibid. 86–87.
15 Ibid. 87.
16 Ibid.
17 Ibid. 92.
18 Ibid.
19 Swinton and Mowat, 90.
20 Ibid.
21 Ibid. 91.
22 Ibid. 92.
23 Karen O'Reilly, *Key Concepts in Ethnography* (London: SAGE, 2009), 187.
24 Samar Kanafani and Zina Sawaf, "Being, Doing and Knowing in the Field: Reflections on Ethnographic Practice in the Arab Region," *Contemporary Levant*, 2 (1), 2017, 5.
25 Ibid.
26 O'Reilly, 187.
27 Andrew Watts, "The Church of Self-Worship: Sunday Morning with the Atheists," *The Spectator*, 22nd February 2014: www.spectator.co.uk/2014/02/so-tell-me-about-your-faith-journey-sunday-morning-at-the-atheist-church/ (accessed 7th January 2020).
28 Elijah Anderson, "The White Space," *Sociology of Race and Ethnicity*, 1 (1), 2015, 11.
29 My sample does contain several Black and Hispanic participants, who took part in ethnographic conversations for this study. However, these participants came from international Assemblies, primarily in the US.
30 Anderson, 19.
31 Ibid.
32 Pew Research Centre, "Racial and Ethnic Composition: Racial and Ethnic Composition by Religious Group," in *Pew Research Centre Religious Landscape Study*, 2014: www.pewforum.org/religious-landscape-study/racial-and-ethnic-composition/ (accessed 7th January 2020).
33 Adam Lee, "Finally: Atheists Are No Longer Just Old White Men," *The Guardian*, 3rd May 2015: www.theguardian.com/commentisfree/2015/may/03/finally-atheists-are-no-longer-just-old-white-men (accessed 7th January 2020).
34 Pranee Liamputtong, *Performing Qualitative Cross-Cultural Research* (Cambridge: Cambridge University Press, 2011), 70–71.
35 Ibid. 70.
36 Faye V. Harrison, "Feminist Methodology as a Tool for Ethnographic Inquiry on Globalization," in Nandini Gunewardena and Ann E. Kingsolver (eds.) *The Gender of Globalization: Women Navigating Cultural and Economic Marginalities* (Santa Fe: SAR, 2007), 24.
37 Ibid.
38 R. F. Ellen, *Ethnographic Research: A Guide to General Conduct* (London: Academic Press, 1987), 124.
39 Ibid.
40 Real name used, with permission.
41 O'Reilly, 65.
42 Terry Arendell, "Reflections on the Researcher-Researched Relationship: A Woman Interviewing Men," *Qualitative Sociology*, 20 (3), 1997, 350.
43 Participants were made aware of my position as a theologian in advance of interviews, via a Participant Information Sheet, containing important information about the study, its intentions, and my academic background.
44 Sunday Assembly, "Tone of Voice," Document, 2.
45 Sanderson Jones, email message to the author, 2nd October 2014.

46 Sanderson Jones, email message to the author, 10th October 2014.

47 Note that the names of all participants in this study, with the exception of Sanderson, are referred to by pseudonyms to protect their anonymity.

48 B. L. Berg and H. Lune, *Qualitative Research Methods for Social Scientists* (Boston: Allyn & Baker, 2004), 24.

49 O'Reilly, 70.

50 Social scientist Robert Yin describes the process of snowballing as involving the selection of new participants for a study through existing ones: "In the course of an interview, you might learn of other persons who can be interviewed. The snowballing occurs when you follow such a lead, and let those new ones result in identifying yet other possible interviewees." Snowballing techniques can be particularly useful in assisting the researcher to broaden the scope of the study. However, Yin cautions that such methods should be used carefully. Researchers must distinguish between having "a purposive reason (e.g., a prospective interviewee is thought to have additional information relevant to your study) and having only a convenience reason (e.g., the prospective interviewee happens to be around and has a free hour to talk with you)." Within this study, snowball sampling proved to be particularly helpful, since I was an outsider to the group, did not attend regularly, did not consider myself to be a member of either community, and did not have physical access to the Sunday Assembly congregation in London on a regular basis. See Robert K. Yin, *Qualitative Research from Start to Finish* (New York: The Guilford Press, 2016), 95.

51 Twenty-two participants were affiliated with the Edinburgh congregation, and eight with the Edinburgh congregation.

52 Steinar Kvale and Svend Brinkmann, *Interviews: Learning the Craft of Qualitative Research Interviewing*, Second Edition (London: SAGE, 2009), 130.

53 Robert Emerson, Rachel Fretz, and Linda Shaw, *Writing Ethnographic Fieldnotes*, Second Edition (Chicago: University of Chicago Press, 2011), 5.

54 I previously outlined a number of Sunday Assembly activities that I became involved in, particularly at the international conference in Utrecht, including (but not limited to): taking part in games, singing, socialising with other members, attending seminars, and partaking in small group discussion. Since these are activities that form the basis of Assembly life, they pertain to what Patricia Adler and Peter Adler describe as a "highly participatory role" for the ethnographer examining community life. See Patricia Adler and Peter Adler, *Membership Roles in Field Research* (London: SAGE, 1987), 40.

55 Emerson, Fretz, and Shaw, *Writing Ethnographic Fieldnotes*, 5.

56 Swinton and Mowat, 70.

57 O'Reilly.

58 Emerson, Fretz, and Shaw, 9.

59 John Loftland, David Snow, Leon Anderson, and Lyn H. Loftland, *Analyzing Social Settings: A Guide to Qualitative Observation and Analysis*, Fourth Edition (Belmont: Wadsworth, 2006), 179.

60 O'Reilly, 75.

61 Direct quotation from a member of the Sunday Assembly London in a branding meeting at the International Conference in Utrecht.

62 David Fetterman, "Ethnography," in Leonard Bickman and Debra J. Rog (eds.) *The SAGE Handbook of Applied Social Research Methods*, Second Edition (London: SAGE, 2009).

63 Despite asking the Sunday Assembly leadership and contacts within the organisation for an up-to-date version of this report, I have been unable to locate one. It is possible that such a report does not exist, at least in the same format of that produced in 2015/16.

64 Sunday Assembly Annual Report Preview 2015, 1.

References

Adler, Patricia and Adler, Peter. *Membership Roles in Field Research*. London: SAGE, 1987.

Anderson, Elijah. "The White Space." *Sociology of Race and Ethnicity*. 1 (1), 2015: 10–21.

Arendell, Terry. "Reflections on the Researcher-Researched Relationship: A Woman Interviewing Men." *Qualitative Sociology*. 20 (3), 1997: 341–368.

Berg, B. L. and Lune, H. *Qualitative Research Methods for Social Scientists*. Boston: Allyn & Baker, 2004.

Creswell, John W. *Qualitative Enquiry and Research Design: Choosing among Five traditions*. London: SAGE, 1998.

Ellen, R. F. *Ethnographic Research: A Guide to General Conduct*. London: Academic Press, 1987.

Emerson, Robert, Fretz, Rachel, and Shaw, Linda. *Writing Ethnographic Fieldnotes*. Second Edition. Chicago: University of Chicago Press, 2011.

Fetterman, David. "Ethnography." In *The Sage Handbook of Applied Social Research Methods*. Second Edition, edited by Leonard Bickman and Debra J. Rog, 543–588. London: SAGE, 2009.

Harrison, Faye V. "Feminist Methodology as a Tool for Ethnographic Inquiry on Globalization." In *The Gender of Globalization: Women Navigating Cultural and Economic Marginalities*, edited by Nandini Gunewardena and Ann E. Kingsolver, 23–31. Santa Fe: SAR, 2007.

Kanafani, Samar and Sawaf, Zina. "Being, Doing and Knowing in the Field: Reflections on Ethnographic Practice in the Arab region." *Contemporary Levant*. 2 (1), 2017: 3–11.

Kvale, Steiner and Brinkmann, Svend. *Interviews: Learning the Craft of Qualitative Research Interviewing*. Second Edition. London: SAGE, 2009.

Lee, Adam. "Finally: Atheists Are No Longer Just Old White Men." *The Guardian*. 3rd May 2015. www.theguardian.com/commentisfree/2015/may/03/finally-atheists-are-no-longer-just-old-white-men

Liamputtong, Pranee. *Performing Qualitative Cross-Cultural Research*. Cambridge: Cambridge University Press, 2011.

Loftland, John, Snow, David, Anderson, Leon, and Loftland, Lyn. H. *Analyzing Social Settings: A Guide to Qualitative Observation and Analysis*. Fourth Edition. Belmont: Wadsworth, 2006.

Migliore, Daniel L. *Faith Seeking Understanding: An Introduction to Christian Theology*. Second Edition. Grand Rapids: Wm. B. Eerdmans, 2004.

O'Leary, Zina. *The Essential Guide to Doing Your Research Project*. Third Edition. London: SAGE, 2017.

O'Reilly, Karen. *Key Concepts in Ethnography*. London: SAGE, 2009.

Pew Research Centre. "Racial and Ethnic Composition: Racial and Ethnic Composition by Religious Group." *Pew Research Centre Religious Landscape Study*. 2014. www.pewforum.org/religious-landscape-study/racial-and-ethnic-composition/

Swinton, John. "Where Is Your Church?" Moving toward a Hospitable and Sanctified Ethnography." In *Perspectives on Ecclesiology and Ethnography*, edited by Pete Ward, 71–92. Cambridge: W. B. Eerdmans, 2012.

Swinton, John and Mowat, Harriet. *Practical Theology and Qualitative Research*. Second Edition. London: SCM Press, 2016.

Tillich, Paul. *Systematic Theology*. Vol. 1. London: SCM Press, 1951.

Ward, Pete (ed.). *Perspectives on Ecclesiology and Ethnography*. Cambridge: W. B. Eerdmans, 2012.

Watts, Andrew. "The Church of Self-Worship: Sunday Morning with the Atheists." *The Spectator*. 22nd February 2014. www.spectator.co.uk/2014/02/so-tell-me-about-your-faith-journey-sunday-morning-at-the-atheist-church/

Yin, Robert K. *Qualitative Research from Start to Finish*. New York: The Guilford Press, 2016.

5 "Celebrating life, passing over suffering"

How the Sunday Assembly responds to adversity

I set out to examine how the Sunday Assembly responds to suffering, including events of global significance and events that are occurring on a personal level. It is evident that the Sunday Assembly and its members *do* acknowledge suffering—both that which is on a global scale and that which is internal to the community. Nevertheless, as will become clear, the movement touches on suffering only *briefly*. Rather than processing grief and pain and allowing the space and time to linger on these, the culture of the Sunday Assembly "passes over" suffering, turning quickly back to the central ethos of "celebrating life." Difficult circumstances are used as building blocks towards self-improvement, and deeper appreciation of what it means to be alive. Rather than responding directly to traumatic events, the Assembly tends to revert to celebration.

In this chapter, I present and weave together stories from the field to create a fuller picture of this key finding. I examine what it means for members to "celebrate life" and consider evidence that this particular adage is employed at the expense of a response to suffering. In the latter half of the chapter, consideration will be given to the Sunday Assembly's silence on, and lack of response to global trauma, using the Middle East as a frame of reference. Throughout, I establish a central claim: that the Sunday Assembly's emphasis on "celebrating life" has created a framework in which it is difficult to respond to suffering. Rather than acknowledging and allowing space for expressions of sadness and grief, the community jumps from a fleeting point of recognition to immediate resolution, employing the central aim of "celebrating life" as its ultimate objective. Within the organisation, there is no language or structure for *holding* suffering; that is, no middle-space in which to acknowledge the pain and confusion which mars the aftermath of a traumatic event. The language I use to describe this is that of "passing over"; the practice that the Sunday Assembly engages in when it either a) acknowledges, but does not "hold" suffering or b) does not acknowledge and is silent about suffering. The implications of this are potentially dangerous; I end this chapter by examining some of the experiences of Sunday Assembly members, who have been negatively affected by its culture of celebration.

Later, I will address the key implications of these findings theologically, arguing that it is important for Church congregations to create a space in which the experiences of trauma and hurt can be held, acknowledged, and grieved over rather than simply released or "passed over" quickly. For now, however, I begin with a particular story, which captures and illustrates the Sunday Assembly's propensity for passing over suffering and reverting to "celebration." It concerns the reaction of the London congregation to the terrorist attacks in Paris in November 2015.

"Three cheers for Paris": a story about "passing over" suffering

A series of co-ordinated attacks took place in Paris, France, on the night of Friday 13th November 2015. Gunmen and suicide bombers targeted a concert hall, a major stadium, restaurants, and bars almost simultaneously. The attacks sent shockwaves across the globe and left 130 people dead and hundreds more wounded.[1] In the aftermath, governments vowed to support France against the Islamic State (IS), who later released a statement claiming responsibility for the attacks. Public vigils were held in major cities, and a number of world landmarks were illuminated in the colours of the French *Tricolore*.[2] Members of the public expressed their solidarity through social media, sharing pictures of the French flag and the "Peace for Paris" symbol, an image created by French graphic designer Jean Jullien, incorporating the Eiffel Tower and a "peace" symbol.[3] Others shared slogans, notably "Pray for Paris" and "*Je suis Paris*," the latter in reference to the phrase "*Je suis Charlie*," which surfaced in the wake of the *Charlie Hebdo* shootings earlier in 2015.[4]

The attacks triggered a widespread reaction from the international community, particularly on social media, and it did not take long for the Sunday Assembly to add its voice to the chorus of popular support. The organisation's international Facebook page proclaimed: "Our thoughts are with Sunday Assembly Paris. *Paris on est avec vous. Votres douleurs sont dans notre couer* [sic]." To the same page, a picture was added, combining the Sunday Assembly logo, the French flag, and an image of the Eiffel Tower, next to the words: "We stand with Paris."

Two days later, the London chapter of the Sunday Assembly held its usual fortnightly gathering. The speaker for the day was Gianna De Salvo, a Cognitive Holistic Therapist. De Salvo's write up of the event on her professional blog is the first of several interconnecting narratives, which together form a picture of the Sunday Assembly's approach to this particular event. She writes:

> I was a bit apprehensive about doing a talk to the Sunday Assembly group about how to wire the brain for joy on the 15th November 2015, just two days after the terrific atrocities that happened in Paris. I was still feeling quite stunned and heavy hearted, as I know so many other people were too. But when I contemplated what my talk was

fundamentally about—simple strategies that anyone can use to move their thoughts and feelings away from being stuck in stress and sadness and pain and back towards joy and awe and wonder—I realised that the timing of the talk couldn't be more perfect. For you see, despite the number of awful things that are happening in the world currently, I still believe, wholeheartedly, that when humans are born they are naturally filled with unconditional love—free from prejudices or judgement of others. They (we) are born with innocence and acceptance and trust and it is only after the world throws at us what it might (and some people get thrown worse stuff that others) that the brain begins to move away from the natural set point of joy towards stress, negative thinking and sometimes far worse.[5]

Note how De Salvo briefly acknowledges the tragedy, alongside her own concerns about speaking so close to the Paris events. She then moves almost immediately to talk about how and why such feelings of grief and emptiness can be overcome. "Despite" the "awful things" that have happened in Paris, De Salvo encourages her audience to think positively. She later relays this advice:

I would like to add to that that when everything seems to be going wrong, look out for what is going right. Even just by noticing the sound of laughter or a flower growing in an unexpected place or the feeling of rain on your face as you walk down the street and recognising for a moment, even just a few seconds, that you can feel grateful for these small things, releases dopamine and serotonin in the brain and brings up a feeling of calm and connection with the world around you.[6]

De Salvo's recommendations seem to assume that the answer to tragedy is to ignore it in favour of positive thinking. Her words seem to jar with the context that she claims to be speaking to. The response to the Paris attacks was international in character; it involved the coming together of people from many different countries, united in their condemnation of the attacks and their support for the city of Paris. By contrast, De Salvo's mindfulness techniques are focused primarily on the self rather than on the global scale of the tragedy. It must also be emphasised that De Salvo does not dwell on the events in Paris in this talk, given two days after the tragedy. She quickly moves on to talk about how feelings of sadness can be moved towards "joy and awe and wonder."[7]

A second account of the movement's response to the Paris attacks comes from Josie, who had been attending the London Assembly for around six months when I spoke with her. When I interviewed Josie, she gave a detailed account of her experience of the post-Paris Assembly. As she walked into Conway Hall, Josie heard French classical music playing softly in the background. Jullien's "Peace for Paris" image was projected onto the large screen at the front of the room. The mood was initially "a little sombre and contemplative." As the service began, Sanderson Jones, who was leading that day, announced a minute of silence for the victims of the attacks. In Josie's words:

> They started with a minute-long silence, and at the end of that, there was a cheer to celebrate the lives of the people who died because . . . Sanderson said, "They are dead now, but they led wonderful lives, so let's all celebrate and give them a big cheer."[8]

According to Josie's account, the suffering of the Paris victims was held, acknowledged, and grieved over within the space of a minute, before the tone shifted rapidly towards one of celebration. It seems that the mood did not remain sombre or reflective for very long. As with De Salvo's talk, resolutions were sought quickly.

Around two months after the Paris attacks, I interviewed Grace, a French woman living in London. She had been attending the Sunday Assembly with her husband and young daughter for two years. When I asked her about the Assembly's responses to suffering, she touched on the recent Paris tragedy:

> We do talk about very serious things . . . without being very dramatic. So, when the Paris attacks happened, it was just before Sunday Assembly. And we did talk about how the world is really dark . . . but that it was important to be really grateful for what we have, and find love even in the darkness.

Because Grace was French, had previously lived in Paris, and had on-going connections with the city, I expected her to be morose when discussing the attacks. Yet her voice remained steady, her tone matter of fact, and her rhetoric in line with that of the organisation. Grace hastily acknowledged that "the world is really dark" before promptly stating the importance of being grateful and celebrating life, all without pause for breath. Again, the deviation from tragedy to celebration was immediate.

Woven together, these three narratives emerging from Assembly in the wake of the Paris attacks illustrate an important finding; that the Sunday Assembly's emphasis on "celebrating life" has created an environment in which it is difficult to respond to suffering. There is not space for the expression of grief (or, in more theological terms, lament). Instead, the community leaps from a fleeting point of recognition and acknowledgement of suffering to immediate resolution. The "celebration of life" is its ultimate objective. Within this framework, whether consciously or unconsciously, the Assembly does not leave space for events of global suffering personal traumas to be fully acknowledged. The theological importance of creating this space will be examined in a following chapter. For now, in order to substantiate the previous assertions, I will first examine what it means within the Sunday

Assembly context to "celebrate life" before drawing together some further examples which illustrate this finding in practice.

What does it mean to "celebrate life"?

> The band finished playing. Sanderson leapt onto the stage against a backdrop of deafening cheers. In the midst of the din, he hollered: "Who's in the mood to celebrate being alive?" Hands reached high, and the congregation roared in response. There was a palpable sense of excitement and anticipation in the hall.

The previous extract from my field notes describes a moment that occurs at every Sunday Assembly service in London.[9] Sanderson Jones, who is typically the master of ceremonies at each event, asks the assembled crowd if they are ready to "celebrate life." His words are echoed in the first of ten points in the Sunday Assembly's Public Charter, a list which is as close to a piece of doctrine as the Assembly comes.[10] It reads:

> The Sunday Assembly is 100% a celebration of life. We are born from nothing and go to nothing. Let's enjoy it together.[11]

The tenth point is a reiteration of the first: "The Sunday Assembly is a celebration of the one life we know we have."[12] The centrality of this idea is bolstered by the organisations' official website. In bold typeface, the home page declares the movement's intent: "Celebrating life together."[13]

In the life and practices of the Sunday Assembly, what does "celebrating life" entail? Points one and ten of the Charter suggest that life should be revered precisely because of its fragility and finitude. Two London members illuminated this idea further when I interviewed them. I met with Rose immediately following a Sunday service at Conway Hall. Early on in the interview, she spoke about attending an Assembly event which was themed around death:

> There was a Sunday Assembly where the entire theme was death. It managed to be incredibly uplifting. Death is . . . it's the leveller. It's what makes our lives extraordinary, because . . . if life didn't end, we might not appreciate what we have.

Rose's words recall the Assembly's Charter, particularly the first point regarding the finality of death and the subsequent need to therefore "enjoy" or celebrate life. Her use of the words "uplifting" and "extraordinary" in relation to death suggest that the content of the service in question was celebratory, as opposed to introspective. Vickie, another member of the London congregation, had inadvertently decided to attend her first assembly on the day that Rose describes earlier. In her own words:

> The first [assembly] that I went to was about death! But it was brilliant the way that it was done, because it wasn't morose, it was sort of . . . hopeful.

Vickie words help to explain and contextualise Rose's comment regarding the death-themed Assembly as "uplifting." She described the Assembly's response to death as "hopeful" and reflective. She continued:

> It's encouraging that curiosity, and maybe thinking about things that maybe people don't want to think about. But the way it's presented . . . it captures that phrase "wonder more." It's something that's worth reflecting on, and maybe it can help you tap into that "living better" idea as well, reflecting on the wonderment of life.

Vickie connects the idea of death with two parts of the Assembly's three-fold motto, namely "Live Better" and "Wonder More." For her, this exploration of death provided an opportunity for reflection on the "wonderment of life." Again, this idea is associated with life's fragility and finitude—such concepts which, ordinarily, provoke introspection and contemplation that is morose or sorrowful in character, being associated with the subject of death. It is therefore prudent to note that the event in question re-packaged and presented as a reason to celebrate and "live well" instead.

Rose and Vickie's descriptions both comply with the Assembly's Public Charter, wherein the celebration of life is intrinsically linked with death and acknowledgement of human mortality, as well as the concept of "living better." I wondered to what extent Sanderson, whose role as Assembly co-founder is to guide the Assembly's outlook, might have been instrumental in this. We had a conversation specifically about death, dying, and the celebration of life, shortly after he conducted the first Sunday Assembly memorial service. The deceased had only attended the Sunday Assembly once but was adamant that he wanted his life to be marked with a ceremony "full of life and celebration." Sanderson described a "cultural glacier" around funeral events, comprised of socially ingrained ideas about how end-of-life ceremonies should look, and what ought to happen at them. For the memorial service, he wanted to provide a different experience—one which was "more uplifting," especially for those "who want something joyful and less serious and morbid."[14] As we discussed this, leaned forward suddenly, and gripped the arm of the chair he was sitting in. "Don't you feel so much more appreciative of life when you think about dying?" he asked, effusively, his eyes glittering.

I invited him to explain further. By way of answer, Sanderson reached for another stock Assembly phrase, which features in its Public Charter: "the one life we know we have." Because the majority of Assembly attendees hold no eschatological outlook, there is no reference to an afterlife.[15] As such, life is viewed as short, ending at the point of death. In response, Sanderson explained, humans should use the concept of death as a "launch pad" through which to remind others "how amazing it is to be alive." For Sanderson: "being alive is so good," and "people just need to be reminded of this." As such, he sees funerals and memorials as one way in which to celebrate life.

The concept of "celebrating life" is, for the Sunday Assembly, an amalgamation of ideas, including recognition of the finitude of human existence ("the one life we know we have") and a resulting desire to "live better" (another key concept, which will be expounded on later). Grace's definition of "celebrating life" is reminiscent of De Salvo's words at the beginning of the chapter. She frames gratitude and positivity as ideal responses to suffering:

> [Celebrating life] means, to me, that . . . there are bad things happening all the time, but that doesn't make the world a bad place. So, finding something to celebrate, or something good coming out of a bad situation. . . . Even the darkest moments will bring something good. I guess. . . . And that life should be. . . . You should go through life with a grateful mind and an open heart. It's about not just looking at the bad parts, but seeing the goodness where you can as well. Even if things are difficult.

Grace did acknowledge that "there are bad things happening" in the world. She added that the Assembly's "celebration" of life:

> is not a naive celebration. It's not, "Oh, everything is beautiful." And good things are not always coming your way. It's more . . . appreciation of everything that surrounds us. As Sanderson says, things shouldn't be taken too seriously.

Within Grace's description lies the basis of my previous assertion. While the Assembly claims not to evade suffering and difficult topics, it *is* primarily focused on celebrating life and retaining a perspective filled with "wonder." The significance and implications of this pattern of thought will be demonstrated in the following section, in which an argument for "holding" and creating space in to acknowledge suffering will be set out from a theological perspective.

The "celebration of life" in practice

Having outlined what the "celebration of life" means to members the Sunday Assembly, I now move to examine what this idea looks like within the life, activities, and practices of the Sunday Assembly. This concept is particularly apparent in talks and presentations at Assembly events, as well as in the movements" "self-improvement" groups. However, this emphasis on "celebration" creates a culture in which it is difficult for Assembly members to acknowledge "ground zero" events, and the real experiences of suffering. This leads to a practice of "passing over" suffering.

"Only space for happy endings": talks and "doing their best"

The focal point of every Sunday Assembly meeting is a sermon-like talk. Typically, talks are delivered by a visiting speaker, though there are exceptions, and members of the community who have special interests, skills, or knowledge may be invited to contribute.[16] Talks are intended to be both thought provoking and informative. At some Assemblies, there is also a slot called "Doing Their Best" or, alternatively (and sometimes less frequently), "These Things I Know." This lasts around five to seven minutes. Though less regular at regional events, this component is usually included in the London Assembly. Unlike the main talk, which is typically more educational or informative in nature, this part of the meeting is intended to be more personal. Official guidelines state that it should be "about someone sharing something they have "done their best" at, or learned, or tried and failed, or about a personal journey they have taken or are currently on." According to the guidelines, the segment normally involves "somebody who can share their struggles, victories and insights from the turmoil of life." The phrase "turmoil of life" piqued my interest. Theodicy begins with a similar recognition that human beings exist within a larger picture of on-going suffering. As such, I wondered if the Assembly's practice of sharing life stories and narratives of struggle might provide some insight into how they were approaching questions related to theodicy.

When Agnes from the Edinburgh organising committee asked if I would fill the "Doing Their Best" slot at one of their meetings, in order to introduce myself and my study to the congregation, I was mildly apprehensive. Having read the guidelines, I assumed that this particular segment was intended for those wrestling with deeply searching questions. In practice, however, this was not the case. In the loosest sense, contributors tend to speak about their "personal journey," which can involve anything from hobbies and interests to short-term goals or future hopes. The first Assembly I observed in London was based on the theme of "Child-like Wonder." It touched on both the "wonder more" aspect of the Assembly's aims, as well as its wish to be more accommodating to its youngest members. In keeping with this theme, the "Doing Their Best" segment focused on an 11-year-old boy, who gave a short, well-rehearsed speech about learning to play the fiddle, followed by a brief recital.

In preparation for my first visit to the Edinburgh Assembly, I set about writing a short talk. It was intended to capture the ethos of "Doing Their

Best," while doubling as an advertisement for my study, so that I could recruit more interview participants. I decided to talk about my doctoral studies and some of the pitfalls that might be encountered on the way. In particular, I spoke about "impostor syndrome," doubting ability, comparing success, and the fear of being "discovered" as academically inadequate. I did so light-heartedly, and on the day, my talk provoked laughter and warm applause from Assembly-goers.

After the service, however, I was approached by several people who expressed concern that I hadn't provided a "solution" to the more negative aspects of my talk. Klaus pressed me for answers: how was I going to improve my self-esteem to get over the impostor syndrome? Had I tried self-help books? Caroline was more rhetorical, telling me that I shouldn't be down on myself and that I had a great deal to "celebrate." My lack of "resolutions" bothered Lisa. She told me not to be so apologetic about my place in academia and added that it made her "sad" to see a young woman so cautious in this way. All three conveyed varying comments, but they were united in their concern: I had not included enough "positives" or points of celebration in my journey.

These encounters appear to illustrate how Sunday Assembly's emphasis on "celebrating life" is leading attendees to expect a narrative involving immediate answers and positive asides, in order to balance out the struggles. It seems that the task is not merely to be aware of one's own shortcomings but also to "get over" them.

At the London Assembly, there appears to be an even more pronounced emphasis on the celebration of life. Both the talks and the "Doing Their Best" segments are, according to Rita, "quite often about dark times, and how people got over them." I wondered if the past tense in Rita's comment was intentional. It may well have been. The speakers that were mentioned by my interview participants were described as having already overcome that which was holding them back; a wide variety of issues, including (but not limited to) physical injury, chronic illness, mental health problems, bereavement, and job loss.[17] As such, their stories always end with a note of celebration.

One such example is Sam Cleasby, a writer and public speaker who has inflammatory bowel disease (IBD). Sam travels across the country talking about her illness in relation to self-esteem and body image.[18] Describing her talk at the London Assembly, Ash said:

> We had a lady come in . . . who [has] a problem with her intestines. She has a colostomy bag, something like that. She came and gave a talk. And it was the week we were talking about loving ourselves and being happy with what we've got, or who we are. And she had done some rather tasteful . . . glamour isn't the word . . . like, "Victoria's Secret" style photo-shoots with the colostomy bag, because it's

attached to her. And she was like: "This is me, and I'm proud of it, this is my life." She was drawing attention to all the people with the disease, who suffer. So, I suppose, negative things . . . they get turned into a positive.

The final line of Ash's description is important. Through the talks and "Doing Their Best," the Assembly "turns negatives into positives" by emphasising instant resolutions to difficult situations. Indeed, for emphasis, he immediately added: "The Sunday Assembly always turn negatives into positives. . . . I suppose they show us reasons to feel lucky."

This is despite Sam's personal blog being replete with examples of the physical and psychological pain and prejudice she has faced because of her IBD. One incident that Sam recounts involves her use of a disabled toilet, and a derogatory comment made by a member of the public who assumed that she would have no reason to use it.[19] In another post, she mentions feeling "extremely depressed and low" while waiting for a formal diagnosis.[20] Yet, because Sunday Assembly attendees were so encouraged to focus on Sam's triumphs, there was no space in which to recognise the other, more difficult parts of her story.

A similar example occurred with another speaker at the London Assembly. Charlotte Roach is a former Olympic trainee cyclist, who was involved in a catastrophic road accident during training. A cyclist ahead of her swerved in the road, and Charlotte fell into the path of an oncoming Land Rover. She punctured her lungs, fractured 12 vertebrae, and broke her ribs and collar bone. As a result of her accident, Charlotte needed emergency spinal surgery and extensive reconstruction work. She slowly learnt to stand and then walk again. A few months later, she was able to return to cycling. Charlotte later completing a 16,000km cycle from Beijing to London to raise money for Derbyshire Leicestershire and Rutland Air Ambulance, who were instrumental in saving her life.[21]

Anne attended the Sunday Assembly on the week that Charlotte spoke. She described Charlotte in this way: "a woman who was a cyclist, almost paralysed in an accident, and then she got better and she cycled all the way back here from China." John, who was also present for Charlotte's talk, elaborated on the same story:

> We had a girl give a talk who was an Olympic triathlete, she got selected for the London Olympics. About seven months short, she was in a horrible training accident, came off her bike and got hit by a [car]. Broke her back, shoulder, ribs, hip . . . lost a lot of blood. Missed the Olympics, but did get back up. She did a bike ride from the China to the UK to raise money for Air Ambulance, which saved her life. And now she's started up a company . . . exercise by playing children's games, like "British Bulldogs" and things like that. Yes, has her own business, and it's going really well.

Both John and Anne shared the same example and took away the same message: Charlotte was catastrophically injured, but she recovered. Not only that, but she went on to achieve something "against the odds." John made a point of emphasising that her life was "going well" again, while Anne didn't pause before mentioning that "she got better."

Yet Charlotte's story is not as triumphant and relentlessly positive as these members of the London Assembly convey. In an interview with Danae Mercer of *The Guardian*, Charlotte explains that she felt "mentally drained, humiliated, defeated and disappointed" as she struggled to recover from emergency spinal surgery. The damage to her spine caused back spasms and left her "in constant agony."[22] To this day, she lives with chronic pain. Attempting to cycle on her road bike again, Charlotte struggled with post-traumatic stress. On her first cycle with a group of young triathletes, she felt "very insecure and uncomfortable" and struggled to hide her "shaking and crying" from them. Charlotte adds that she saw "everything as a hazard," and that encountering aggressive drivers would reduce her to tears.[23] While Mercer's interview with Charlotte commends her for her charity work and touches on her abiding love for cycling, it ends with a sobering observation:

> Today, the impact of those few seconds in November can still be seen on Roach. She has scars across her shoulders, her elbow, her back. Her Olympic opportunity never fully materialised. And every day, she has pain.[24]

From this, it is clear that, while she may have completed a charity bike ride and founded a business,[25] both the physical and psychological trauma that Charlotte experienced from her accident is, in some sense, enduring. However, this was not touched on by Sunday Assembly members. The prevailing culture of celebration shifted Charlotte's narrative, so that she was portrayed as one who had been healed, and one who had "conquered" her injuries. The darkness of her slow and painful recovery was minimised.

The portrayal of "happy endings" to narratives of struggle is reflected both in the Assembly's response to the Paris attacks, which opened this chapter, and in the way in which the lives and experiences of visiting speakers are portrayed. This outlook does not accommodate a space in which to discuss the actual suffering that occurred or continues to occur. There is no mention of any intermediary or on-going (perhaps even open-ended) struggles experienced by the injured triathlete or the girl with the colostomy bag. It is because of this that I claim that their experiences of suffering were "passed over" by the Sunday Assembly.

"Everyone celebrates each other": Live Better groups

The Sunday Assembly's motto is "Live Better, Help Often, and Wonder More." According to long-term London attendee Jack, "the 'Live Better' is probably the most fundamental bit." What does it mean to "live better"? The Assembly's website states: "We aim to provide inspiring, thought-provoking and practical ideas that help people to live the lives they want to lead and be the people they want to be."[26] As previously mentioned, one aspect of this involves the content of Assembly meetings, and in particular the speakers. But there is another element of the life of the community to consider. In London,[27] the Assembly runs Live Better groups, previously referred to as "Resolve groups." According to a Sunday Assembly webpage, which has since disappeared, "Live Better" groups bring people together to help one another "achieve their goals [and] fulfil their ambitions." It appears that these groups underwent a hiatus in London (circa 2016/17), but were relaunched in September 2019 as a monthly pub meeting, which has been running ever since.[28] In what follows, I discuss these groups with reference to their previous format (pre-2016). These peer-to-peer support groups were initially run periodically for eight weeks, meeting once a week for an hour, and were overseen by a "trained facilitator."[29]

As with the talks, I wondered if some form of implied theodicy or meaning making might materialise within these meetings, as people shared their stories and struggles with one another. Indeed, when I asked Rita from the London Assembly about what measures the Assembly took to respond to suffering, she cited "the Live Better groups" as the primary point of reference for help and support for the community, especially for those experiencing personal problems. Others implied that these groups had the potential to deal with particularly arduous issues. Having taken part in several cycles of Live Better groups, Tony described the process as "very emotional" and "exhausting." He added, "Some of the people who go have got quite difficult things going on in their lives." Ellie, who was in the same group as Tony, added:

> Our group can get into the hard stuff. In our group, at least, it's very open. Which I think is really good. And often we'll go, "Woah, this is a therapy session tonight."

While Tony and Ellie's particular group had the capacity for problem sharing at a deeper level, theirs seems to be an anomalous example. Officially, the groups were not and are not intended as a support-service. Rather, they are goal-oriented, focusing on those "starting a new habit or hobby or trying to complete a project."[30] As Trish clarified:

> They have these Live Better groups where people try to work through their own personal issues, but that's more [about] trying to accomplish goals as opposed to going through a rough time.

Alistair gave some examples of the kind of aims attendees might have, while also noting the "self-interested" nature of this system:

[Live Better] seems very self-interested, where people have something they want to resolve. It might be, like, they want to change their career, they want to get a new job, they want to get 'round to filling in years of uncompleted tax returns, or they want to lose weight.

Felicity attended a series of meetings with what she described as "a very concrete problem." She felt overwhelmed with work and emails and went along to get some perspective from her peers. Felicity referred to the groups as supportive and "helpful in a low-key manner," adding that "everyone celebrates each other." Felicity's use of the term "celebrate" in relation to the Live Better groups is significant. As I have already noted, the Sunday Assembly's emphasis on "celebrating life" seems to drive a culture of resolution, wherein any struggles are viewed as issue to be solved or as examples from which others can learn. There seems to be no space in which such issues can be acknowledged, addressed, or wrestled with; nor is there any Assembly vernacular pertaining to this idea.

A striking and practical example of this arose in a discussion I had with Alice, who had, at the time, completed three cycles of Live Better groups. The latest incarnation of this had involved a "buddy system," in which attendees were split into pairs and encouraged to check in with and support one another outwith meeting times. Alice's experience of Live Better coincided with a period of turbulence in her personal life. Both of her parents became seriously unwell. Her father suffered from encephalitis (inflammation or swelling of the brain), and around the same time, her mother was diagnosed with breast cancer. Being separated from them geographically put a strain on Alice. In her words, she suffered from a "life crisis" due to "all the stress that it brought on." I was curious to know if Alice's group provided any kind of support for her during this time, and so I asked her about this directly. She replied: "No, I wouldn't say so." Elaborating, she said that she was grateful for the presence of the Sunday Assembly during this time, and the distraction that it provided her. "But," she added, "there was no official kind of . . . help available." When I asked her to speak more about this, Alice seemed uncomfortable. She responded by diverting the focus back towards a discussion of her aims and goals within the Live Better context, telling me about how she and her "buddy" would organise get-togethers in order to motivate one another. She added that the groups ultimately provide advice, encouragement, and support with resolutions, but that there was no help specific to her own personal experience. Like the speakers Charlotte and Sam, Alice's suffering was not addressed, but "passed over."

"Alright, my Gran is getting close to dying": a story from the field

At the Assembly's international conference in 2016, I attended a session on the "Life Course," described as a "brand new way of helping people through the big (and small) questions." It appears that this model did not ultimately supplant the format and existence of "Live Better groups," but in terms of their intentions, the two seem largely similar. The Life Course is founded on the evidence-based work of Martin Seligman and makes use of his PERMA model of positive psychology,[31] combined with "Sunday Assembly wisdom." Structurally, it echoes the traditional format of the Alpha Course: a shared meal, a short talk, and a time of discussion.[32] The Assembly had completed one three-month prototype cycle of the Life Course at this point. The session was intended to be a "taster" of what the Life Course could provide. Sanderson began by giving a short talk about how "we so often don't appreciate how fortunate we are in our lives." Thereafter, we were asked to think about and write down the "story" of the past year of our lives. If we had faced any "challenges" or "difficult times," we were to write about these positively.

After doing this alone, we were told to pair up with someone we had never spoken with before. I was paired with Jennifer: a petite, purple-haired Londoner. Jennifer was particularly enthusiastic about the task. She told me in detail about the positive changes she had made to her life in the past year after splitting from her long-term partner. She had become vegan, qualified as a Pilates instructor, started studying Eastern philosophy, and had begun attending the Sunday Assembly. After listening to our partner, we were asked to give a minute of feedback. According to notes that I made about this encounter in my field journal, I "wasn't sure what to say." As a researcher, I was "beginning to feel quite exposed and vulnerable," since I was taking part in a task which was so personal. As such, I kept my comments to Jennifer brief, and gave as little detail as possible.

When it was my turn, I kept my story simple. I used much of the same rhetoric as I did in my talk to the Sunday Assembly in Edinburgh, drawing on my life as a doctoral student. I presented this in a positive way, telling Jennifer how grateful I was to have the opportunity to study. This only took a few moments to say. I paused and sat in silence. Jennifer leaned in towards me, nodding. "Go on, what else?" she encouraged. "Um . . . I don't have much!" I replied, shrugging. "That's basically it." But Jennifer would not be sated. "What challenges have you had to face?" she asked, moving her chair closer to mine. I tried to stave off the question, but Jennifer persisted. She leaned forward, tilting her head to the side. She caught my eye and wouldn't look away. I felt compelled to add something else, and so I began to speak about my (now) late grandmother. I was very close with my Granny, and at the time in which this conversation took place, she was struggling with the effects of old age. As I began to describe some of the everyday tasks that my Granny now needed help with, Jennifer cut in. For accuracy, I audio-recorded our conversation, with Jennifer's permission. Included here, in full, is her response to my moment of contemplation:

> Oh, yeah, I know what you mean. When people get closer to death, though, they, like, think about their lives and what's happened, and they

try and look back on stuff positively. And like . . . I bet that's what your Gran is doing now. I bet she's looking back on an *amazing* and full life and thinking, "Wow! Look what I did with my ninety-odd years," you know? And Katie, you can use that, too. You could say, umm . . . "Alright, my Gran is getting close to dying," so maybe you could use her situation to think about your own mortality. Like, what is it you want to look back on when you're 90? What do you want to see in your life? You don't want regrets, you know? You want to be like, "Yes, I lived my life to the full! That's amazing, I'm going to celebrate that."

I found it striking that Jennifer didn't hesitate before turning my situation on its head, from a struggle to a celebration, without knowing any of the salient details. Jennifer's "bet" that Granny was looking back on a life well lived was, in some ways, tragically wrong. From a childhood spent cowering in an Anderson shelter, as bombs rained down on Clydebank during the Blitz of World War Two, to years of segregation in convalescent homes for contracting tuberculosis, to being widowed at the age of 52, Granny's life had been anything but easy. As I noted in my field journal:

> Jennifer's presumption that Granny would be looking back on her life through rose-tinted spectacles could not be further from the truth. The reality of old age pains and frustrates her, and I doubt that she is spending all of her time "celebrating" and reminiscing on happy times as she slowly loses her essential faculties.

I was also struck by Jennifer's suggestion that I use my fading grandmother's mortality to think about what *I* want to achieve with my life. Again, the emphasis was not on suffering, but on how to view the situation in a positive capacity.

As we re-joined the larger group, I thought about what Jennifer had said. It seemed that the exercise had caused a lot of scenarios to be pinched, pulled, and manipulated into "positives," where situations were more complex and not so easily reducible. Some fit the level that the task was "pitched" at quite well; these examples concerned taking up a new hobby and moving to a new job. Others, including those that dealt with depression or mental illness, were not so easily condensed and solved within a five-minute conversation. Before, the Assembly's emphasis on "finding the positives" and moving towards a celebration of life was simply a concept identified as important through my interviews. In my interaction with Jennifer, it lifted off the page, came to life, and was embodied within our dialogue. In this activity, I understood more fully the impact of the rhetoric of "celebrating life." In this way, the Assembly's propensity to "pass over" suffering was heightened and became a part of my own experience in a small but significant way.

In the previous discussion, the Assembly's emphasis on "celebrating life" has been evident in its response to Paris (the immediacy of the applause to "celebrate" the lives of the dead) and in the talks and content of its services (the resolutions required in "Doing Their Best" and the "happy ending" narratives of speakers). In relation to Live Better groups, the same phenomenon is at work. Attendees strive towards a goal, aiming at the resolution of problems or issues. They are seeking to minimise negative aspects of their lives, choosing instead to focus purely on what is good and praiseworthy. This was also the case in the short story I shared from my experience in the field earlier. When considering the place of theodicy, meaning making and responses to suffering, this leap from acknowledgement to immediate resolution is curious. More crucially, as will be explained in due course, it is also problematic and potentially even dangerous.

The silence of the Sunday Assembly

Thus far, it is evident that the Sunday Assembly responds to suffering in part by stressing the "celebration of life." In doing so, it "passes over" suffering, in other words, acknowledging a trauma or event, then quickly moving back to a point of celebration, wherein the positives and "wonder" of life can be emphasised. Nevertheless, it is not always possible for the Assembly to relate suffering to celebration. In those times, the movement falls silent, preferring not to speak about global issues or "ground zero" events. This results in a skewed, almost polarised attitude to suffering: one which eagerly seeks solutions to some events and problems, while clearly avoiding others. I move now to examine this phenomenon at work in the Sunday Assembly, supporting my assertions with evidence from my gathered data.

In each of the 30 semi-structured interviews I conducted, I asked participants whether the Sunday Assembly has any particular way of responding to suffering. Alice answered my question ("Does the Sunday Assembly respond to suffering?") in the following way:

> No. Not so much. That . . . as far as I know, that has not happened. It has certainly not happened at any of the ones that I've been to. It hasn't really tackled like, big horrible stuff about the world.

Indeed, while the Assembly *did* acknowledge the Paris attacks in November 2015, it appears to have evaded discussion of other tragic occurrences. What are the noticeable exceptions? The members I spoke to only gave a few examples, but most alluded to the on-going conflict in the Middle East. The Syrian civil war, the refugee crisis, and the rise of the Islamic State (IS) in particular have been constant fixtures in global headline news since the Assembly's conception in 2013. The example of Middle East tensions (loosely defined) was not mentioned or introduced by myself as part of an interview question or otherwise. I suspect that a number of interviewees reached for this as a frame of reference because of on-going and intensive media coverage of the political situation there. Taking the Middle East (again, loosely defined) as an initial point of reference, I will now examine some of the reasons given by interviewees for the organisation's silence on, and lack of response to, tragic events.

"It isn't ideological, so it isn't confrontational": no cohesive ideology

Returning to the Sunday Assembly Public Charter, point two states that: "The Sunday Assembly has no doctrine."[33] Related to this assertion is point nine: "we won't tell you how to live, but will try to help you do it as well as you can."[34] The latter half of this statement alludes to the ideals of "celebrating life" and "living better," which have already been expounded. Beyond these central tenants, however, the former part of point nine asserts the Assembly's supposed lack of ideology. Earlier (in Chapter 3), I challenged the Sunday Assembly's assertion that they are a movement with no doctrine, pointing out several key beliefs in their motto and Public Charter, including "live better, help often, wonder more," as well as "radical inclusivity" and the "celebration of life." I suggested that these guiding principles were "doctrinal" in character, given that they appear to constitute a set of beliefs and "truth claims."[35] Nonetheless, it is important to note that attendees and organisers abide by the Charter statement and continue to claim that the movement has no doctrine. Because of this, as will become evident shortly, certain decisions are practices are made with this assumption in mind.

For Clive, a long-term attendee from London, the Sunday Assembly is "almost deliberately non-ideological." When I asked him why this was, he replied:

> That's its appeal to so many people, that it doesn't take a stand. . . . It's what appeals to many, many people there. That's the whole point, that's why they go, because it isn't ideological, so it isn't confrontational.

This claim appears to be intentional, insofar as it intends to establish space for the core concept of "radical inclusivity." Under this objective, the Assembly is attempting to create a climate which "welcome[s] people from all walks of life." The facilitation of such a broad spectrum of opinions within one community has many repercussions, but one in particular is of interest here; because the Assembly does not have a coherent approach to suffering (as a result of its emphasis on the "celebration of life"), it tends to "pass over" or ignore it.

References to on-going war and political turmoil in the Middle East by Assembly members illustrate this silence in more concrete terms.[36] As Felicity stated when asked about the Assembly's response to suffering: "No, we don't have people coming to talk about what's happening in Syria, and let's all raise money for the Syrian refugees, for instance." The same was true for

Clive, who stated that the Assembly "could not be expected" to acknowledge the suffering occurring in the Middle East. He alluded to problems of agreement on such issues, since the Sunday Assembly is a "diverse" grouping:

> If it's much more complex, like the refugee crisis or the Middle East, I can't see how Sunday Assembly could say anything. Within the Sunday Assembly there would be incredibly divergent views on that, the issues are so complex.

Clive rightly points to the complexity of the issues at stake in such matters. However, he fails to account for why a broad range of views would prevent the organisation from responding to the situation, or even discussing it.

The minimising of suffering is not unique to the London chapter. Frank, an attendee from Edinburgh, commented that the organisation was still in the process of growing and developing a sense of identity, leaving it unclear as to how they would discuss such issues:

> When times are really rough and you find people discussing these kinds of issues, you would find individuals having their own point of view. There wouldn't be one collective notion coming out of that.

I asked Frank to clarify this statement. He explained that there was "nothing in place" and no language with which to discuss "suffering or bad things" in the Sunday Assembly.

For Tony, it made sense for the Assembly to avoid engaging with and responding to such matters, since: "ISIS [the Islamic State] is in the news all the time, and by the time we get to Sunday Assembly, we've all read the news." It seemed from his comment that Tony was attending the Assembly to escape bad news. This attitude is consistent with the Assembly's more corporate desire to celebrate life, and not to wrestle with more difficult aspects of human existence. Tony continued: "If Sanderson talked about that stuff every week, every time we met . . . you'd feel he had some sort of axe to grind." By this admission, it seems that making a response to this kind of suffering might threaten the stability of the Assembly's perceived "radical inclusivity."

Joan, a long-term attendee of the London Assembly, also cited the Middle East in reference to the Assembly's response to suffering. She answered my question about this somewhat tersely:

> There's no official response. I wouldn't have thought so . . . we don't have a committee sit down and ask, for example, "What's our response to Syria going to be?"

I asked her if there was any particular reason for this. She replied: "We don't get involved, unless something is clearly illegal." When I pressed her further for an example (simultaneously wondering if war crimes didn't count as illegal), Joan snapped angrily: "I don't know, it's just too difficult to think about. That's it in my view, that's all I want to say." In relation to the views of other Assembly members on the same matter, her response, while blunt and defensive, seems in some ways to encapsulate the Assembly's attitude towards such issues.

"We're just there to celebrate life": not the place to discuss suffering

Why, exactly, has the Assembly has been able to make reference to some kinds of suffering (for example, the terrorist attacks in Paris in November 2015), while minimising discussion about others (the Middle East)? A recurring reason stated by interviewees is that the Assembly is "not equipped" for dealing with such suffering, or that it "isn't the place" for these issues.

For Maggie, who sits on the organising committee in Edinburgh, the Assembly is a place where "people can come and just enjoy themselves, and forget all the bad stuff for a while." It is not somewhere "that addresses people's issues." In fact, when asked directly about the Assembly's response to suffering, and how it handles the more difficult aspects of life, Maggie said:

> Well, I don't know that it necessarily does, and I'm not even sure that that's its job. I'm not sure it's there to address people's issues, per se. I am aware that there are. . . . Like any other public group, it does attract people who I would say possibly have . . . whatever the term is, "things going on." And you can tell. But as far as I'm concerned, we are just there to celebrate life and have fun.

In Maggie's answer, the celebration of life appears to be the Assembly's primary objective, to the exclusion of any discussion about suffering. Her words further strengthen my claim that the framework put in place by the elevation of this objective leaves little space to deal with suffering on a personal level, or with "ground zero" events.

In London, Joan had similar opinions on the remit of the Assembly. In her characteristically abrupt tone, Joan explained:

> We're not a psychiatric group. We don't have any specialists on hand to help with people with their problems, nor do we claim to have. So, if there are people who have difficulties . . . I imagine we would encourage them to seek help elsewhere, but . . . um, it's people who just want to make friends with people, essentially.

For Joan, as for Maggie, the Assembly is primarily for enjoyment. It is not a place in which issues of individual suffering could be resolved. Agnes concurred: "Some people don't see it as that kind of community. It might put some people off. It has to be quite a light touch." She expressed concern that openly talking about the difficulties of life could "repel folk from coming through the door" and reiterated Joan and Maggie's position that the Assembly "is mostly about coming together and sharing the good parts of life."

It is evident that boundaries for discussion exist, since some instances of suffering are appropriate for discussion at Sunday Assembly, while others are not. Thus far, this is true specifically of the Assembly's reaction to the Paris attacks, and its lack of comment regarding the Middle East. Tony provided another example. For him, the Assembly's focus on the theme of death was acceptable as a one-time event, but he was wary of death and dying being discussed too much in the context of Sunday meetings. He referenced the *Charlie Hebdo* shooting in January 2015, which Sanderson "touched on a little bit" in his regular address to the congregation. According to Tony, this was well-received. Those gathered found it "touching and moving." However, he was quick to designate this response as "appropriate," saying: "It was right to do it *then*. You don't want to be banging on about . . . you know, fire and brimstone and death all the time. You know, when it's appropriate, you do it." It is clear, therefore, that some Assembly members are simply not willing to allow or conceive of a space in which a deeper discussion of global events of suffering might occur. Richard, a long-term Assembly-goer in London, acknowledged this, saying "people try to avoid that . . . the negative side of life." However, to this statement, he added:

> But I think it's something that'll be done more effectively in future. I think people could expect that sort of thing, especially when you've got a group of several hundred people. I think we probably need to do that sort of thing.

Indeed, some members did seem to be aware of the way in which the Assembly "passes over" suffering, and the on-going need to challenge this.

"We can't just block it out and sing Queen": acknowledging the need to respond

When I spoke with Alice, she admitted that the movement "hasn't really tackled . . . big horrible stuff about the world." Nonetheless, she found the Assembly event themed around death to be "very powerful" and explained that there was "power in publicly, collectively confronting something horrifying, frightening and awful." She continued:

> I think the Assembly *should* talk about suffering more. I think [that] needs to be developed. I think that the [assembly on the theme of death] shows that it can work. I mean obviously, it's difficult because . . . I think, partly because sometimes they're mindful of what it's going to be like if it's the first one that somebody comes to. But, I mean, the world

is, like, in a shocking state at the moment. We can't just block it out and sing Queen, can we? Forever? We can't. We have to have some kind of discussion and . . . yeah. I think [the Sunday Assembly] is amazing. I think being . . . it's taught me to be a more positive person. But I think, at the same time, it can't just be kind of . . . jumpy up and down and just celebrate life all the time! Because really horrible, scary things happen in life.

Alice's statement clearly acknowledges the Sunday Assembly's tendency to "pass over" suffering. Further still, she challenges the legitimacy of this approach, referring to the prevalence of "ground zero" events in twenty-first-century life; for her, this should prompt the Assembly into speaking about the more difficult parts of life. As someone who does not believe in any kind of deity or afterlife, Alice was at pains to add that she is not looking for "certainties" or for "comfort." "I don't necessarily want that," she declared. "But to have that collective acknowledgement of the bad things in life—that's something. That's something I do want."

In a similar vein, Linda from Edinburgh pointed out that "people who don't embrace religion . . . have stopped going to churches, so they will begin to look for other alternatives." As such, she agreed with Alice that dealing with suffering and tragedy "is definitely a role that the Sunday Assembly . . . will need to step into." From Tony's perspective, this is "inevitable." He explained that the demographic of the London Assembly is "very young," and as such, "there hasn't been a significant death or loss within the community as yet." "But as it grows," he mused, "it'll have to find ways to deal with things like that." Referring also to death and bereavement, Alistair added: "You've got to talk about it. To not talk about it. . . . Well, logically, you're looking to your community to make sense of things that are difficult."

Steve, an Edinburgh member, suggested that the Assembly had touched very lightly on difficult subjects, particularly through the content of talks given by visiting speakers. However, he felt that this wasn't enough, and that members should "recognise what [speakers] are mentioning." Examples he gave included "helping others in a time of need, environmental awareness, social issues like homelessness or hunger or food banks." He added that there was some discussion amongst the organising committee in Edinburgh about what topics to include in future sessions. "One way I could see life issues being mentioned in Assembly is to invite more speakers along, who could talk about those," Steve suggested. For him, the content and outlook of the Assembly seemed to hinge almost entirely on what the visiting speakers would have to say on the matter.

Like Steve, Trish gave a suggestion for how the current lack of discussion surrounding suffering and trauma might be remedied. Previously, Trish attended New York City Atheists.[37] The organisation held meetings "with a social worker once a month" in order to "talk about various topics, and to help people talk through their personal problems." Trish reminded me that the Sunday Assembly's Live Better groups are not intended for this type of "deep, soul-searching self-help," since they are "more about resolutions." She wondered aloud whether setting up sessions akin to what the New York City Atheists offered might work in London, as a potential outlet for those struggling with personal issues needing a supportive environment.

From this, it is clear that while some are comfortable for the Assembly to function as a place for celebration, others have noted the need for, and "inevitability" of, some kind of co-ordinated response to suffering. Indeed, after conducting his first funeral, Sanderson appeared to be acknowledging the need for a more developed outlook on suffering, imploring his congregation to "build Sunday Assembly so that we can help people in trying times."[38] He noted that congregational communities, such as churches, mosques, and synagogues, "come into their own at moments of crisis, pain and transition," but that there has historically been "no alternative to these providers of community and care." As such, he wrote, "We need to be there for deaths and injuries, as well as naming ceremonies and marriages."[39] From this, it seems that the Assembly's focus could be on rituals and ceremonies rather than sporadic care and response in the future.

The dark side of celebration: the dangers of "passing over" suffering

At the beginning of this chapter, I outlined some of the ways in which the Sunday Assembly cultivates a climate of celebration. I explained that the idea of "celebrating life" is not inherently wrong. However, when it becomes the default response to difficult questions, leads to the act of "passing over" suffering, and, in doing so, results in a failure to acknowledge or respond to pain and trauma, it can become dangerous.

Several stories from members of the Sunday Assembly support this claim. The first is extracted from a thread on the Sunday Assembly Nashville members board, on the website meetup.com. The author of the leading post is anonymous but attended the movement's international conference in Atlanta in 2015. At the time of writing, the post is still live and publicly accessible. It points to the constant "pressure" to celebrate life at the Sunday Assembly:

> Insisting upon the positive runs counter to the ethic of radical inclusivity and will most likely result in a gentle and gradual excluding of those who cannot muster up the continuous positivity. The requirement to cheer, to be positive constantly, erodes and narrows life, narrows experience, narrows the full complexity of humanity. In talk after talk at [the conference] and more, at the big Sunday Assembly service itself, I was immersed in a constant exhortation of how wonderful everything was and how I should cheer and applaud harder, longer, louder. I felt immersed, in other words, in a weekend of fake orgasms.[40]

The writer continues, describing the conference as a place in which "every clap must be cranked up into an ovation that will blow off the roof and in which every emotion must be the greatest." The problem with this is that the "demand for extreme feeling and reaction pushes out the genuine for the manufactured." In other words, the author of the post, who claims to have since left the Sunday Assembly, is concerned that the movement is unable to accommodate anything which detracts or deviates from the prevailing culture of celebration. On its own, the post may be said to contain a specific and individual grievance, which has no weight or bearing on the realities of Sunday Assembly culture. However, when placed in context alongside the other narratives I have included in this chapter, it reinforces the claim that the Assembly's climate of celebration can at times encourage attendees to present an almost unnaturally happy exterior, at the expense of also addressing the more difficult parts of their lives.

A final story from the field adds further weight to the opinions of the anonymous poster. When I attended the movement's international conference, an assembly was held on the final morning. This is the same type of event which the member from Nashville refers to earlier as "the big Sunday Assembly service." It included all the trappings of a normal Sunday service in London: communal singing, a talk, a short meditation, and a "Doing Their Best" segment. This was filled by Carmen, who had travelled from the US to attend the conference. I noted an atmosphere of "tangible excitement" in my field journal. Despite the collective tiredness from three days' worth of activities, those gathered cheered and clapped loudly throughout and danced and sang energetically with each song. However, when Carmen reached the front of the room to deliver her reflection, she was not so excitable. In fact, she looked visibly upset. I watched as the paper between her hands shook, and her eyes clouded with tears. She began to speak, but her voice faltered more than once. It was clear that Carmen was about to share something which had grieved her enormously. The room was eerily silent. Eventually, one member in the front row stood up to embrace Carmen and offer her a tissue. The audience was roused from their stupor, applauding the act.

Carmen exhaled several times and then began her talk. She explained that the Sunday Assembly is a place in which people gather to celebrate, but that there are "stories behind that exterior" which are important, too. Carmen began to speak about her life and the suffering she had been living through. A young member of her Assembly had died, and she had been heavily involved in the situation. Her mother had been severely ill. She had recently lost her job. Her sister's husband had walked out on his family. Her uncle had been diagnosed with terminal cancer. She had been diagnosed with diabetes. All of this had taken space within the span of just a few short months.

"Sometimes, we are not aware of the things that make us feel like ourselves, that make us feel normal," Carmen explained tearfully. "But after this series of events, I was very much aware that I did not feel normal.

I didn't have enough time or energy between events to understand them, or process them, or really do much about them." She described her brain as being "hijacked" by dark thoughts during this time. "All of my support systems seemed to be in need of a support system," she continued. "And so, I had no support, whatsoever." Carmen went on to talk about how angry she had felt to have so many challenging and life-altering events take place all at once. While she spoke, I glanced around the hall. While some attendees were listening attentively, others shifted uncomfortably, staring at their hands or at the floor. One or two pulled their phones from their pockets and began scrolling through them, as if the talk was boring or in some way not of significance to them.

Carmen wrapped up by speaking about "returning to normality" after having dealt with so much. She talked about the signs that life was "moving forward," ending by saying:

> One morning recently, I woke up at 6 a.m. . . . and I had this wild, unstoppable desire and urge to go vacuum the car. And something clicked. I just knew my "normal" was just around the corner.

At this, laughter and applause broke out around the room. Relief seemed to wash over the crowd. One man further down the row to my right exhaled dramatically and mimed wiping his brow. Just like Charlotte and Sam, the speakers in London, Carmen's story had had a "happy ending." Her narrative had fit within the boundaries of acceptable discussion of suffering at a Sunday Assembly event because it had ended with a reassurance that everything had returned to "normal." Sanderson, who was leading the event, led the applause for Carmen. He described her talk as "powerful and inspiring." He then asked us to speak with someone nearby about "the things that make us feel normal," adding that: "We can celebrate everything, even the mundane!" It seemed that this was a spontaneous segment rather than a planned interlude. I had a brief conversation with a woman to my immediate left, before excusing myself to go and refill my coffee cup at the back of the room.

On my way across the hall, I felt compelled to search for Carmen. I noticed her sitting alone in a seat at the back. She was still wiping the tears from her eyes, as energetic discussion and laughter swirled like rising tides around her. It was jarring to see her alone and crying, having just bared her soul to the room. Her suffering was not held for any length of time. Her grief made those gathered appear visibly uncomfortable, and so it was passed over quickly. The take-away message from her talk was, according to Sanderson, that we should be grateful for that which makes us feel "normal" and comfortable. A tone of celebration was re-introduced as swiftly as possible; the assembly moved forward with reflections on the weekend's events, plans for the conference the following year, and an energetic rendition of "Uptown Funk" as the closing song.

At coffee time after the service, I approached Carmen. I did so tentatively, and acutely aware of my position as a researcher. I drew level with her, and saw that she was still crying a little, and she looked exhausted. We spoke, and I thanked her for her honesty. Carmen embraced me tightly. I felt her shaking; she sniffled and patted me on the back. "Thank you," she said. "That was hard." Feeling that the noise in the room was too much, I stepped outside for a moment and sat down on a nearby bench. Perhaps it was tiredness, or Carmen's story, or being overwhelmed by several days of constant pressure to smile and celebrate that wracked my body with sobs; whatever caused my own tears then, I knew better than to show them to the people gathered inside. I had learnt, even as a researcher and an "outsider," to hide my sadness from view.

Conclusion

In this chapter, I have examined the boundaries of the Sunday Assembly's responses to suffering, both on official and individual levels. These boundaries contain responses to events such as the Paris attacks and the *Charlie Hebdo* shootings. At the same time, they do not seem to incorporate reactions to more complex political situations, such as the Middle East, or instances of more serious personal suffering. Where the Assembly *has* acknowledged trauma, it has done so by emphasising fragility and finitude of life, and as such, the need for its "celebration." At other times, it has minimised suffering, "passed over" it, or remained silent rather than making any kind of response.

How does the Assembly make this leap from fragility and finitude to celebration? The implied logic behind the notion of "celebrating life" is largely unclear. During an "Open Space" session at the Assembly's international conference, I conducted a series of informal conversations with members of the international Sunday Assembly community. I asked ten people: "What exactly is the significance of "celebrating life?" Answers ranged from "because we can" to "it's just a nice thing to do." Three people did not answer the question, since they were not sure. This small snapshot lines up with a larger issue: the Assembly relies heavily on the concept of "celebrating life," and they can define and practice this in many ways, which have been discussed within this chapter. Yet the significance of this, and the reasoning behind this jump from suffering to celebration, remains unclear.

The Sunday Assembly is a fairly new organisation. It may it still be tracing the perimeters of its aims and objectives, and indeed it has faced a number of challenges including the closure of several of its congregations. Because of this, it remains to be seen whether meaning making in the face of suffering and trauma will become officially included in time, which is still a possibility. Amongst some of the attendees, however, there is simmering dissatisfaction with the current state of affairs. As Linda from the Edinburgh congregation realised, non-religious people are actively seeking alternative communities for solace and support. Whether its numbers rise or fall, the Assembly exists within a wider where instances of human suffering and disaster are unceasing. These communities cannot shelter themselves from pain and trauma indefinitely.

Thomas Brudholm and Thomas Cushman suggest that responses to instances of suffering typically involve a "religious dimension."[41] In the wake of destruction, people reach for cultural "reservoirs" of meaning, often located in religious beliefs and practices.[42] Within Christian theology, theodicies, or theological explanations of suffering, are developed in order to explain the existence of a divine being in relation to the existence of suffering in the world. However, as established in the opening chapters of this book, many traditional approaches to theodicy have proven both ineffective and pastorally damaging. As such, a more holistic approach is needed, in response to both the problem of historically inadequate Christian theodicy and the findings contained within this chapter relating to the Sunday Assembly and its attempts at meaning making.

Notes

1 BBC News, "Paris Attacks: What Happened on the Night?," 9th December 2015: www.bbc.co.uk/news/world-europe-34818994 (accessed 7th January 2020).
2 The Guardian, "Paris Attacks: Buildings around the World Are Lit Up in Honour of the Victims of Friday 13," 14th December 2015: www.theguardian.com/world/gallery/2015/nov/14/paris-attacks-memorials-victims-friday-13 (accessed 7th January 2020).
3 Robbie Gonzalez, "Meet Jean Jullien: The Artist Behind the 'Peace for Paris' Symbol," *Wired*, 14th November 2015: www.wired.com/2015/11/jean-jullien-peace-for-paris/ (accessed 7th January 2020).
4 Mukul Devichand, "How the World Was Changed by the Slogan 'Je Suis Charlie'," *BBC Trending*, 3rd January 2016: www.bbc.co.uk/news/blogs-trending-35108339 (accessed 7th January 2020).
5 Gianna De Salvo, "May the Joy Be with You: Rewiring the Brain towards Joy, Sunday Assembly London: 15th Nov 2015," *Inner Balance Therapies*, 5th January 2016: https://inner-balance-therapies.com/2016/01/05/may-the-joy-be-with-you-rewiring-the-brain-towards-joy-sunday-assembly-london-15th-nov-2015/ (accessed 7th January 2020).
6 Ibid.
7 Ibid.
8 A further, perhaps superfluous, question regarding Josie's description concerns Sanderson's assertion/assumption that those who died led "wonderful" lives— how can we know this? What impact do these words have on the congregation's collective perception of the tragedy?
9 The language of "celebrating life" is also used at the start of gatherings in local Assemblies. At the Edinburgh chapter, this is normally packaged as part of the introduction, wherein a short description of the Sunday Assembly is offered to those who are visiting for the first time.
10 I outlined the Assembly's "doctrine" in detail in Chapter 3, where I also touched on the idea of "celebrating life" as being somewhat integral to the movement's outlook. Nevertheless, prior to conducting research in London and Edinburgh, I was unaware of how much of an impact the concept of "celebrating life" had in practice, at a congregational level.

11 The Sunday Assembly, "About Sunday Assembly": https://sundayassembly.online/about-sunday-assembly/ (accessed 7th January 2020).

12 Ibid.

13 The Sunday Assembly, "Celebrating Life Together": www.sundayassembly.com/ (accessed 7th January 2020).

14 Sanderson is likely speaking about mainstream Anglican approaches to funerals here. Culturally, not all funerals can be described as "serious and morbid." One specific example is Nigerian Christian funerals. F. Eyetsemitan points out that these are often characterised by singing, dancing, and music, in order to ensure that the deceased has a successful afterlife. See F. Eyetsemitan, "Cultural Interpretation of Dying and Death in a Non-Western Society: The Case of Nigeria," in *Online Readings in Psychology and Culture*, 3 (2), 2002.

15 This is a majority opinion, but it doesn't account for the outlook of all members. For example, Ash, a member of the London Assembly, displayed some eschatological views. He explained his beliefs in a kind of cyclical rebirth, saying: "I feel that there is something more. I think our soul moves to another life." He went on: "I suppose I'm comfortable with the idea reincarnation, but I don't see the whole coming back as an animal thing. I just think we come back as ourselves in a new body." While this particular form of eschatology is not of the Christian tradition, it is prevalent within a number of Eastern religions. The concept of Samsara—an endlessly repeating cycle of birth, life, and death characterised by Karmic interference—can be found within the holy writings and traditions of Hinduism and Buddhism.

16 An example of this in my own research came from a visit to the Edinburgh Assembly, where Linda, an Assembly member and professional psychologist, spoke about her work on the science of attraction.

17 Note these phrases, particularly "mental health" and "chronic illness" are umbrella terms, covering a vast range of experiences. The use of such terms here reflects the wording used by Assembly participants. Examples relating to experience of physical injury and chronic illness are given presently.

18 Sam Cleasby, "My Story," *So Bad Ass* (blog): www.sobadass.me/my-story/ (accessed 7th January 2020).

19 Sam Cleasby, "To the Woman That Tutted at Me Using the Disabled Toilets . . .," *So Bad Ass* (blog): www.sobadass.me/2015/02/17/to-the-woman-who-tutted-at-me-using-the-disabled-toilets/ (accessed 7th January 2020).

20 Cleasby, "My Story."

21 Danae Mercer, "After the Crash: The Triathlete Who Got Back on Her Bike and Gave Back," *The Guardian*, 7th October 2013: www.theguardian.com/environment/bike-blog/2013/oct/07/after-accident-triathlete-giving-back (accessed 7th January 2020).

22 Ibid.

23 Ibid.

24 Mercer, "After the Crash."

25 Elizabeth Hotson, "Putting the Fun Back into Fitness," *BBC News*, 31st October 2016: www.bbc.co.uk/news/business-37727456 (accessed 7th January 2020).

26 The Sunday Assembly, "About Sunday Assembly."

27 These groups were, for some time, exclusive to London. In 2020, it appears that this is still the case, although there is some evidence to suggest that a "Live Better" group was started in Portland (US) at one point.

28 Current information about events at the London Assembly can be accessed at: www.sundayassembly.com/events/category/meetup/

29 According to Tony, an attendee of the London Assembly, all training for "Live Better" group leaders was conducted internally. During the fieldwork component of this research, I could not find any evidence or examples of what such

training might involve, and the interview participants I spoke with were largely unable to elaborate.

30 The Sunday Assembly London, "Live Better Groups."
31 As noted in Chapter 3, Seligman's PERMA model draws on positive emotions "to help individuals . . . find lives of happiness, fulfilment, and meaning." See Slavin J. Slavin, Debra Schindler, John T. Chibnall, Ginny Fendell, and Mindy Schloss, "PERMA: A Model for Institutional Leadership and Culture Change," *Academic Medicine*, 87 (11), 2012, 1481.
32 The Alpha Course is a "series of interactive sessions that freely explore the basics of the Christian faith." Centrally, these involve a short talk or presentation, which is followed by discussion time. See Alpha Course, "What Is Alpha?": https://alpha.org/about/ (accessed 7th January 2020).
33 The Sunday Assembly, "Public Charter for the Sunday Assembly": www.sundayassembly.com/public-charter-for-sunday-assembly/ (accessed 7th January 2020).
34 The Sunday Assembly, "About Sunday Assembly."
35 See Alister McGrath, *Studies in Doctrine* (Grand Rapids: Zondervan, 1997), 244.
36 It is worth noting that what is true of this particular example is also true of the Assembly's silence on tensions, conflicts, and traumas in the local community. For example, the London Assembly was silent after the Grenfell Tower fire on 14th June 2017 at the 24-storey Grenfell Tower block of public housing flats in North Kensington in West London. No official statement was released, and it appears that the central London chapter did not dispatch any of their volunteers to help with relief efforts. While it is possible that the Assembly's proximity to Grenfell (it being located in Central London, and Grenfell some 40 minutes away) meant that this was not exactly a "local" tragedy, it is worth considering that help and assistance in the aftermath of the fire came from much further afield than London. Owen Bowcott of *The Guardian* notes that volunteers came from as far as Birmingham to help residents and local groups with aid operation. See Owen Bowcott, "Grenfell Tower Fire: Army of Volunteers Join Relief Effort," *The Guardian*, 17th June 2017: www.theguardian.com/uk-news/2017/jun/17/grenfell-tower-fire-food-donations-kensington-chelsea-relief (accessed 7th January 2020).
37 See New York City Atheists, "About Us": http://nycatheists.org/about-us/ (accessed 7th January 2020).
38 Sanderson Jones, "My First Funeral," *The Sunday Assembly* (blog): www.sundayassembly.com/my-first-funeral/ (accessed 7th January 2020).
39 Jones, "My First Funeral."
40 Anonymous user, "Thoughts on a Conference Called Wonder, part 2," 27th June 2015: Meetup.com; Sunday Assembly Nashville Message Board: www.meetup.com/Sunday-Assembly-Nashville/messages/boards/thread/49062421 (accessed 7th January 2020).
41 Thomas Brudholm and Thomas Cushman (eds.), *Religious Responses to Mass Atrocity: Interdisciplinary Perspectives* (Cambridge: Cambridge University Press, 2009), 2.
42 Ibid. 3.

References

The Alpha Course. "What Is Alpha?" https://alpha.org/about/
Anonymous. "Thoughts on a Conference Called Wonder, Part 2." *Meetup.com Sunday Assembly Nashville Message Board*. 27th June 2015. www.meetup.com/Sunday-Assembly-Nashville/messages/boards/thread/49062421

BBC News. "Paris Attacks: What Happened on the Night?" 9th December 2015. www.bbc.co.uk/news/world-europe-34818994

Bowcott, Owen. "Grenfell Tower Fire: Army of Volunteers Join Relief Effort." *The Guardian*. 17th June 2017. www.theguardian.com/uk-news/2017/jun/17/grenfell-tower-fire-food-donations-kensington-chelsea-relief

Brudholm, Thomas and Cushman, Thomas. *Religious Responses to Mass Atrocity: Interdisciplinary Perspectives*. Cambridge: Cambridge University Press, 2009.

Cleasby, Sam. "My Story." *So Bad Ass* (blog). www.sobadass.me/my-story/

———. "To the Woman That Tutted at Me Using the Disabled Toilets." *So Bad Ass* (blog). www.sobadass.me/2015/02/17/to-the-woman-who-tutted-at-me-using-the-disabled-toilets/

De Salvo, Gianna. "May the Joy Be with You: Rewiring the Brain towards Joy, Sunday Assembly London: 15th Nov 2015." *Inner Balance Therapies* (blog). 5th January 2016. http://innerbalance1.wordpress.com/category/neuroscience-concepts/

Devichand, Mukul. "How the World Was Changed by the Slogan 'Je Suis Charlie'." *BBC Trending* (blog). 3rd January 2016. www.bbc.co.uk/news/blogs-trending-35108339

Eyetsemitan, F. "Cultural Interpretation of Dying and Death in a Non-Western Society: The Case of Nigeria." *Online Readings in Psychology and Culture*, 3 (2), 2002.

Gonzalez, Robbie. "Meet Jean Jullien: The Artist Behind the 'Peace for Paris' Symbol." *Wired*. 14th November 2015. www.wired.com/2015/11/jean-jullien-peace-for-paris/

The Guardian. "Paris Attacks: Buildings around the World Are Lit Up in Honour of the Victims of Friday 13." 14th December 2015. www.theguardian.com/world/gallery/2015/nov/14/paris-attacks-memorials-victims-friday-13

Hotson, Elizabeth. "Putting the Fun Back into Fitness." *BBC News*. 31st October 2016. www.bbc.co.uk/news/business-37727456

Jones, Sanderson. "My First Funeral." *The Sunday Assembly* (blog). 1st October 2017. www.sundayassembly.com/my-first-funeral/

McGrath, Alister. *Studies in Doctrine*. Grand Rapids: Zondervan, 1997.

Mercer, Danae. "After the Crash: The Triathlete Who Got Back on Her Bike and Gave Back." *The Guardian*. 7th October 2013. www.theguardian.com/environment/bike-blog/2013/oct/07/after-accident-triathlete-giving-back

New York City Atheists. "About Us." http://nycatheists.org/about-us/

Slavin, Stuart J., Schindler, Debra, Chibnall, John T., Fendell, Ginny, and Schloss, Mindy. "PERMA: A Model for Institutional Leadership and Culture Change." *Academic Medicine*. 87 (11), 2012: 1481.

The Sunday Assembly. "About Sunday Assembly." https://sundayassembly.online/about-sunday-assembly/

———. "Celebrating Life Together." www.sundayassembly.com/

———. "Public Charter of the Sunday Assembly." www.sundayassembly.com/blog/public-charter-for-sunday-assembly

6   "Pause a while"

Middle space, Holy Saturday, and theological "holding" of suffering

In studying the Sunday Assembly, I sought to determine how those involved in this particular configuration of non-religious congregational activity respond to tragic events that occur both within their communities and on a global scale. In the previous section, a collation and analysis of observational and interview-related data showed that the Assembly does not practice any one official form of response to suffering. If the Sunday Assembly has any form of theodicy, it is a defence of the "celebration of life" rather than the goodness of God. The act of celebrating life has its merits. It is clearly very meaningful to some members, impacting positively on their mental health and wellbeing. However, it is also clear that the Assembly's emphasis on celebration has an effect on its ability to address suffering. The organisation's continued focus on this common goal leaves little room for its members to work through difficult events and can instead promote fast resolutions.

In this chapter, I provide a theological response to the Sunday Assembly's culture of celebration and its tendency to "pass over" pain and trauma and to deal with globally significant catastrophic events only fleetingly. In doing so, I turn to two theological works, which advocate a space in which to "hold" suffering; that is, to fully inhabit the painful tension between horror and hope, and to wrestle with the implications of trauma *before* responding or moving forward. Rowan Williams's response to the terror attacks of 9–11, and Shelly Rambo's work on Holy Saturday, are held together by this common thread, which I suggest constitutes a theological challenge and point of resistance to the practice of "passing over" suffering. I will also consider propensity of the Christian Church to also "pass over" suffering, drawing on the work of John Swinton, as well as two personal narratives relating to my own experiences of church on a local level. The reflections of Williams and Rambo, as well as a consideration of the Church as a place which, all too often, does not deal well with tragedy, will prepare the ground for further work in the proceeding chapter, in which I offer suggestions for the Church on resisting the denial and avoidance of suffering.

A note on this reflection

Having identified some answers to my initial query, I now move to reflect on these findings theologically. For the Church, and for theologians, what can be gleaned from this study of a "secular congregation"? In the process of responding to my findings, I will not be attempting to construct a "traditional" theodicy. There are several reasons for this, some of which have already previously been identified and explained in earlier chapters. While perhaps repetitive (and in many ways, obvious), these are worth a brief reiteration here.

At the beginning of this book, I outlined the intrinsically problematic nature of theodicy, from theological inconsistencies to the inadequacies of theoretical solutions. In addition, theodicy often arises in response to a particular event, and throughout this book, I have referred to both historical examples and current affairs to strengthen my arguments. A "one size fits all" theodicy is neither possible nor desirable. Since this book does not deal with one particular instance or event but draws upon many experiential examples of the realities of suffering, it is neither right nor possible to offer one generic explanation which encompasses them all. Finally, this study is an inquiry rather than actively concerned with apologetics. I set out to answer a theological query *regarding* theodicy and to critique it, as opposed to gathering information for such an approach.

Resisting "passing over"

In the previous chapter, I made the case that the Sunday Assembly's current practice of "passing over" suffering can be pastorally dangerous, leading to the isolation of individual members and failing to engage with catastrophic events. By way of evidence, I engaged with an anonymous post by a member of the Sunday Assembly from Nashville, who felt that they had been pushed to "celebrate life" to the extent that they left the movement. I also introduced the story of Carmen, whose suffering was turned to celebration in the space of a few moments. It is evident that this practice of celebration, where it fails to consider the lived realities of difficult experiences, can be one-sided at best, and dangerous at worst.

As such, in responding to the Sunday Assembly's current practice (as well as the propensity of the Church and Christians to "pass over" suffering), it is instructive to consider which parts of this might be challenged and resisted. One particular characteristic of this action is the speed at which the Assembly moves forward after acknowledging an event of mass suffering. Two examples from the previous chapter illustrate this; in the case of the Paris attacks in November 2015, the London congregation held a minute's silence, after which they applauded those who had died. Carmen, who shared her suffering with those gathered at the international conference, had her narrative taken and used as an exercise in "reasons to be grateful" just moments later. From these, and from other examples, it is apparent that the Sunday Assembly moves from acknowledgement of suffering back to a mood of celebration as quickly as possible; sometimes, not even accommodating more than a few minutes in which these difficult topics might be discussed and grieved over, or "held."

As has been made clear, the Assembly's actions of "passing over" suffering have the potential to cause hurt. In resisting an immediate move from suffering to celebration, I argue that a space must be created between the initial source of trauma, and any recovery or healing, if appropriate or even possible. In setting aside the time to "hold" suffering, to experience it, to live in the pain of the "not yet," and to wrestle with hard questions, a more holistic approach emerges: one which is neither problematic traditional theodicy nor hasty acknowledgement nor endless silence. Later, I suggest that it is within such a space that Church communities can come together and support one another, creating a "culture of lament" in preparation for times of hardship, so that narratives of suffering are recognised rather than rejected.

Here, I turn to two particular works of theology, which lay the ground for my later practical suggestions about how such a "culture of lament" might be created and sustained. Each work has been chosen for its emphasis on the importance of space and time after a catastrophic event or personal trauma, in which to fully encounter the suffering of individuals and communities. The suggestions they contain challenge a culture in which suffering is "passed over," and instead, advocate for a "middle space" between trauma and potential healing or moving forward. Rowan Williams's response to the terror attacks of 9–11, and Shelly Rambo's work on Holy Saturday, advocate a theological space in which to "hold" suffering—to fully inhabit the painful tension between horror and hope, and to wrestle with the implications of trauma *before* responding or moving forward. For Williams and for Rambo, suffering must be acknowledged, grieved over, and lamented, and human beings must take time to process difficult events. Engagement with these works will prepare the ground for the next chapter, in which more grounded, practical theological suggestions for churches responding to suffering will be offered.

Writing in the Dust: Rowan Williams on pausing after 9–11

As adults weep,
And babies
wake and smile,
a long way down,
in the places of my breaking.
I pause a while,
and take some time to
think of cruelty
and breathe.[1]

This extract from Pádraig Ó Tuama's atmospheric meditation, "September the Twelfth Two Thousand and One," captures something of the devastating aftermath of the globally impactful 9–11 disaster. Ó Tuama ends with a pause, reflecting on the destruction in silence. Yet the kind of reaction contained within this poem is at odds with the extensive media coverage and clamouring din of news bulletins that followed 9–11. The events of 11th September 2001 elevated tragedy into public conscious in a unique and far-reaching manner.[2] Images of passenger planes hitting the Twin Towers of the World Trade Centre and of crumbling, smoke-filled buildings were beamed across the world at relentless pace. The worldwide press ensured that there was no space for silent contemplation after 9–11.

The impact of 11th September was made tangible because of the speed of modern technologies which allowed many to watch the disaster unfold in real-time. Theologian Serene Jones was amongst those who followed the tragedy as it was broadcast on television:

> When I turned on the television on the morning of September 11, I and most of North America and indeed much of the world watch thousands of people die before our very eyes. We saw the real—not merely the threatened or feared—annihilation of people who were or could have been our family, friends, neighbours. . . . At first as I watched, I thought, "There are few people in the history of the world who have witnessed, in the moment of its occurrence, such massive death, a witnessing now made possible by our current telecommunications technology."[3]

The devastation of 9–11, as Jones describes it, was broadcast in real-time. The disaster was made available for public consumption even before the second plane had hit, before the towers had fallen, while people were still scrambling to escape buildings. Almost as immediately as pictures of the attacks had been broadcast, opinions and explanations for the tragedy were being plied. Jones adds that these events took place on a Tuesday. By Sunday of the same week, she was back in the pulpit, attempting to preach about what had happened. Just a week later, she was scheduled to give a presentation on trauma and violence. However, she struggled to re-order her thoughts in light of what had happened:

> Every time I sat down to write, I was overwhelmed with feelings of confusion, a sense of uncertainty, blurriness; it was hard to breathe, and my stomach hurt. I knew it was crucial in times like those, for powerful theological words to be spoken; but I, like so many others around the world, was scared and quite literally could not bring order to my thoughts. When I finally presented the lecture on September 18, it was still unfinished: the text was ragged, its words halting, its ideas scattered.[4]

Jones later admits that neither the sermon she delivered on 16th September, nor the lecture on theology and trauma she gave on 18th September, could be construed as exhaustive and consummate pieces of thought. She could not begin to articulate a theology of 9–11 immediately. Indeed, her background in trauma studies prevented her from rushing to explain away the place of God in this moment of terror.[5]

Christian ethicist Stanley Hauerwas admits that he faced a similar struggle when trying to write a theological response to 9–11. At the beginning of his essay "September 11, 2001: A Pacifist Response," written just a few months after the attacks took place, Hauerwas explains:

> I want to write honestly about September 11, 2001. But it is not easy. Even now, some months after that horrible event, I find it hard to know what can be said or, perhaps more difficult, what should be said. Even more difficult, I am not sure for what or how I should pray.[6]

For Hauerwas, as for Jones, words did not come easily in the aftermath of 9–11. The personal narratives of these two American theologians convey a sense of the difficulty involved in constructing hasty theological responses after a traumatic event takes place.

While Jones and Hauerwas struggled to gather their thoughts, Rowan Williams, a Welsh theologian and the former Archbishop of Canterbury, began to reflect quietly on his own experiences of 11th September. Williams was in a building used by Trinity Church in New York at the time of the attacks, having been scheduled to take part in discussions surrounding spirituality with church staff members. In *Writing in the Dust: Reflections on 11 September and its Aftermath*, Williams begins with his personal experience of this particular incident of devastation, subsequently moving towards a broader contemplation about how Christians might respond in similar situations of violence. Williams's approach embodies the words from Ó Tuama's poem; he chooses not to locate God in a time of adversity, but to "pause a while," "take some time to think of cruelty, and breathe."[7]

Like Jones and Hauerwas, Williams found it difficult to reach for answers. He describes an encounter he had with a young Catholic airline pilot in the street shortly after the disaster. The young man caught sight of Williams's clerical collar and approached him, demanding to know "what the hell God was doing when the planes hit the towers."[8] Williams admits that he could provide no comforting answer. While in the midst of devastation, he reached for platitudes about divine intervention, but ultimately found these to be lacking when face to face with a distraught and emotional young man.

Reflecting on his struggle for answers, Williams suggests that hasty dialogue and religious explanations are the opposite of what is required in the aftermath of a traumatic event.[9] Indeed, he offers no theodicy or religious platitudes of his own in response to 9–11 and actively discourages the construction of traditional theodicies (the kind explored in detail in Chapter 1 of this book). He explains that Christians should avoid the temptation to gravitate towards the most immediate option of response, as this may not necessarily be correct, or helpful to those who are experiencing the trauma first-hand. Relatedly, Williams is conscious of the risk of "binding" God to his own purposes. By this, he is referring to the shaping of an understanding divine providence, to portray God as "useful" in times of terror. Where God is contorted to suit individual preferences in the wake of disaster, the danger of exploiting selfish interests is realised. Williams heeds caution: "When we try to make God useful in crises . . . we take the first step towards the great lie of religion: the God who fits our agenda."[10]

One need not look further than a few days after the attacks to see what Williams means. Recall the conversation between Pat Robertson and Jerry Falwell on *The 700 Club* (mentioned in Chapter 1), which took place just two days after the attacks. This platform was used by both men to tie the actions of God to their particular conservative agenda, attacking and holding accountable "all of them who tried to secularise America." The conversation ended with both Robertson and Falwell imploring their listeners to "render their hearts," praying and fasting in response.[11] In doing so, they "bound God to their own agenda," pushing for a religious revival and using the suffering of many to further their cause.

Hasty reactions to 9–11 were not confined to the religious sphere. George W. Bush, US president at the time of the attacks, admitted that his initial reaction to the news was to wish for vengeance on the perpetrators, and for God to intervene and "send them to hell." On a visit to the former World Trade Centre site three days after the attacks, Bush described a "palpable bloodlust" present in those who gathered, and an overwhelming urge to exact violent revenge. Furthermore, he recalled the declaration of bystanders that God would be "on their side" as they sought to avenge the attacks. Jewish philosopher Alan Mittleman points out that the problem of inciting religious violence in God's name is an ancient concept, but one which is given "new salience" in the wake of 9–11.[12] This is because the name of God was used not only in conjunction with the "holy war" of al-Qaeda, by those who flew planes into the World Trade Centre and the Pentagon, but also within the rhetoric of Western (American) retaliation. This particular case of immediate theodicy in the wake of 9–11 was one amongst other factors which led to the later devastation of the Iraq War.

How, then, to respond in the face of such unforeseen violence, when the shock waves of an event threaten to demand answers from some and immediate action from others? Williams suggests a time of silent contemplation. He is wary of theologians and other social commentators speaking too soon, lest they form a picture of God that simply suits their own needs (just as Robertson, Falwell, and Bush did). The title of Williams's short reflection,

Writing in the Dust, is taken from an exegetical exploration of chapter eight of John's gospel.[13] In the text, an "adulterous" woman is hauled before Jesus, who is asked to pass judgement on her. When Jesus is questioned about the woman's fate, he does not reply immediately, rather pausing to stoop and write in the dust with his finger. He hesitates and does not respond for some time, appearing to consider the situation before replying. In Jesus's silence, Williams sees a space in which those gathered can begin to reflect and "see themselves differently."[14] Within this space, there are no fixed answers, and there is no immediate move forward.

After traumatic events, Williams advises Christians to learn to live in the "void" of silence. Such acts of terror—and indeed, God's presence or lack thereof within them—can never be adequately explained. Traditional theodicy cannot hope to justify such horrors. However, a pause for contemplation in the wake of tragic circumstances can "allow some of our demons to walk away."[15] In other words, Williams encourages pause for thought so that damaging words and actions are not taken in haste. At the very least, a moment of stillness can ensure that some of the potentially harmful vitriol that can come packaged with the first knee-jerk responses to tragedy is filtered out.

"A suffering beyond death": Shelly Rambo and the "middle space" of Holy Saturday

The work of Williams on 9–11 points towards a space between the initial shock, grief, and anguish which accompany an event of mass suffering and implies a future move towards speech, answers, and reconfigurations of God's presence. But for theologian Shelly Rambo, there is a further element to the experience of such moments of rupture. In *Spirit and Trauma: A Theology of Remaining*, Rambo describes trauma as "the suffering that does not go away."[16] While both Williams and Rambo reflect on the events of 11th September 2001, Rambo's text is not a concentrated reflection on any one particular even. Rather, she draws widely from the field of trauma studies, and on her own experiences through her life and work in the Church.[17]

Rambo's text opens with a personal narrative of a visit to New Orleans, two and a half years after Hurricane Katrina struck the Gulf Coast. The hurricane, which made landfall in August 2005, was destructive and deadly; it swept through the Gulf of Mexico, causing catastrophic damage in several major cities. The death toll climbed to 1,833 people, who were killed either directly or indirectly.[18] It is estimated that Katrina caused US$108 billion worth of total damage to homes, schools, roads, vehicles, and businesses across five US states: Louisiana, Mississippi, Florida, Georgia, and Alabama.[19] In New Orleans, Rambo met with a group of churches, who were discussing their collective role in the rebuilding of the city. Julius Lee, a deacon, spoke up in the meeting about the "great push to claim that New Orleans is back to normal."[20] Rambo explains that: "The language of restoration, of rebuilding, can make people forget the existing reality of what people are experiencing."[21] Lee spoke further about life being profoundly changed for people in the Gulf after the storm. Rambo describes the tension between "the public uneasiness with trauma, and the push to move beyond it," as well as "an impatience with suffering, revealing a timeline on public attention and sympathy."[22]

Inadvertently, Rambo's words here are descriptive of the Sunday Assembly's response to suffering. In the previous chapter, I explained the way in which the Assembly can at times be "impatient" with suffering, pushing to move beyond it to a point of celebration as quickly as possible. I drew on the narrative of the 2015 Paris attacks, as well as a story of personal suffering from Carmen. In both situations, the Assembly's response was one which might be described as "public uneasiness." This is a similar to that which Rambo describes in her work. Indeed, when listening to Carmen's talk at the Assembly's international conference, I noted that members of the congregation appeared palpably unsettled. The collective desire of those gathered to move beyond her suffering as quickly as possible was compounded by the leadership's decision to change the direction of the conversation and use her story to ask attendees what they were "most grateful for." Yet I noticed that Carmen was still visibly upset about her experiences, and that she continued to cry. For Rambo, Carmen's reaction is part of the lived reality of trauma, a kind of suffering which is hallmarked by a sense of "ongoingness."[23] Rambo herself points to the ways in trauma "persists in the present . . . in symptoms that live on in the body."[24]

Theologically, the continuous presence of trauma can be discerned in many parts of the Christian scriptures. Rambo chooses to draw on the particular example of Easter, as a lens through which her ideas regarding trauma might be expressed theologically. Christ's death on the cross on Good Friday is analogous of the immediate shock, chaos, and searing darkness that comes from a traumatic event. This pain is not immediately released; Rambo refers to the cross as "haunting" event, which casts a shadow over the Christian tradition.[25] Then comes Holy Saturday:

> Positioned between Good Friday and Easter Sunday in the Christian liturgical calendar, Holy Saturday is often overshadowed by the two days and remains, in many traditions, a day that merely marks a turn between the events of Jesus's death and resurrection. . . . [T]here is a biblical silence in the aftermath of the crucifixion; the Gospel accounts do not reveal much about the activities between cross and resurrection. . . . Yet the middle develops in the Christian tradition into a rich literary and liturgical landscape of the underworld, filled with images of Christ's post death travels to hell.[26]

In her exploration of Holy Saturday as a lens through which to examine trauma theologically, Rambo turns to the writings of Hans Urs von

Balthasar, a Swiss theologian and Catholic priest, and Adrienne von Speyr, a contemporary mystic, who wrote extensively on Holy Saturday in relation to her experiences of "participation in Christ's descent into hell."[27,28] Speyr reports that she would experience "intense migraine headaches, as if the crown of thorns was being pressed into her temples," and that she would often physically bleed "as if the wounded heart of Christ was her own."[29] Yet on Holy Saturday, her active suffering would cease. Rambo explains that "another, more inexplicable form of suffering" would begin for Speyr: "a suffering that extended beyond death."[30] The uniqueness of the suffering of Holy Saturday, for Speyr and for Christ's followers in the biblical account, lies in the joins between life and death. On this middle ground, the immediate trauma is over; the initial shock and physical pain subsides and yet suffering still remains. In the aftermath of death, Rambo describes the nearness of the Holy Spirit, "remaining" and "persisting" with love in a space which offers no immediate redemption, and in which there is a "mixed picture of life and death."[31] This, she says, is the experiential reality of life after traumatic events.

What are some of the "Holy Saturdays" of our time; the spaces in which immediate suffering is over, yet lingers in the on-going trauma experienced by those closest to it? I have already drawn on the example of Carmen, from my own study on the Sunday Assembly. Rambo mentions New Orleans, which, as she witnessed herself, was "not restored" immediately in the wake of Hurricane Katrina.[32] Jones, whose description of the real-time 9–11 broadcast was mentioned earlier in this chapter, points to the on-going suffering of those who witnessed and (either directly or indirectly) experienced the events of these attacks. She suggests that the events left many in a "disassociated playback loop," wherein the violence was "re-enacted again and again."[33] Indeed, many of those living and working in New York, who had witnessed and lived through the collapse of the World Trade Centre towers, displayed classical symptoms of PTSD in the aftermath of the disaster. Once the initial shock and horror of the attacks had passed, residual anguish clung to survivors, witnesses, and those who were bereaved. Likewise, Chilean liberation theologian Mario Aguilar identifies a "period of exhaustion" after the 1994 Rwandan genocide.[34] In the space of 100 days, an estimated 800,000 Rwandans were killed, the majority (but not all) of whom were Tutsi peoples;[35] most (but not all) of those who perpetrated the violence were Hutus, part of the country's largest ethnic group.[36] The Rwandan people, who had been exposed to a campaign of systematic slaughter, and who had, in many cases, lost members of their families to the relentless bloodshed of the machete, were traumatised by what they had lived through. Aguilar describes a post-traumatic mood in Rwanda in the aftermath of the genocide, explaining that "Rwanda was a nation of silence."[37,38] The corpses of those killed were left untouched because most Rwandans were immersed in the actions of either killing or fleeing the violence.[39,40] A study by psychologists Heide Rieder and Thomas Elbert on the survivors of the genocide found that their exposure to the violence and the "cadavers" of the deceased had resulted in "high rates of mental health and psychosocial problems due to the inconceivable, dehumanised brutality that the majority of them had been exposed or witness to."[41] In all of the mentioned cases—from New Orleans to New York to Rwanda—the "end" of immediate suffering did not necessarily mark the end of the trauma experienced by those who lived through it. After 9–11, bodies and rubble were cleared from the wreckage of the Twin Towers. After the genocide in Rwanda, machetes were set down and bones retrieved. But thereafter, a new form of suffering began, a kind of suffering "beyond death."[42]

Rambo is aware of this particular dynamic, and she emphasises the importance of witnessing to this kind of on-going suffering. For her, Christians cannot simply focus on the promises of the future, contained within the "Easter morning." They must learn to linger on the reality of on-going devastation; "the cracks within the peaceful running of the world, which highlight the 'not yet' of the Kingdom of God."[43] Instead of passing over suffering, Christians are called to participate in this "suspended middle territory, between life and death" and to recognise the brokenness of those who live their lives on this middle ground.[44] This is, specifically, a Christian vocation; for Rambo, Christians are "oriented to suffering in a particular way" in the "aftermath of the cross."[45]

The Church "passes over": silence and suffering

In responding theologically to the findings from my study of the Sunday Assembly, a further consideration has emerged. The words of Serene Jones and Stanley Hauerwas earlier in this chapter communicated something of the struggle of responding theologically to 9–11; additionally, Jones found it difficult to preach in church on the weekend of the events. Rowan Williams, too, found it hard to answer the immediate questions he faced about the same event; as a member of the clergy, he was stopped in the street and asked about God's intentions and whereabouts. Could it be that theologians and the Church also find it difficult to respond to catastrophic events? If this is the case, could the Church, too, be prone to "passing over" suffering?

It is crucial to state that is not necessarily the case in all churches and denominations. In fact, it is primarily a white, Protestant church problem. In her classic text *African American Christian Worship*, Melva Wilson Costen writes that Black church worship is effused with lament "in the midst of struggles."[46] This can be traced back to the singing of African American spirituals; unaccompanied, monophonic unison songs, which both imparted Christian values which also describing and lamenting the evils and hardships of slavery. For R. Clifford Jones, spirituals "protested the social conditions in which Blacks were locked even as they pointed to a better day of freedom and justice."[47] Black Christians have long been forced to live in the shadow of Good Friday under white supremacy. Worship in Black churches and communities is therefore steeped in a history of oppression and marginalisation. Because it is so much a part of the story of Black Christianity, suffering cannot be "passed over" in Black worship. Indeed, it is a particular form of white privilege to be able to "pass over" (or even talk about avoiding) suffering.

There are other denominations in which suffering is directly addressed within a worship setting rather than circumvented. Russian, Greek, and other strands of the Eastern Orthodox Churches practice public lament during Great Lent. The Matins of Lamentation, usually celebrated on Good Friday, resembles the Byzantine Rite funeral service. It involves the chanting of Psalm 118. Each verse is interspersed with laudations (*ainoi*) of the dead Christ.[48] Year-round worship is modelled on this, and Sunday services call on God for mercy and forgiveness.

However, in majority-white Protestant churches, lament and discussion about suffering has, for Soong-Chan Rah, become "a lost discipline."[49] Glenn Pemberton points out that while laments constitute 40% of the Psalms, Protestant church hymnals in the US do not reflect this. In the hymnal for the Churches of Christ, laments make up 13%. In the Presbyterian hymnal, this figure is 19%, and in the Baptist hymnal, 13%.[50] Additionally, Rah observes that of the top 100 worship songs, according to Christian Copyright International, only five fall into the category of "lament."[51]

Later, I will examine this particular phenomenon in greater detail. For now, it should be noted (if briefly) that the issues of "passing over" suffering and avoidance of lament that I am talking about are primarily the kind that affect white Protestant churches in the Western hemisphere. To that end, there are several narratives which help to explain exactly what I mean when I suggest that some churches have a problem with the act of avoiding suffering.

In his work *Raging with Compassion*, John Swinton gives an account of a local Church of Scotland service he attended in August 1998. The service took place one day after the Irish Republican Army (IRA) detonated a car bomb in Omagh, Northern Ireland. The bomb killed 28 people and injured 220 others. Swinton describes the "unrelenting" television coverage of the event, showing images of a street strewn with wreckage and the "blood-stained testimonies of the injured."[52] He explains that the events affected him "even as a distanced onlooker," and that they caused him to think on "deep and penetrating questions about the goodness and fairness of God."[53] As such, going to church was a chance for him and others to "receive some guidance as to how, together, we might deal with our confusion, orientation, and anxiety." He details the service:

> The first hymns went by; nothing was said. We were told to worship, to praise the Lord, to life our hearts heavenwards and appreciate the wonderful things that God has done for us. We did. And still nothing was said. The prayers went by and we thanked God for his [sic] great mercy

towards us; nothing was said about the bombing. The sermon was narrated. We were instructed to have faith and be thankful that God was still God and has reached down in love to us despite our sinfulness . . . still nothing was said. The prayers of intercession came . . . and went . . . silence. The entire service came and went with no recognition of the tragedy that had happened in our country to our own people.[54]

Throughout the service, Swinton had waited for the tragedy in Omagh to be spoken of. He reflects that "there was no room in our liturgy and worship for sadness, brokenness, and questioning," adding that:

> We had much space for joy, love, praise and supplication, but it seemed that we viewed our acknowledgement of sadness and the tragic brokenness of our world as almost tantamount to faithfulness.[55]

In Swinton's church, this particularly traumatic event, still raw and unfolding, was not acknowledged; the church was silent. Just as the Sunday Assembly favours celebration over suffering, to the extent that it "passes over" that which is tragic or painful, this church favoured "joy, love, praise and supplication" but found no room in which to meet with the questions and crises arising from the bombing. In this way, Swinton's church engaged in "denial and avoidance" of the suffering of the people of Omagh.[56]

Swinton's story is one such example of how the Church, like the Sunday Assembly, can fail to recognise and "hold suffering." But has this changed in almost two decades? Could it be that the Church of the twenty-first century, in a constant climate of war, violence, terror, and disaster, has learnt to engage the suffering around it and to draw on the Christian tradition of lament which encourages expression of pain and loss? Two experiential accounts, pertaining to my own experiences of church during the duration of my doctoral study, suggest otherwise.

A few years ago, I attended a Pentecost service for a cluster of city churches. The service took place on 4th June 2017, the morning after a van mounted a pavement on London Bridge and was driven into a group of pedestrians. The van crashed, and its three male occupants ran to nearby Borough Market, where they stabbed people with long knives.[57] Eight people died, and a further 48 were injured.[58] This was the third terror-related attack in the UK in just over two months, following a similar attack in Westminster in March and a bombing in Manchester in May. Like Swinton, in the aftermath of the Omagh bombing, I felt the need for some leadership and guidance about faith on the morning after the London Bridge attacks. Even as a "distanced onlooker," I felt a sense of shock and horror; there had been so many recent attacks, one after the other. The thought of the rising body count tied my stomach in knots.

Pentecost is about the coming of the Holy Spirit and is a celebration of the birth of the worldwide Church. As such, the majority of the service I attended focused on the Church throughout the world. There was a triumphalist message about the spread of God's word across the globe, communicated in the hymns and sermon. Mention of the attacks in London was notably absent from every part of the service, and it was clear that no last-minute amendments had been made to accommodate them.

Finally, in the prayers of intercession near the end, the attacks were mentioned fleetingly; the congregation was asked to "pray silently" and individually for the victims in London. But there was no sign of leadership, no genuine outpouring of grief, and no effort to create a space in which this suffering could be acknowledged and held. Prayers quickly gave way to the singing of a celebratory chorus of "Shine Jesus Shine"; a somewhat jarring and unpalatably triumphant finale on what was an otherwise sombre day. The Church, it seems, is not just susceptible to the kind of silence that Swinton describes. It is also prone to the same action of "passing over" suffering as the Sunday Assembly.

A second narrative relates to a church congregation I found myself a part of during my doctoral studies. It was a wealthy, suburban church, located on the western edge of the city where I live and a short distance from one of the highest-performing secondary schools in Scotland. My attendance at this church was largely tied to my husband Peter's job there as a youth worker. It was on a dark October evening when I was driving to pick him up from work that I first that I first heard about a pupil from the school near the church having been killed. Sitting in traffic, I listened to the radio: the 16-year-old boy had been stabbed at lunchtime. He had been rushed to the local hospital but died shortly afterwards. The faces of people in the cars next to me were just as drained and shocked as mine. It was clear that this terrible news was spreading quickly.

I picked Peter up, and we made our way to the school. Entrances were cordoned off, and police cars blockaded the surrounding roads. Groups of pupils had begun to gather at the gates. They clustered together; the sounds of their sobs intermingled with the steady crackle of police radios. The wind and rain began to pick up, but there was nothing the police could do. They would not let anyone inside the building, and so those who had come seeking answers could only wait, shivering outside in the steadily darkening night.

I wondered aloud if our church building had been opened. It seemed obvious that it should be; logistically speaking, the church was five minutes away and would be passed by many of those beginning to make their way up to the school. The space was large enough to hold several hundred people at once, it could be heated to keep those who had been standing outside warm, and there would be food and drink and quiet places to sit for those in shock. Standing watching the groups of pupils, huddled together, mourning their friend, it seemed obvious what the best and most caring course of action should be.[59] I wanted to be at the church, to make a warm and safe space for those who were hurting from the day's events.

When we arrived at the church, however, it was dark inside; the door was bolted, and there was no one else around. By this point, several hours had passed since the news of the young boy's death had broken. His tragic story was, by now, a local and national headline. Peter carried a set of keys for the sanctuary, and so the two of us made the decision to go inside, turn on the lights, and open the doors for those passing by. It was only once we had done this that we alerted other members of our congregation. Some understood what we had done and made their way down to help us. Others stayed away, conscious of the mounting presence of the press on the street or of the outpouring of grief from the school pupils.

Moments after I had wedged open the heavy double-doors at the front of the building, battling against the rising winds and rain, I heard footsteps at the entrance. A woman and her teenage son, still wearing his school uniform, asked if they could come inside and sit awhile. The boy was shivering; whether from the cold or the shock, it was not clear. I invited them to make themselves comfortable, and asked them to let us know if there was anything else they might need. Within the hour, the church was half-full; those who had been gathered at the school gates had congregated in the sanctuary. Members of the church had arrived. Most were occupied with making tea and coffee or stemming the tide of photographers and reporters in search of tear-stained faces and eye-witness accounts. The minister busied himself with the press, leading them in their droves to the vestry, to deliver platitudes about the shock and horror of the event on camera. Peter and I were left to usher in the school pupils, parents, teachers, and locals, who were searching for a place of peace and solitude, as the fate of one of their number became an evening headline across the country.

As Peter and I worked together to try and create a safe and welcoming space, we were approached, numerous times, by members of the congregation, who were concerned that we had not "tried to cheer the children up." Some implored us to hand out leaflets about our teenage ministries to "up our numbers." Others wanted us to interrupt the clusters of pupils to "talk to them about how they were feeling." In all of these different approaches, one thing was abundantly clear; an unbridled outpouring of grief would not be tolerated. The space to weep and lament might have been intended, but it was to be punctuated at regular intervals by parishioners who, uncomfortable in the face of such visible suffering, were intent on "fixing" and "righting" the situation.

I wondered whether such actions might have been the product of immediate collective shock, yet I noted similar behaviour throughout the rest of the week, as the church doors stayed open. Further, words of lament were difficult to come by. As we prepared for a candle-lit vigil for the boy in the following days, a member of the church told me that they had been struggling to find hymns or readings which appropriately captured the mood in the church. "We never sing anything sad," he explained. "And our worship is always upbeat and happy." Just as in Swinton's local church, where "love, joy, praise and supplication" were afforded a central place in worship, there was no space in the worship at this church for sadness, brokenness, and questioning of faith. In other words, there was not a "culture of lament."

Conclusion

This study has identified a phenomenon of "passing over" suffering within the experience of the Sunday Assembly community. In this chapter, I have outlined some of the ways in which a similar phenomenon might be noted in the behaviours and actions of the Church. This may point towards the evasion of suffering as an inherently human response. Nonetheless, the intention of this study, as one grounded in practical theology, is to be "transformational." In other words, the findings of this research must be grounded and relayed in a way which can, specifically, help the Church in some way to think about its response to suffering.

As I have explained in this chapter, a theological response must challenge a hasty move from suffering to celebration or reconciliation. The Sunday Assembly's rush towards celebration reveals an impatience with suffering, and, in Rambo's words, "a timeline" on attention and sympathy. In the examples given in Chapter 5, it is apparent that the Assembly's action of "passing over" both globally traumatic events and instances of individual suffering is both incomplete and potentially dangerous. Rambo's work in particular reveals the tension of on-going suffering in a post-traumatic frame of reference; something which, if left unacknowledged, can be incredibly damaging. In Christian tradition, there are numerous examples of "pause" between trauma and response to be found. Williams draws on Christ's action of "writing in the dust" in the Gospel of John, while Rambo explores the mysticism of the Easter narrative and Holy Saturday through a lens of trauma.

The shape of the "middle-space" after suffering, which I have begun to outline theologically here, is primarily needed by white Protestant churches, and must be detailed further. At the beginning of this book, I explained that the Church and theologians needed to move beyond the construction of potentially damaging theodicies and explanations for suffering. It is clear from the narratives at the end of this chapter that the Church must *also* be wary of responding to suffering by "passing over," minimising, or avoiding it. In what follows, I will explore ways in which the Christian traditions of lament and Christ-centred community can be used in practice. The ultimate resistance to the denial and avoidance of suffering is to create what I will call a "culture of lament."

Notes

1 Pádraig Ó Tuama, *Readings from the Book of Exile* (Norwich: Canterbury Press, 2012), 67 (emphasis added).

2 Scottish theologian John Bell cautions against setting this particular event apart from other instances of suffering, explaining that the "continuous outpouring of grief around 9–11" often fails to take into consideration "similar unwanted and unexpected violations of a nation's borders and security" which have taken place outwith the immediate US context. In doing so, Bell is careful "not to belittle the USA experience" but simply to locate 9–11 in a wider global context, and to advocate for the inclusion of non-Western narratives of suffering in discourse. He argues that the other "ground zero" events are "no less important to the psyches of these nations and no less important in the eyes of God than what happened to the USA on one day in 2001." In her own exploration of 9–11, theologian Tina Beattie appears to support Bell's re-contextualisation of these events. She locates the attacks historically, suggesting that: "The violent killing of 2,752 human beings barely registers in the slaughterhouse of modernity." (See John Bell, *Hard Words for Interesting Times: Biblical Texts in Contemporary Contexts* (Glasgow: Wild Goose Publications, 2003), 92–93, and Tina Beattie, "Fragments: Reflections in a Shattered Screen," *Political Theology*, 5 (12), 2011, 674). In noting this, and in the interests of reflexivity, it is important to acknowledge the use of Western-centric narratives in this chapter; this work is located within the boundaries of Western theological learning and thinking. The events of September 11th are dealt with here as an example of a catastrophic event, since 9–11 was a such an epoch-defining moment. It has been theologically compelling (with numerous works in addition to those mentioned in this chapter being produced), significant for the study of suffering and trauma (which will become evident later in this chapter when examining the work of Shelly Rambo), and also a catalyst for the rise of New Atheism (as mentioned previously in Chapter 2).

3 Serene Jones, *Trauma and Grace: Theology in a Ruptured World* (Kentucky: Westminster John Knox Press, 2009), 28.

4 Ibid. 24.

5 Ibid.

6 Stanley Hauerwas, "September 11, 2001: A Pacifist Response," in Stanley Hauerwas and Frank Lentricchia (eds.) *Dissent From the Homeland: Essays after September 11* (Durham: Duke University Press, 2003), 425.

7 Ó Tuama, 67.

8 Rowan Williams, *Writing in the Dust: Reflections on 11th September and Its Aftermath* (London: Hodder and Stoughton, 2002), 7.

9 Ibid. 8.

10 Ibid. 8–9.

11 Pat Robertson and Jerry Falwell, "Transcript of Pat Robertson's Interview with Jerry Falwell, Broadcast on the 700 Club, September 13th 2001," in Bruce Lincoln (ed.) *Holy Terrors: Thinking about Religion after September 11th* (Chicago: University of Chicago Press, 2010), 107.

12 Alan Mittleman, "The Problem of Religious Violence," *Political Theology*, 5(12), 2011, 722.

13 The text from John's gospel, which Williams draws on, reads: "But Jesus went to the Mount of Olives. At dawn, he appeared again in the temple courts, where all the people gathered around him, and he sat down to teach them. The teachers of the law and the Pharisees brought in a woman caught in adultery. They made her stand before the group and said to Jesus, 'Teacher, this woman was caught in the act of adultery. In the Law Moses commanded us to stone such women. Now what do you say?' They were using this question as a trap, in order to have a basis for accusing him. *But Jesus bent down and started to write on the ground with his finger.* When they kept on questioning him, he straightened up and said to them, 'Let any one of you who is without sin be the first to throw a

stone at her.' *Again, he stooped down and wrote on the ground.* At this, those who heard began to go away one at a time, the older ones first, until only Jesus was left, with the woman still standing there. Jesus straightened up and asked her, 'Woman, where are they? Has no one condemned you?' She said, 'No one, sir.' And Jesus said, 'Neither do I condemn you. Go your way, and from now on do not sin again.'" John 8: 1–11, *The Holy Bible New Revised Standard Version* (London: Harper Collins, 2011) (emphasis added).

14 Williams, 77.
15 Ibid. 81.
16 Shelly Rambo, *Spirit and Trauma: A Theology of Remaining* (Kentucky: Westminster John Knox Press, 2010), 15.
17 Rambo explores, for example, the aftermath of Hurricane Katrina for those living in New Orleans (Rambo, 1), the post-traumatic stress of those involved in the Iraq War (Rambo, 18), and the survivors of the Holocaust (Rambo, 24).
18 CNN, "Hurricane Katrina Statistics Fast Facts": http://edition.cnn.com/2013/08/23/us/hurricane-katrina-statistics-fast-facts/index.html (accessed 7th January 2020).
19 Ibid.
20 Rambo, 1.
21 Ibid. 1–2.
22 Ibid. 2.
23 Ibid.
24 Ibid.
25 Ibid. 158.
26 Ibid. 45.
27 Ibid. 47.
28 Balthasar recounts that Speyr experienced visions "every year after the passion ended on Good Friday, at about three o'clock in the afternoon." Shortly after "began the 'descent into hell' (which lasted into the early morning hours of Easter Sunday) about which Adrienne gave detailed accounts year after year." Hans Urs Von Balthasar, *First Glance at Adrienne Speyr*, trans. Antje Lawry and St. Sergia Englund (San Francisco: Ignatius Press, 1981), 65.
29 Rambo, 49.
30 Ibid.
31 Ibid. 140–141.
32 Ibid. 9.
33 Jones, *Trauma and Grace*, 29.
34 Mario Aguilar, *Theology, Liberation and Genocide* (London: SCM Press, 2009), 42.
35 Aguilar notes that "moderate Hutus" also comprise some of the number killed, though it is difficult to say exactly how many.
36 It should be recorded that Aguilar believes these classifications to be "fictitious" and within the "imagination of the media." He rightly points out that the categories of "Hutu" and "Tutsi" are not as rigid as the worldwide press have made them out to be, and that many moderate Hutus lost their lives in the killings as well. Nonetheless, these labels, while limited, still provide a way of understanding some of Rwanda's historic tensions, and some of the internal perceptions which clashed in the lead up to the 1994 genocide (see Aguilar, 19–20).
37 Aguilar, 33.
38 It should be noted that the "silence" being referred to here is not the same as the silence of the Sunday Assembly in response to "ground-zero" events, as explored in the previous chapter. The silence in Rwanda was post-traumatic.
39 Charles Kambanda, "Display of Human Remains in Rwanda's Genocide Memorial Sites: Who Is Reaping from the Atrocious Tragedy?," *Veritas Info* (blog):

www.veritasinfo.fr/article-display-of-human-remains-in-rwanda-s-genocide-memorial-sites-who-is-reaping-from-the-atrocious-trag-74738267.html (accessed 7th January 2020).

40 The Rwandan Patriotic Front (RPF) passed official legislation to leave the skulls and bones of the dead in place. Paul Kagame, leader of the RPF who assumed the presidency of Rwanda in 2000, stated that "the genocide memorial sites and the human remains therein are proof that world leaders failed to prevent and/or stop Tutsi genocide."

41 Heide Rieder and Thomas Elbert, "Rwanda: Lasting Imprints of a Genocide: Trauma, Mental Health and Psychosocial Conditions in Survivors, Former Prisoners and Their Children," *Conflict and Health*, 7 (6), 2013, 1.

42 Rambo draws on Hans von Balthasar's interpretation of Adrienne von Speyr's telling of the Christian story. Von Speyr had visions of Christ's time in hell and described the suffering there as being more of a "soul-condition": a psychological rather than physical period of trauma. This would certainly correspond with the phenomenon of post-traumatic stress, which constitutes a period of psychological turmoil after initial, physical suffering has ceased. Rambo, 49–50.

43 Rambo, 60.

44 Ibid. 25.

45 Ibid. 159.

46 Melva Wilson Costen, *African American Christian Worship*, Second Edition (Nashville, TX: Abingdon Press, 2010)—see Chapter 7 in particular for a more in-depth discussion of this.

47 R. Clifford Jones, "African-American Worship: Its Heritage, Character, and Quality," *Ministry*: www.ministrymagazine.org/archive/2002/09/african-american-worship-its-heritage-character-and-quality.html (accessed 7th January 2020).

48 Greek Orthodox Diocese of America, "Great and Holy Friday": www.goarch.org/holyfriday (accessed 7th January 2020).

49 Soong-Chan Rah, *Prophetic Lament: A Call for Justice in Troubled Times* (Downers Grove: InterVarsity Press, 2015), 23.

50 See Glenn Pemberton, *Hurting with God: Learning to Lament with the Psalms* (Abilene, TX: ABU Press, 2012).

51 Rah, 23.

52 John Swinton, *Raging with Compassion: Pastoral Responses to the Problem of Evil* (Grand Rapids, MI: Wm. B. Eerdmans, 2007), 92.

53 Ibid.

54 Ibid.

55 Ibid.

56 Ibid.

57 BBC News, "London Attack: What People Saw," 4th June 2017: www.bbc.co.uk/news/uk-40149159 (accessed 7th January 2020).

58 BBC News, "London Attack: What We Know So Far," 12th June 2017: www.bbc.co.uk/news/uk-england-london-40147164 (accessed 7th January 2020).

59 In Matthew 25, Jesus, as part of His Oliviet Discourse, addresses his followers, in part saying: "When the Son of Man comes in his glory, and all the angels with him, then he will sit on the throne of his glory. All the nations will be gathered before him, and he will separate people one from another as a shepherd separates the sheep from the goats, and he will put the sheep at his right hand and the goats at the left. Then the king will say to those at his right hand, 'Come, you that are blessed by my Father, inherit the kingdom prepared for you from the foundation of the world; *For I was hungry and you gave me food, I was thirsty and you gave me something to drink, I was a stranger and you welcomed me, I was naked and you gave me clothing, I was sick and you took care of me, I was in prison and you visited me.*' Then the righteous will answer him, 'Lord, when was

it that we saw you hungry and gave you food, or thirsty and gave you something to drink? [3] And when was it that we saw you a stranger and welcomed you, or naked and gave you clothing? And when was it that we saw you sick or in prison and visited you?' *And the king will answer them, 'Truly I tell you, just as you did it to one of the least of these who are members of my family, you did it to me.'"* Matthew 25: 35–40, *The Holy Bible New Revised Standard Version* (London: Harper Collins, 2011) (emphasis added).

References

Aguilar, Mario I. *Theology, Liberation and Genocide*. London: SCM Press, 2009.

BBC News. "London Attacks: What People Saw." 4th June 2017. www.bbc.co.uk/news/uk-40149159

———. "London Attack: What We Know So Far." 12th June 2017. www.bbc.co.uk/news/uk-england-london-40147164

Beattie, Tina. "Fragments: Reflections in a Shattered Screen." *Political Theology*. 5 (12), 2011: 672–677.

Bell, John L. *Hard Words for Interesting Times: Biblical Texts in Contemporary Contexts*. Glasgow: Wild Goose Publications, 2003.

Clifford Jones, R. "African-American Worship: Its Heritage, Character, and Quality." *Ministry*. www.ministrymagazine.org/archive/2002/09/african-american-worship-its-heritage-character-and-quality.html

CNN. "Hurricane Katrina Statistics Fast Facts." http://edition.cnn.com/2013/08/23/us/hurricane-katrina-statistics-fast-facts/index.html

Greek Orthodox Diocese of America. "Great and Holy Friday." www.goarch.org/holyfriday

Hauerwas, Stanley. "September 11, 2001: A Pacifist Response." In *Dissent From the Homeland: Essays after September 11*, edited by Stanley Hauerwas and Frank Lentricchia, 181–194. Durham: Duke University Press, 2003.

Jones, Serene. *Trauma and Grace: Theology in a Ruptured World*. Louisville: Westminster John Knox Press, 2009.

Kambanda, Charles. "Display of Human Eemains in Rwanda's Genocide Memorial Sites: Who Is Reaping from the Atrocious Tragedy?" *Veritas Info* (blog). www.veritasinfo.fr/article-display-of-human-remains-in-rwanda-s-genocide-memorial-sites-who-is-reaping-from-the-atrocious-trag-74738267.html

Ó Tuama, Pádraig. *Readings from the Book of Exile*. Norwich: Canterbury Press, 2012.

Pemberton, Glenn. *Hurting with God: Learning to Lament with the Psalms*. Abilene, TX: ABU Press, 2012.

Rah, Soong-Chan. *Prophetic Lament: A Call for Justice in Troubled Times*. Downers Grove: InterVarsity Press, 2015.

Rambo, Shelly. *Spirit and Trauma: A Theology of Remaining*. Louisville: Westminster John Knox Press, 2010.

Rieder, Heide and Elbert, Thomas. "Rwanda: Lasting Imprints of a Genocide: Trauma, Mental Health and Psychosocial Conditions in Survivors, Former Prisoners and Their Children." *Conflict and Health*. 7 (6), 2013.

Robertson, Pat, and Falwell, Jerry. "Transcript of Pat Robertson's Interview with Jerry Falwell, Broadcast on the 700 Club, September 13th 2001." In *Holy Terrors:*

Thinking about Religion after September 11th, edited by Bruce Lincoln, 108–112. Chicago: University of Chicago Press, 2010.

Swinton, John. *Raging with Compassion: Pastoral Responses to the Problem of Evil.* Grand Rapids, MI: Wm. B. Eerdmans, 2007.

Von Balthasar, Hans Urs. *First Glance at Adrienne Speyr*. Translated by Antje Lawry and Sr. Sergia Englund. San Francisco: Ignatius Press, 1981.

Williams, Rowan. *Writing in the Dust: Reflections on 11th September and Its Aftermath*. London: Hodder and Stoughton, 2002.

Wilson Costen, Melva. *African American Christian Worship*. Second Edition. Nashville, TX: Abingdon Press, 2010.

7 Creating a culture of lament
How the Church can resist "passing over" suffering

The phenomenon of "passing over" suffering has been identified in the research contained within this book, with particular regards to the Sunday Assembly; a godless congregation that "celebrates life." Thus far, the Sunday Assembly has acted as a lens through which to scrutinise deeper questions relating to theodicy and Christian responses to suffering. Now, as well as tentatively suggesting possible methods for the Sunday Assembly, the findings from this investigation will speak directly to the life and work of the Church, and its handling of suffering at the grassroots level. In what follows, lament and community practice, two particular aspects of the Christian life, will be explored. Together, I suggest that these actions lead to the creation of what might be termed a "culture of lament": an on-going accumulation of resources and practices, which create space within the life and worship of the Church for the articulation of grief and suffering. Infusing the practices of the Church with lament is one way to equip and prepare congregations to respond to suffering and to resist the human urge to ignore or move away quickly from it.

A response to the Sunday Assembly

As a work of practical theology, this study has been written throughout with the Church in mind. Nonetheless, there has been light shed upon practices which take place, at present, within the Sunday Assembly. As such, before moving to consider what the findings of my research mean for the Church, I will briefly conclude my work on the Assembly, suggesting what my findings might indicate for those who have been involved in this study.

It is, in some ways, unsurprising that the Sunday Assembly chooses to "pass over" and avoid discussion of suffering. As touched on in the previous chapter, Christian communities, too (particularly white, Protestant churches) are susceptible to ignoring or evading the realities of global trauma. Later in this chapter, the works of Walter Brueggemann, Soong-Chan Rah, and John Swinton will outline the church's reluctance to lament and to address suffering. Collectively, this evidence suggests that the propensity to move quickly past suffering is one which is, more widely speaking, a human trait, as opposed to one unique to, or inextricably bound up in, the practices of the Sunday Assembly. Laterally, it is important not to blame the Sunday Assembly's lack of response to traumatic events purely on its lack of faith in a divine being, as the previous writings indicate that Christians, too, are susceptible to "passing over" suffering.

Additionally, the Sunday Assembly's position as a fairly new organisation must be taken into consideration. The Assembly is a group still in its early years. Initially, the organisation experienced unprecedented attention and demand for replication of its non-religious "church" model. It was therefore forced to adapt and pull together a structure and remit within a relatively short space of time. This has been reflected in its changing priorities, group structures, and schemes, which have undergone some refinement since its establishment in 2013.[1] Further, in distancing itself from the labels of "atheist" and "church," the Assembly has had to inhabit new ground. What this new position might constitute is not entirely clear. The works of "temperate atheists," such as Alain de Botton, Phillip Kitcher, and Andre Comte-Sponville, go some way to hinting at what a contemporary atheistic position incorporating aspects of religious art, ceremony, festival, and ritual might look like.[2] Yet these thinkers have not been responsible for creating and maintaining congregations of their own, and the Sunday Assembly does not draw on the ideas of any one source or set of writings. To an extent, the Sunday Assembly is continuing to develop, and discovering and outlining its priorities as an organisation. Practically speaking, it may simply be too early in the life of the organisation for a coherent plan or set of instructions for responding to suffering to develop.

Nonetheless, the passing over of human trauma does have consequences. I have observed the consequences of this in my fieldwork at the Sunday Assembly. Two examples, which I have drawn on several times, concern the Paris attacks in November 2015, and the story of Carmen. In both of these situations, suffering was not "held"; it was not sat with, lived in, or allowed to shroud the congregation in sadness. Instead, a move towards elation and celebration was encouraged at the very earliest opportunity.

There have been some vague conversations regarding the need for pastoral care, and some Assembly members are aware that this still needs to be addressed.[3] Recall the words of Alice, an attendee of the London Assembly, who explained that the Assembly had not yet tackled the realities of global catastrophic events:

> I think the Assembly *should* talk about suffering more. I think [that] needs to be developed. . . . [T]he world is, like, in a shocking state at the moment. We can't just block that out and sing Queen, can we? Forever? We can't. We have to have some kind of discussion and . . . yeah. I think [the Assembly] is amazing. . . . It's taught me to be a more positive

person. But I think, at the same time, it can't just be kind of . . . jumpy up and down and just celebrate life all the time! Because really horrible, scary things happen in life.

Alice's words encompass both the Assembly's emphasis on celebration, and its reluctance to face the darker parts of human existence, as well as her own desire for a focus on global news. Concurrently, Richard, also from the London Assembly, explained that the organising committee has looked in to "getting more involved in pastoral care, and dealing with those kinds of issues." However, he added that "a lot of people have mentioned that it's not something we necessarily do particularly well." While he explained that the organisation was "trying to get some people that are trained in that sort of thing," Richard did not outline any concrete proof of the Assembly's commitment to expanding its remit to include pastoral care.

When I enquired about such outlets for pastoral care, Assembly officials directed attention towards Live Better groups: small groups set up to help members "reach their full potential."[4] Nonetheless, these gatherings tend to be narrowly concentrated on individual "life improvement" goals. As London member Felicity explained, Live Better groups are intended to "[help] people with problems in their lives in a very gentle, low-key manner." She indicated that issues raised in this environment might include: "struggling with work-life balance, finding time for family and friends, or wanting to complete a task; taxes, emails, that sort of thing." As Trish surmised, these gatherings are "where people try to work through their own personal issues" and that they were focused "more [on] trying to accomplish goals" as opposed to helping those "going through a rough time." Tony clarified that the groups "seem very self-interested, where people have something they want to resolve." His examples of topics that might be raised at these meetings were similar to those Felicity gave: "It might be that [someone] wants to change their career, they want to get a new job, they want to get around to filling in years of uncompleted tax returns, or they want to lose weight." Such activities are not so much about holding the immense suffering associated with personal traumas, or global, far-reaching events of suffering. Rather, they tend to point back to the celebration of life, encouraging self-improvement and reflection on the positive aspects of life.

Is the Sunday Assembly declining because it "passes over" suffering?

Despite members of the Assembly having expressed a need for the acknowledgement of suffering, and for future pastoral care, nothing like this has yet materialised. In fact, at time of writing, the Sunday Assembly is facing a challenging predicament: its numbers are falling. In her 2019 article about the Sunday Assembly for *The Atlantic*, Faith Hill estimates that the number of global attendees has fallen by around 3,500 in the last four years (it was previously approximated to be around 5,000 in 2016).[5] At the same time, the number of Sunday Assembly congregations has reduced from 70 in 2016 to around 40 in 2019.[6] Hill describes some of the problems that Assemblies have faced: logistical issues, competing groups, and a lack of a unifying non-religious "identity." Beyond this lies the question: can the Sunday Assembly's more recent deterioration be attributed to its lack of response to suffering?

For her article, Hill spoke to Richard Sosis, an anthropologist at the University of Connecticut who has extensively studied the makeup of religious and non-religious communes. According to Sosis, what the Sunday Assembly lacks at present is a sense of transcendence. For him, "transcendence is what gives the community a higher level of meaning than going to Johnny's Little League game."[7] Over time, he suggests that the Sunday Assembly might develop a sense of transcendence by creating its own rituals. For Hill, "It might mean that ideals they already espouse—such as helping others, or finding wonder in nature—get elevated to a sacred level."[8] Hill's mention of "helping others" is interesting. I take this to mean that the Sunday Assembly *could* make space to listen to its members through all the complexities of their lives. Of course, this would still mean "celebrating life" and drawing attention to those moments that are full of wonder and miracle and awe. But it would also mean walking alongside those—like Carmen, Alice, and so many others—whose suffering needs to be acknowledged and heard.

In response to Hill's article, Giles Fraser, journalist and Rector of St. Mary's Newington Church in London, wrote a piece that was published by UnHerd just a few days later. In his article, Fraser critiques the Sunday Assembly's particular brand of "happy-clappy atheism"[9] and its tendency towards relentless celebration. This brings him to a particular concern:

> It's all very well celebrating the best of the world. But what about the worst. The real challenge for a God-less church is how it deals with the problem of evil.[10]

A worthwhile query—in fact, one which this very book has attempted to explore. Fraser continues:

> On one level, of course, they can do this just as easily as traditional churches. When something terrible occurs in the world, the Assemblies can of course analyse its causes, commit to making the world a better place, and take a collection to relieve the suffering of those affected. But there's another sort of evil: the darkness within. How do they address that? My acid test, then, for a godless church is this: how would they tackle the funeral of a paedophile? Or: what do they say at the eulogy for a racist?[11]

Fraser seems to believe that churches have the answer to these issues: "In church we can say: *Lord, have mercy* and *Father, forgive* [sic]." As will become evident, I am convinced that the church should adopt a dynamic and active "culture" of lament, which extends beyond simply answering such complex issues with words from tradition. While I may not agree with Fraser's proclamations about the Church, his comments are interesting for the discussion at hand. Fraser goes on to explain that the Church holds ways of acknowledging and addressing the "inherent brokenness" of humankind. In this, there is both a space to hold suffering and potential for hope and for healing, however this may look. He ends his article by bluntly stating that:

> if you cannot accommodate failure—your own or that of your congregants—then you don't have enough to exist for. And you deserve to perish.[12]

In other words, Fraser is suggesting that if the Sunday Assembly cannot find a way to address suffering and acknowledge the imperfections of its members, it should not be allowed to continue operating.

Taking Fraser's reasoning together with the research contained within this book, it is reasonable to suggest that the Sunday Assembly's failure to find a way in which to deal way with the "brokenness" of its members and of the world *could* be contributing to its falling numbers. It is worth noting that Sanderson Jones wrote a rebuttal to Fraser's piece, which addressed the difficulties of financial sustainability, sourcing volunteers, and opening new chapters. This goes some way to addressing the other issues which the organisation has been challenged with in recent years, and these should certainly be taken into consideration.[13]

The practice of celebrating life is not wrong; indeed, there is a great deal about it which is admirable; but it *is* incomplete. The Sunday Assembly is a gathered community of human beings, and suffering is an ever-present shadow on the fabric of human life. In a gathering of people like the Sunday Assembly, there will be those who fall outwith the boundaries of celebrating life at any given time. Alice experienced a "life crisis" as she struggled to come to terms with her parent's illnesses. Carmen lived through a particularly difficult time, facing multiple different trials in her personal life. As such, if the Assembly is to survive and carry on in a climate where suffering, both global and personal, is an ever-present reality, it must find a way to tackle suffering for its members. Indeed, the Assembly itself claims to be committed to "helping often": another reason to give this some consideration.

How might the Sunday Assembly address suffering?

In suggesting some ways that the Assembly might move forward, I do so tentatively. For one, I do not identify as a member of the Sunday Assembly community. Further, this book is a work of practical theology, and so it is ultimately concerned with directing its findings towards the Church. As such, the following proposals are made primarily in relation to my research findings, with the understanding that the organisation would not necessarily choose to adopt them in practice, and with the intention that the reader treats the suggestions I make for the Church with greater weight.

Later in this chapter, I draw on the Christian tradition of lament. Grounded in the scriptures, lamentation commonly takes the form of prayer out of pain. It expresses the confusion, hurt, and brokenness which comes from witnessing or being part of an experience of suffering. Is lament something which could be co-opted by the Sunday Assembly, or used in non-religious settings? John Swinton and Walter Brueggemann (whose work will be referred to in due course) emphasise the direction of lament and its petitioning of God. In this sense, their suggestions are directed at, and fit best within, a Church environment. Yet there is work within the area of lament which, although not entirely transferrable, might hold some wisdom for the Sunday Assembly.

The work of Emmanuel Kantongole and Chris Rice presents lament as a resource for Christian communities but might also speak to the Sunday Assembly's habit of "passing over" suffering. Kantongole and Rice outline a three-pronged approach, which begins with the concept of "pilgrimage." They explain that "the goal of a pilgrim is not to solve, but to search, not so much to help as to be present. Pilgrims do not rush to a goal, but slow down to hear the crying."[14] Here, Kantongole and Rice offer a theological response to suffering, which resists the "rush" for answers and slows down to "hear the crying" and listen to those who have experienced trauma. For the Church, this stance heeds Rambo's caution to resist a premature shift towards "rebuilding" and "reconciliation." For the Sunday Assembly, the use of pilgrim language may not be suitable, but the image of slowing to listen to the anguish of those at the heart of traumatic events is still relevant.

Related to this is the second part of Kantangole and Rice's practice of lament, which concerns relocation: "The practice of relocation [means] taking our bodies to the hard places and tarrying long enough to be disturbed."[15] This suggestion might be interpreted as allowing ourselves space in which to grieve and meet with the source of our pain, to speak to our experience, and to allow ourselves to realise the extent of our hurting. Again, it reinforces the idea of "coming alongside" those who are hurting, encountering the pain of the other in the space of lament. The third aspect of this pattern of lament concerns confession. Kantongole and Rice explain that, in a broken world, "the challenge is to keep naming the truth, keep being disturbed" and keep remembering "the awful depth of brokenness."[16] At present, neither the Sunday Assembly nor those churches which reject the practice of lament can claim to be doing this. The act of rapidly "passing over" suffering does not allow for the extent of human brokenness to be understood. Kantongole and Rice add that:

> The prayers of lament in the Psalms were public prayers, intended to be read and inserted into the corporate life of worship in a way

that helps us tell the truth and confess to the brokenness of our own contexts.[17]

The shape of lament which Kantongole and Rice press for is both outward looking, and self-reflective, challenging congregations not only to join together in recognition of the darkness of the world, but in meditation on their place within it. To both the Church and groups like the Sunday Assembly, theirs is a call to resist becoming immune to disturbing events and bad news, and to consider their own involvement and practical response in any given situation.

Similarly, the work of theologian Nancy Duff introduces three primary values of the lament psalms, which, although chosen for their value for Church congregations, might contain some transferable wisdom for groups like the Sunday Assembly. For Duff, the lament psalms challenge human inability to acknowledge the intense emotions that grief can entail.[18] This is something which the Sunday Assembly currently struggles with, since the act of "passing over" suffering doesn't allow them to linger for long on the true extent of the consequences of human brokenness. Second, Duff explains, the lament psalms free us to make bold expressions of grief in the presence of others.[19] The Sunday Assembly does have small groups in which lament might be enacted, but have yet to declare "boldly" the true depths of individual suffering.[20] Finally, the lament psalms allow us to rely on the community to carry hope on our behalf, when we have none left in us. A corporate sense of hope is something which might already be at play within the Sunday Assembly's culture of celebration but could be harnessed to support individuals who are struggling with personal situations of suffering.

Practically speaking, it is unlikely that the Sunday Assembly will choose to draw directly on the Psalms(!). However, there are existing aspects of Assembly services into which lament might be incorporated in a non-religious sense. Most Assembly gatherings begin, end, and have at their centre a range of popular songs, sung by the congregation. The Assembly could incorporate music suitable for periods of meditation. Kitty Empire of *The Guardian* describes Leonard Cohen's song "Hallelujah" as "the perfect secular lament":

> Referring to a number of Old Testament stories,[21] Cohen's song is a perfect secular hymn, alluding to religiosity, but not explicitly indulging in it. The "hallelujah" itself is Hebrew for "praise God," but the song deals with a failed relationship, constructing parallels between surrender in love and religious feeling.[22]

The inclusion of such songs, whether drawing on religious imagery or otherwise, would indicate a shift in tone; a space in which to hold and recognise the realities of evil and trauma. The same could be achieved in the time set aside for poetry readings at Assembly gatherings. William Wordsworth's

"Lines Written in Early Spring," for example, captures a melancholy mood regarding the fate of humanity, and contains the line, "Have I not reason to lament?"[23] Similarly, "The Song of Despair" by Chilean poet Pablo Neruda captures something of the sadness and fragility of human relationships. It contains lines such as: "Oh pit of debris, everything fell into you; what sorrow did you not express, in what sorrow are you not drowned!"[24]

At present, only one "tone" is accommodated at the Sunday Assembly: a high-octane attitude of celebration-driven positivity. If the Assembly is truly to abide by its founding declaration to "help often," it must help those within its midst who are suffering. I have suggested that this might be done by adopting some of the guiding principles—rather than the content, direction, or structures—of lament psalms, and by creating pockets within Assembly gatherings in which sadness might be acknowledged or addressed through song or poetry, in addition to (and not instead of!) the prevailing narrative of celebration. I must reiterate that there is nothing inherently wrong with celebrating life. Indeed, this is a practice from which many people could learn. It can instil and reawaken a sense of wonder where it is lost; it can remind us of the fragility and awe-inspiring experience of life. Where the "celebration of life" becomes problematic is where it becomes all-consuming, to the extent that it neglects the brokenness and pervasive evil of the world we live in today.

The use of the Sunday Assembly in this book has, however, been for one end: to examine responses to suffering in order to shed new light on theological problems bound up in the practice of theodicy. It is time, now, to depart from consideration of the Sunday Assembly and to gather the strands of this book together in a response to those for whom it was primarily written: the Church.

"You will not dread what darkness brings": a response to the Church

I began this exploration with an examination of some of the ways in which the church has used theodicy. As explained in the previous chapter, the Church has not found itself immune to the "passing over" of suffering. From the book of Lamentations, to the Psalms, to Christ's weeping on the news of the death of his friend Lazarus, the Christian scriptures are replete with instances of lament. Nevertheless, as Swinton found in his local church after the Omagh bombings, and as I witnessed multiple times in the writing of this book, lament remains an underused resource in much of Christian liturgy and worship in the twenty-first century. This is not a particularly new observation. In his work, *The Psalms and the Life of Faith*, Old Testament scholar Walter Brueggemann observes that:

> The Lament Psalms offer important resources for Christian faith and ministry, even though they have been largely purged from the life and liturgy of the church.[25]

Similarly, theologian Soong-Chan Rah frames lament as a "lost discipline."[26] He notes that while laments constitute around 40% of the Psalms, the practice of lament is conspicuously absent from modern church worship. In evidence, Rah observes that of the top 100 worship songs, according to Christian Copyright International, only five fall into the category of lament.[27] The majority reflect themes of celebratory praise; for example: "Happy Day," "Here I Am to Worship," "Glorious Day," "Marvellous Light," and "Victory in Jesus." Speaking to his own context of American churches, Rah writes that worship "reveals what Christians prioritise," concluding that: "The American Church avoids lament."[28] As a result, "the underlying narrative of suffering that requires lament is lost in lieu of a triumphalist, victorious narrative." Rah's point is that the church has a long history of lament resources upon which it can draw, but that congregations rarely make full use of these. His evidence points to a further question, which I have previously raised: does the church, like the Sunday Assembly, have a problem with the "passing over" of suffering? This idea will be examined in further detail in due course. Meanwhile, Brueggemann asks:

> What happens when appreciation of lament as a form of speech and faith is lost, as I think it is largely lost in contemporary usage? What happens when the speech forms that redress power distribution have been silenced and eliminated? The answer, I believe, is that a theological monopoly is reinforced, docility and submissiveness and engendered, and the outcome in terms of social practice is to reinforce and consolidate the political-economic monopoly of the status quo.[29]

For Brueggemann, the avoidance of lament within churches is both pastorally and socially dangerous. In the context of this study, which is so concerned "ground zero" events, Brueggemann's words may be carried over as a reference to the church's lack of protection of victims of such events. A lack of lament is not simply a liturgical deficiency; it prevents Christians from hearing and giving voice to those who suffer.

What, then, is to be done about the church's failure to include lament in its liturgy and praise? I turn now to examine the works of Brueggemann and Swinton in greater detail, paying particular attention to the propositions made by each for use at the grassroots congregational level.

Emphasising lament: practical suggestions for the Church

In the Christian tradition, lament constitutes an address to God, descriptive of the suffering and anguish from which one seeks relief. In the Book of Psalms, laments constitute a group of Psalm Forms and tend to take one of two different formats: those that are communal and those that are individual. In communal laments, the nation reflects collectively on natural disasters, plague, or the oppression of Israel by surrounding nations. In individual laments, the individual who is speaking grieves their own fate and circumstances. Michael Coogan provides a description of the typical structure of biblical laments, which might be applied to either communal or individual laments:

1   An address to God
2   A description of the suffering involved
3   Cursing of the persons or party responsible for the suffering
4   Either a protestation of innocence, or an admittance of guilt
5   A petition for divine assistance
6   An expression of faith in God's receipt of prayer
7   An anticipation of divine response
8   A prayer of thanksgiving or a vow of praise to God.[30]

Brueggemann suggests several ways in which lament psalms might be used and appropriated within the life of the church. He claims that the psalms give "form" and expression to grief. In other words, they provide a language in which to hold on to and express suffering.[31] They also have an "affirmative" ending. The psalmist addresses God in anger, yet towards the end they tend to point to their own (or their communities') loyalty to and trust in God.[32] In order to explain this, Brueggemann draws on the work of Elisabeth Kübler-Ross, whose theory of the "Five Stages" of grief has been particularly ground breaking in the field of psychiatry.[33] While not engaging closely with the specific of Kübler-Ross's thesis, Brueggemann explains that the "five stages" she identifies "can be correlated with the movement in Israel's laments."[34] Four of her stages (denial, anger, bargaining, and depression) speak of plea, whereas one (acceptance) speaks of affirmation.[35] In this respect, Brueggemann views the psalms as part of a rich resource which can be drawn upon by both individuals and communities in times of suffering. This suggestion does have some merit, but it should be noted that the grief stages, as expounded by Kübler-Ross and others in the field of psychiatry, cannot always encompass the realities of grief. Human beings are susceptible to moving back and forth through the "stages" of grief, and, at times, grieving cannot be fully contained within such a modern medical framework. Recall Shelly Rambo's warning that, for some, suffering "does not end" and continues to linger in the body for years.[36]

For Swinton, lament can occur at congregational level, but is even more effective when practiced in small groups. Like Brueggemann and Rah, Swinton is aware of "a culture within our churches that denies sadness and anger at world events."[37] As such, the church has to remember how to lament. Swinton develops his practical suggestion regarding the use of lament psalms within a small group structure in dialogue with the work of Erhard Gerstenberger. Swinton writes:

> The creation of small pastoral care communities within the larger life of the church enables the church to provide a level of care and develop a depth of community which would not be possible within the traditional

pastor centred model of pastoral care. . . . The goal of small groups is to respond to the felt needs of a particular group of persons in the congregation, and to enable people to experience community in a real and tangible way. In doing so, people are enabled to develop a deeper understanding of themselves and of what it means to live within a caring community which hears, listens, understands, and notices.[38]

Small groups can become places where people's pain and honest rage can be felt, where victims of suffering can be listened to and "heard into speech," as Swinton describes it.[39] This idea also speaks to the brief discussion of post-traumatic silence in the previous chapter, in which I explained the importance of silence ultimately being brought to voice. It also points back to the Sunday Assembly's own attempts to create small group gatherings in order to combat loneliness.

Besides using lament in small group settings, Swinton also suggests the creation of new laments. Within the small gatherings he advocates, "it is possible for people to learn how to use the psalms as a language to express their sadness and anger."[40] Swinton continues: "It is also a place where people can learn how to create new lament psalms that reflect their own personal or communal pain and experiences of suffering."[41] He gives the particular example of Ann Weems, a Christian author of poetry, songs, and meditations, whose son, Todd, was murdered on the night of his twenty-first birthday. In her text, *Psalms of Lament*, Weems uses the structure and shape of the lament psalms to communicate the grief that she is experiencing at the sudden loss of her young son.[42] In a series of moving and personal petitions to God, Weems writes lines such as: "Then they killed him, whom I loved more than my own life (even that you taught me)."[43] For Swinton, Weems's approach is a good model to begin with when practising lament in small groups. He provides a six-point structure for lament:

1   An address to God, in which the community can choose to God any name deemed suitable for the divine.
2   A complaint, in which the undesirable situation is recounted.
3   An expression of trust; a simple statement which expresses faith in spite of the complaint.
4   An appeal or cry for God to intervene.
5   An expression of certainty, in which the community "assures God that it does not doubt, even in the midst of its doubt."[44]
6   A conclusion; normally a vow of praise in which the community "assures God of its love."[45]

Swinton points out that there are many ways in which lament can be enabled, including a need to "reflect on how we preach about sadness . . . how we might teach our young people to understand it, and how we might incorporate lament into our counselling practices." He lingers, however, on the concept of community lament, which he describes as a practice that can "begin to absorb pain and enable perseverance."[46]

A *"culture of lament"*

The practice of lament can take place individually, as in the case of Weems on the death of her son, or in small groups, as suggested by Swinton. It may also take place more widely, in community. Indeed, where practices of lament and community presence are combined, a "culture of lament" is created. What do I mean by this, and what does such a scenario look like in practice?

In the previous chapter, I explored various theologies which advocate for a "middle ground" between trauma and recovery (if recovering and healing are at all possible). The suggestions of Williams and Rambo are important because they discourage Christians from reaching too quickly for explanations in the face of suffering. They create a metaphorical space in which solutions do not have to be immediately forthcoming, and in doing so, resist the creation of harmful theodicies. Their suggestions also caution people from "passing over" suffering. Yet while these are strong ideas, both Williams and Rambo miss the final step, which is lifting these concepts from the theological thought space into the local congregation. It is not enough to simply state a need for pause. Because of this, I want to begin to consider how this "middle space" might be created at grassroots level within churches, through the gradual creation of an active culture of lamentation. As stated before, the churches I am referring to here are, specifically, white, Protestant, Western churches, where Rah points out that lament is often lacking in the landscape of worship. In order that congregations are equipped to draw on the language of lament, particularly in the event of a global news story, I suggest that they must prepare by incorporating lament into the vernacular of their worship services, and the practices of their communities. It is the continued practicing of lament in these ways that leads to a lament culture; one in which lament is routinely considered and included in the work and worship of the church, so that it can be drawn on in times of suffering.

What are some ways in which a "culture of lament" might be created? I grew up in a small village on the West Coast of Scotland. In our local parish, we relied heavily on sung rather than spoken lamentation. Arguable, the singing of hymns and psalms of lament does not render their content any less salient. Indeed, Ian Bradley suggests that hymns are a "tremendous vehicle"[47] for carrying across aspects of doctrine, and that churchgoers tend to assimilate much of their theology through the medium of singing. Nonetheless, Scottish hymn-writers John Bell and Graham Maule point out that sung lament is often repressed by "limp musical settings of . . . ancient texts, or presumed over-familiarity with them," which has "dulled our senses to the direct, raw pleading and complaining, which is as necessary for healthy faith as adoration."[48] It is because of this that Bell and Maul have worked to paraphrase the psalms of lament, so that they can be more clearly under-stood by those who are to sing them. Some of their most commonly sung hymns refer to Gods presence in times of suffering, and to the comfort of divine immanence. The majority of these paraphrased psalms cover a wide range of grievance, such as illness and injury, bereavement, death, and anger at God.

In addition to paraphrased psalms, there are a wealth of congrega-tional sung refrains, which encompassed lines of petition and lament. Typi-cal examples include chants from the Taizé community, a French ecumenical monastic order. One such refrain, titled *O Lord hear my prayer*, is a direct petition, calling on God to hear and answer the prayers of those gathered.[49] Another example of a sung response, also from Taizé, is the ostinato "Jesus, remember me when you come into your Kingdom." This is a similar plea for divine mercy, paraphrased from Luke 23:42.[50] Other laments encourage Christians to wait for God, and to be strong in their time of waiting.[51] Sung laments such as these can be incorporated into liturgical or non-liturgical traditions. They can also provide a simple way in which to approach lament language without changing the structures of an existing worship service.

Spaces can be created within worship services for global news to be held and acknowledged in prayer. Many churches already direct their attention towards global news from the week during prayer time. It may be possible for further space to be created, either within or after the worship service, for people to sit in contemplation and reflection of this. Perhaps there are points of action that can be taken. I attended a small church in the Inner Hebri-des during the 2019–2020 Australian bushfire season. Immediately after the service, there was space set aside to discuss the congregation's response to the crisis; would they donate money? If so, where to? Were there known contacts at Australian churches who could advise? It was not the answers to these questions that really mattered, but the space that was created for all people in attendance to consider how they might respond to the on-going crisis, both as individuals and in community.

Beyond this, there is a need for ritual and for marking certain events as and when they happen. Back in my childhood church in the West of Scot-land, this practice has been incorporated in one form or another for many years. One particularly memorable example is from 1995. On Wednesday 13th March that year, 16 primary school children aged five and six, along with their teacher, were killed by a gunman who entered Dunblane Primary School in Stirlingshire.[52] The congregational response to this particular trag-edy is summarised by Sheila, who led the youth group at the time:

> There was a sense of shock after Dunblane. . . . Straight away, though, we thought, "We have to do something." We wanted to make the church into a place where people could come and remember the children, reflect on what had happened. . . . I remember we discussed it at Youth Group. I think it was the next week. . . . We made a circle, a kind of wreath

of candles, one for each of the children who had died, and we placed it right at the front of the church. We, the Youth Group . . . we held a kind of reflective, night-time service. We played some calm music, we let people come up to the front and light candles.

Sheila's words capture something of a culture of lament in practice the Dunblane shootings. Rather than quickly acknowledging and then moving past this devastating event, which had wide-ranging repercussions in the weeks and months that followed,[53] the parishioners chose to pause. They "held" the pain and anguish that they and others in Scotland felt in a reflective service. Within this space, no immediate answers were sought. Lamentation was spoken and sung, and the community came together to express their and acknowledge their shock. These were simple gestures, and were not always delivered perfectly. However, they were made possible through on-going, weekly attention to the practice of lament.

The practical suggestions given here are tentative rather than prescriptive. They in some ways sparse and incomplete; intended as conversation starters rather than the final say on how lament "ought to" look and sound. This is because the adoption of such practices will, of course, depend upon individual congregations and denominations, who will have their own traditions and patterns of worship to contend with. Because of this, it is difficult to be too closely prescriptive. It bears noting that none of these are unique or new ideas! Indeed, many churches will incorporate pieces of lament into their life and work already. However, I include these suggestions here in the context of my wider discussion. They are presented that they might be seen anew, as ways in which to resist "passing over suffering" within the context of a carefully considered, regularly practiced culture of lament.

Conclusion

In this chapter, I have outlined several practices which might help Christians to stop or interrupt the phenomenon of "passing over" suffering; an action which, though identified through interviews with and observation of the Sunday Assembly, is apparent, too, in the church, and particularly in what Brueggemann, Rah, and Swinton identify as a "reluctance" to lament. I have expounded the collation of both lament and community response, and termed this a "culture of lament"; a Church context in which small spaces are made to hold suffering week on week, so that when larger events occur, the community is able to draw upon the rich lament resources which it has already practiced and rehearsed.

It is important to note that a "culture of lament" is not the antithesis of the Sunday Assembly, and that it is not wholly at odds with the Assembly's practice of "celebration." The Church need not spend all of its time wailing and gnashing teeth at the state of the world, and, indeed, it cannot, since the Christian life is underpinned by hope and the promise of Christ's defeat of death through the Resurrection. But, as a repercussion of this specific study, it is important that the Church begins to determine ways in which to return to, and even embrace, the practice of lament.

When catastrophic events occur, Williams and Rambo agree that Christians must pause to create time and space in which to process tragedy. Both draw on theological hermeneutics and paradigms to state their case. Ultimately, this study acknowledges that it is not enough to simply state a need for pause. The suggestions and conclusions contained within this chapter have (tentatively) begun to push at more detailed ways in which this "middle space" might be created at the grassroots level within churches through the gradual creation of a culture of lament.

Notes

1 See Chapter 1 and the conclusion for information about the Sunday Assembly's changings structures, with particular reference to the shifting format of small group meetings.
2 See Chapter 2 for more on what I term "temperate atheism."
3 In an article on the Sunday Assembly's Edinburgh congregation, I outline some of the "vestiges" of Christian life and practice apparent in that particular community. The term "vestiges" here "refers centrally to aspects of Christianity, whether ritualistic, identity-driven, or otherwise, which are carried over, unconsciously retained, or actively incorporated into a secular perspective, even where faith in a divine being is not." Pastoral care is one such example of a Christian practice which members of the Assembly look to retain. See Katie Cross, "The Sunday Assembly in Scotland: Vestiges of Religious thought in a Secular Congregation," *Practical Theology*, 10 (3), 2017, 253.
4 Previously "Smoups," later incorporating "The Life Course." Refer to Chapters 3 and 5 for more information on the evolution of the Assembly's small group structures.
5 Faith Hill, "They Tried to Start a Church without God: For a While, It Worked," *The Atlantic*, 21st July 2019: www.theatlantic.com/ideas/archive/2019/07/secular-churches-rethink-their-sales-pitch/594109/ (accessed 7th January 2020).
6 Ibid.
7 Ibid.
8 Ibid.
9 Giles Fraser, "The Pointlessness of Happy-Clappy Atheism," *UnHeard*, 25th July 2019: https://unherd.com/2019/07/the-pointlessness-of-happy-clappy-atheism/
10 Ibid.
11 Ibid.
12 Ibid.
13 Sanderson Jones, "22 Reflections On The Atlantic Article About Sunday Assembly and Secular Congregations," *Medium*, 22nd July 2019: https://medium.com/@sandersonjones/22-reflections-on-the-atlantic-article-about-sunday-assembly-and-secular-congregations-437088b6eb9e (accessed 7th January 2020).
14 Emmanuel Kantongole and Chris Rice, *Reconciling All Things: A Christian Vision for Justice, Peace and Healing (Resources for Reconciliation)* (Downers Grove: InterVarsity Press, 2008), 91.
15 Ibid. 91.
16 Ibid. 92–93.
17 Ibid. 93.

18 Nancy Duff, "Recovering Lamentation as a Practice in the Church," in Sally Brown and Patrick Miller (eds.) *Lament: Reclaiming Practices in Pulpit, Pew, and Public* (Louisville: Westminster John Knox Press, 2005), 3.
19 Ibid. 14.
20 See Chapter 5 for examples of topics covered in Sunday Assembly peer support sessions, such as the Live Better groups and Life Course.
21 In a sense, "Hallelujah" is not as "secular" as Empire might suggest; it contains references to, and is still clearly in dialogue with, the Jewish tradition.
22 Kitty Empire, "Leonard Cohen's Lament Has Become a Perfect Secular Hymn," *The Guardian*, 14th December 2008: www.theguardian.com/music/2008/dec/14/leonard-cohen-hallelujah (accessed 7th January 2020).
23 William Wadsworth, "Lines Written in Early Spring," in Stephen Gill (ed.) *William Wordsworth: The Major Works* (Oxford: Oxford University Press, 1984), 80–81.
24 Pablo Neruda, "The Song of Despair," in Pablo Neruda (ed.) *Twenty Love Poems and a Song of Despair* (San Francisco: Chronicle Books, 1993), 72.
25 Walter Brueggemann, *The Psalms and the Life of Faith* (Minneapolis: Fortress Press, 1995), 84.
26 Soong-Chan Rah, *Prophetic Lament: A Call for Justice in Troubled Times* (Downers Grove: InterVarsity Press, 2015), 23.
27 Ibid.
28 Ibid.
29 Brueggemann, 102.
30 Michael M. Coogan, *A Brief Introduction to the Old Testament: The Hebrew Bible in Its Context* (Oxford: Oxford University Press, 2009), 370.
31 Brueggemann, 86.
32 Ibid. 88.
33 See Elisabeth Kübler-Ross, *On Grief and Grieving: Finding the Meaning of Grief through the Five Stages of Loss* (London: Simon and Schuster, 2005).
34 Brueggemann, 89.
35 Ibid.
36 Rambo, 1–2.
37 John Swinton, *Raging with Compassion: Pastoral Responses to the Problem of Evil* (Grand Rapids, MI: Wm. B. Eerdmans, 2007), 121.
38 John Swinton, *From Bedlam to Shalom* (New York: Peter Lang, 2000), 120.
39 Swinton, *Raging with Compassion*, 122.
40 Ibid. 126.
41 Ibid.
42 It was, in fact, Walter Brueggemann who directed Weems to the lament psalms and suggested that she compose her own psalms of lament to express her feelings upon the death of her son.
43 Ann Weems, *Psalms of Lament* (Louisville: Westminster John Knox Press, 1995), 1–2.
44 Swinton, *Raging with Compassion*, 128.
45 Ibid.
46 Ibid.
47 Ian Bradley, *Abide with Me: The World of Victorian Hymns* (London: Faber & Faber, 2011), 2.
48 John L. Bell and Graham Maule, *When Grief Is Raw: Songs for Times of Sorrow and Bereavement* (Glasgow: Wild Goose Publications, 1997), 7.
49 Jacques Berthier, "O Lord Hear My Prayer," in *Songs of God's People* (Oxford: Oxford University Press, 1998), 85.
50 The Taizé Community, "Jesus, Remember Me": https://hymnary.org/text/jesus_remember_me (accessed 7th January 2020).
51 The Taizé Community, "Wait for the Lord Whose Day Is Near": https://hymnary.org/text/wait_for_the_lord_whose_day_is_near (accessed 7th January 2020).

52 Peter Wilkinson, "Dunblane: How UK School Massacre Led to Tighter Gun Control," *CNN*, 30th January 2013: http://edition.cnn.com/2012/12/17/world/europe/dunblane-lessons/index.html (accessed 7th January 2020).
53 The events in Dunblane provoked widescale public debate regarding gun laws in the UK and led to fundamental changes in the laws regarding possession of firearms. See Wilkinson, "Dunblane: How UK School Massacre Led to Tighter Gun Control."

References

Bell, John L. and Maule, Graham. *When Grief Is Raw: Songs for Times of Sorrow and Bereavement*. Glasgow: Wild Goose Publications, 1997.

Berthier, Jacques. "O Lord Hear My Prayer." In *Songs of God's People*. Oxford: Oxford University Press, 1998.

Bradley, Ian. *Abide with Me: The World of Victorian Hymns*. London: Faber & Faber, 2011.

Brueggemann, Walter. *The Psalms and the Life of Faith*. Minneapolis: Fortress Press, 1995.

Cross, Katie. "The Sunday Assembly in Scotland: Vestiges of Religious Thought in a Secular Congregation." *Practical Theology*. 10 (3), 2017: 249–262.

Duff, Nancy. "Recovering Lamentation as a Practice in the Church." In *Lament: Reclaiming Practices in Pulpit, Pew, and Public*, edited by Sally Brown and Patrick Miller, 3–14. Louisville: Westminster John Knox Press, 2005.

Empire, Kitty. "Leonard Cohen's Lament Has Become a Perfect Secular Hymn." *The Guardian*. 14th December 2008. www.theguardian.com/music/2008/dec/14/leonard-cohen-hallelujah

Fraser, Giles. "The Pointlessness of Happy-Clappy Atheism." *UnHeard*. 25th July 2019. https://unherd.com/2019/07/the-pointlessness-of-happy-clappy-atheism/

Gill Stephen. *William Wordsworth: The Major Works*. Oxford: Oxford University Press, 1984.

Hill, Faith. "They Tried to Start a Church without God: For a While, It Worked." *The Atlantic*. 21st July 2019. www.theatlantic.com/ideas/archive/2019/07/secular-churches-rethink-their-sales-pitch/594109/

Kantongole, Emmanuel and Rice, Chris. *Reconciling All Things: A Christian Vision for Justice, Peace and Healing (Resources for Reconciliation)*. Downers Grove: InterVarsity Press, 2008.

Neruda, Pablo. *Twenty Love Poems and a Song of Despair*. San Francisco: Chronicle Books, 1993.

Rah, Soong-Chan. *Prophetic Lament: A Call for Justice in Troubled Times*. Downers Grove: InterVarsity Press, 2015.

Swinton, John. *From Bedlam to Shalom*. New York: Peter Lang, 2000.

———. *Raging with Compassion: Pastoral Responses to the Problem of Evil*. Grand Rapids, MI: Wm. B. Eerdmans, 2007.

The Taizé Community. "Jesus, Remember Me." https://hymnary.org/text/wait_for_the_lord_whose_day_is_near

———. "Wait for the Lord Whose Day Is Near." https://hymnary.org/text/wait_for_the_lord_whose_day_is_near

Weems, Ann. *Psalms of Lament*. Louisville: Westminster John Knox Press, 1995.

Wilkinson, Peter. "Dunblane: How UK School Massacre Led to Tighter Gun Control." *CNN*. 30th January 2013. http://edition.cnn.com/2012/12/17/world/europe/dunblane-lessons/index.html

Conclusion

This book began with a particular concern; that the pursuit of theological explanations for suffering and evil has, in practice, proved to be problematic. Theodicy, whether academically construed or offered in a pastoral context in a church setting, holds the potential to be pastorally damaging. It abstracts, sanitises, and generalises the particular pain of individuals, in order to fit suffering into a neatly edged, theoretical framework. In doing so, it produces "solutions" and "answers" to the problem of evil, which are largely inapplicable to the human experience. In some forms, it creates a culture of blame, wherein people are targeted and made scapegoats for the "wrath" and anger of God. Having established this at the beginning of the book, I argued that the more practical Christian approaches are needed in place of theodicy.

The purpose of my research, therefore, was to suggest how the Church and the theological community might be equipped with creative and grounded approaches to suffering, particularly in light of the context of the twenty-first century, characterised by increasing secularisation and the near-constant mass communication of radical suffering in the form of modern technology. I highlighted the growing focus amongst scholars of religion and sociology on the spaces between observant orthodoxy and overt manifestations of non-religion. In particular, sociologists Linda Woodhead and Grace Davie underline the urgency of addressing this "middle ground" in academic research, given that it could comprise at least half of the British population.[1,2] I explained that this space has not yet been examined in any substantial detail by theologians. Since the growing prevalence of those who neither identify as religious or non-religious has impacted upon church attendance and may, as such, influence the role of theology in the public sphere, it is important for theologians to acknowledge and interact with those who inhabit this curious new ground. Because of this, I made the decision to examine these theological through the lens of the Sunday Assembly: a congregational movement, whose events have the appearance of religious worship, yet are decidedly irreligious. In doing so, I listened to those who had left the Church for this new community and questioned more specifically how the problem of evil and suffering was being dealt with in this context. I anticipated that data gathered from interviews and observation with the Sunday Assembly in London and Edinburgh would act as a lens of critical interpretation, shedding light on current perceptions of theodicy in the public sphere. Perhaps, in turn, findings would hint towards new ways in which suffering might be encountered and responded to in a Church setting.

The findings of this book

Upon examining the Sunday Assembly, I found that its leadership and members were, at times, acknowledging suffering, both at a global scale and within their own communities. Nonetheless, the movement touches on traumatic events and individual pain only briefly. Rather than processing grief and allowing time to linger in spaces of hurt, I found that the Sunday Assembly "passes over" suffering. By this, I refer to the action of either ignoring, overlooking, or remaining silent about world events or instances of personal suffering, or turning quickly away from them, and back to the movement's central ethos of "celebrating life." I explained that difficult circumstances are often turned into opportunities for members to work towards self-improvement, and a deeper appreciation of what it means to be alive. As such, I found that the Assembly's concern with its statement and practice of "celebrating life" is what often overrides its engagement with suffering. I suggested that the dismissal of suffering can be a human trait, one which affects both the Assembly and the Church. Nevertheless, I found that this practice results in the anguish of Sunday Assembly attendees being overlooked, since there is no space in meetings, or vernacular language, in which to hold their grief.

What is unique about these findings? Broadly, I have amassed a collection of findings relating to the Sunday Assembly, a group still in its infancy, which has not yet garnered a great deal of academic attention within any discipline.[3] As such, this book represents one of the first sustained insights into the presence and practices of this community. By virtue of using this yet unstudied group as a lens of interpretation for critical, theological reflection, I have contributed new knowledge regarding the Sunday Assembly in London and Edinburgh.

More specifically, this book has pointed to a key ethos within the Sunday Assembly—that of "celebrating life." I have outlined the ways that this ethos is realised in the rhetoric and practices of the movement. In doing so, I have noted some of the consequences that this focus on "celebrating life" can have, relating to my research questions regarding meaning making and theodicy in contemporary context. I have suggested that the "celebration of life" is the movement's default way of responding to both catastrophic events of a global magnitude, and to individual experiences of pain and hardship.

My findings have been drawn into conversation with observations on theology and the Church. As explained, I began this study by establishing some of the ways in which theodicy can be a dangerous method of responding to suffering—both theologically, within the confines of the academy but also, more crucially, in Church congregations, where it threatens to generate blame, guilt, and suspicion. I set out to find what other approaches were being taken in the twenty-first century, and whether and how social attitudes towards suffering and responses to it have any bearing on the contemporary Church. In putting forth the Sunday Assembly's approach, I have been able to reflect on the practices of the Church, which also struggles to "hold," acknowledge, and respond to suffering. Like the Sunday Assembly, the Church is also susceptible to "passing over suffering."

While this particular conclusion is not wholly new or unique (I previously mentioned Swinton's narrative of his local Church avoiding discussion of suffering in the aftermath of the Omagh bombing), it has been reached in this book in a new and different way. Using a synthesis of practical theology and a non-religious lens of critical interpretation, I have reached theological conclusions by a new method and from a distinct perspective. The examination of a self-proclaimed "secular group" within a practical theological framework is something which I have not had the scope to develop in detail beyond my own findings, but it is a topic and practice which merits much greater future attention. The discipline of practical theology has engaged in the past with the voices and stories of those who exist outwith the church.[4] However, there has not been a great deal of work on self-identifying non-religious communities. It is important for practical theologians interested in doing theology publicly to hear the narratives of those who exist in the "middle" of religion and non-religion, given that their numbers are becoming more statistically significant in contemporary Britain. This work offers one example of how such groups might be approached from a practical theological perspective, in order to offer insight into the life and work of the Church in present times.

The significance of this study

The findings of this study have broad significance. For one, while this work was intended to reflect critically on, and drawing conclusions for, Church practice, my findings have some implications for the Sunday Assembly. I identified the ways in which members had been hurt by the inability of the movement to properly acknowledge their suffering. I observed, first-hand, the results of the Assembly's practice of turning pain into celebration. If the Assembly is, as it claims to be, "radically inclusive," then it must also include narratives which challenge its philosophy of "celebrating life."

This study is particularly timely, since the realities of global suffering are so increasingly pervasive. These are now simply a click away, communicated at an ever-quickening pace. With such vast quantities of news, it is not possible to assimilate and respond to every instance of suffering. Nevertheless, there is also an inherent human need to acknowledge death and destruction, and a sense that something should be said.

Regardless of the downturn in religious adherence in recent years, events of suffering provoke the need for response in society at large. In light of this, the Church remains relevant, with its rich tradition of holding suffering through the practice of lament. Rather than constructing philosophical answers, I suggest that the Church should focus its attention on the accumulation of resources and practices, which create space within its life and worship for the articulation of grief and suffering. An on-going commitment to the application of lament, both spoken and sung, can create a way of life in which church leaders and attendees are equipped with a language in which to "hold" and address both globally significant events and instances of individual suffering. The creation of a culture lament can also help Christians to resist reverting to silence, or "passing over" trauma.

The limitations of this study

In concluding this work, it is prudent to note some of the ways in which it is limited. The Sunday Assembly is a relatively new movement, having launched 2014. I studied the Assembly's congregations in London and Edinburgh over a period of three years, during which time the movement underwent a great deal of internal change.[5] I have made a concerted effort to track developments in the group's policy and practice in as much detail as possible. Due to the rate at which the organisation has developed its leadership structures, accreditation procedures, and the form of its peer support groups, there will inevitably be some gaps in this research relating to Sunday Assembly policy.

Further, while the Sunday Assembly has a global reach, only two congregations from within this movement were examined in detail. The research I conducted at the Assembly's international conference conveyed some sense of the international Assemblies, yet time and scope only allowed for a two-site ethnographic study to be conducted. It is possible that other Assemblies within the movement's global reach have begun to develop their own responses to events of suffering. However, since this book has concentrated on the flagship congregation in London, and one "satellite" assembly in Edinburgh, the conclusions drawn will inevitably focus on these communities to the exclusion of others.

Scope for further study

This book holds broader implications for further study in a number of areas. Since the Sunday Assembly is still a relatively new community and is continuing to develop and change its structures and practices, it is possible that it might yet adopt an official response to suffering on a global and individual scale. Indeed, I spoke with several members of the Sunday Assembly, whose words provide evidence that there is an appetite within the movement for this. Alice from London said that she would like to see a "collective acknowledgement of the bad things in life," while Linda from Edinburgh agreed that dealing with suffering and tragedy "is definitely a role that the

Sunday Assembly . . . will need to step into." Tony explained that the demographic of the London Assembly is currently "very young," and as such, "there hasn't been a significant death or loss within the community as yet." However, as the community grows, Tony acknowledged that "it'll have to find ways to deal with things like that." Referring also to suffering related to death and bereavement, Alistair said: "You've got to talk about it. To not talk about it. . . . Well, logically, you're looking to your community to make sense of things that are difficult." Should the Sunday Assembly begin to adopt official mechanisms of response to suffering, further work on their movements within this area could take place, building on the basis of the work contained within this book.

It is worth noting that I did uncover some findings related to what might be described as the "ecclesiology" of the Assembly. In footnotes, I have referred to an external piece of work I undertook relating to what I term the "vestiges" of Christian life and practice apparent in the Edinburgh congregation of the Sunday Assembly. Within this particular context, the term "vestiges"

> refers centrally to aspects of Christianity, whether ritualistic, identity-driven, or otherwise, which are carried over, unconsciously retained, or actively incorporated into a secular perspective, even where faith in a divine being is not.[6]

Examples of the Sunday Assembly's "religious memory" include a desire for pastoral care, as well as funerals and "life celebrations." While these were referenced as part of my wider data findings, there is space to develop and discuss these further. From a theological perspective, it may be questioned *what* members of the Sunday Assembly "carry over" from their experiences of Church, and *why* they select activities such as communal singing and gathering in a congregational formal. The Sunday Assembly's assertion that these are the "best parts of Church" may have more to bring to light about public attitudes towards the Church more generally. As such, there is scope for a further, more in-depth comparative study in this area, which might note the Assembly's rejection of practices such as sacraments and liturgy, while concurrently retaining a generic Church service format and style of congregational meetings.

In 2020 (at the time of writing), the Sunday Assembly is experiencing something of a downturn in its membership, which I have referred to at several points throughout this book. While I noted some early signs of decline in 2016, this particular topic was the focus of a great deal of media speculation in the summer of 2019, upon the publication of Faith Hill's article for *The Atlantic*. The article exposed the Sunday Assembly's struggle to keep its congregations open, including its problems with logistics, volunteer power, finances, and other Sunday morning social options. "For those who stick with Sunday Assembly," Hill writes, "the challenge now is to make the community last beyond their own generation."[7] Will the Sunday Assembly appeal to future generations? Or will its downturn continue? It is simply too soon to tell. Regardless, in theological terms at least, the Assembly remains a fascinating site of study, and one ripe for further investigation.

Conclusion

In this book, I have engaged with the Sunday Assembly, a community which constitutes a microcosmic example of a much wider shift in British society, from Church membership and participation to growing numbers of people who reject both religious and "secular" labels. I began with the intention of finding alternative practices to theodicy, which has been a problematic theological enterprise. In doing so, I journeyed from a place of celebration to a "culture of lament."

The Christian faith is not one deprived of celebration. Christians celebrate the incarnation, life, and resurrection of Jesus Christ, as the revelation of God's love and goodness. There is much to celebrate within the Church, and yet human life is filled with suffering and tribulation. While celebration is not wrong, it is not always pastorally appropriate for the Church to engage in it. Further, my reflections on the Sunday Assembly have led me to consider that the Church, just as much as those who are non-religious, can be guilty of "passing over" suffering, and moving quickly onwards to that which is more triumphant and more celebratory. Because of this, a space for grief is needed—a place in which the pain of the human experience might be held and acknowledged.

This work began as one concerned with the philosophical dangers of theodicy. It ends with a set of suggestions for the transformation of Church practice. Lament is not a new phenomenon; passionate expressions of grief and sorrow directed at God are older than the Christian faith itself, and this book is certainly not the first to suggest lament as a pastoral coping mechanism. Despite this, with each day that passes, human suffering does not relent or dissipate. There is much to lament in this world, which is uncertain, ever-changing, and witness to on-going suffering with each day that passes. Terrorism reigns; the climate crisis threatens our planet's future; human beings continue to wound one another in untold ways. Lament is one of our oldest solutions, but it may still be our most compelling. As the earth groans under the weight of trauma, an emphasis on lament within the Church is more important and more pressing than ever before.

Notes

1 Linda Woodhead, "The Rise of 'No Religion' in Britain: The Emergence of a New Cultural Majority," *Journal of the British Academy*, (4), 2016, 249.
2 Grace Davie, "Vicarious Religion: A Response," *Journal of Contemporary Religion*, 25 (2), 2010, 262.
3 I have, however, highlighted existing contributions regarding the Sunday Assembly in the field of sociology in this work, namely from Jacqui Frost of Portland State University and Tom Mortimer and Melanie Prideux of the University of Leeds.

4 Some recent examples of practical theologians noting contemporary culture in their work include Eric Stoddart, who explores the topic of surveillance in twenty-first-century society (see Stoddart, *Theological Perspectives on a Surveillance Society: Watching and Being Watched* [London: Ashgate, 2011]), Doug Gay, who points to current debates surrounding Scottish nationalism (see Gay, *Honey from the Lion: Christianity and the Ethics of Nationalism* [London: SCM Press, 2013], and Leah Robinson, who has written on sectarian violence in sports (See Robinson, "Separation of Church and Soccer: The Impact of Secularization on Religion-Based Violence in Sports," in J.-G. A. Goulet, L. D. Murphy, and A. Panagakos (eds.) *Religious Diversity Today: Experiencing Religion in the Contemporary World* (Praeger Publishing: Santa Barbara, 2016).

5 I have noted, for example, the changes which have taken place within the London Assembly's peer-to-peer support groups. These began as Smoups, intended to help members achieve New Year's resolutions, but were later rebranded as Live Better groups, with a greater focus on the movement's ethos of "living better." The Life Course was introduced as a potential extension or replacement of Live Better groups. Most recently, in 2017, the London Assembly has launched an "urban retreat" called "Retreat to the Future," which claims to give attendees "an opportunity to work through your outlook, beliefs, values and actions in the experimental, joyful, creative, multi-sensory Sunday Assembly way." It is advertised as "the next version of the Sunday Assembly's Life Course." See "Sunday Assembly Presents: Retreat to the Future": www.sundayassembly.com/retreattothefuture (accessed 7th January 2020).

6 See Katie Cross, "The Sunday Assembly in Scotland: Vestiges of Religious Thought in a Secular Congregation," *Practical Theology*, 10 (3), 2017, 253.

7 Faith Hill, "They Tried to Start a Church without God: For a While, It Worked," *The Atlantic*, 21st July 2019: www.theatlantic.com/ideas/archive/2019/07/secular-churches-rethink-their-sales-pitch/594109/ (accessed 7th January 2020).

References

Cross, Katie. "The Sunday Assembly in Scotland: Vestiges of Religious thought in a Secular Congregation." *Practical Theology*. 10 (3), 2017: 249–262.

Davie, Grace. "Vicarious Religion: A Response." *Journal of Contemporary Religion*. 25 (2), 2010: 261–266.

Gay, Doug. *Honey from the Lion: Christianity and the Ethics of Nationalism.* London: SCM Press, 2013.

Hill, Faith. "They Tried to Start a Church without God: For a While, It Worked." *The Atlantic*. 21st July 2019. www.theatlantic.com/ideas/archive/2019/07/secular-churches-rethink-their-sales-pitch/594109/

Robinson, Leah. "Separation of Church and Soccer: The Impact of Secularization on Religion-Based Violence in Sports." In *Religious Diversity Today: Experiencing Religion in the Contemporary World*, edited by J.-G. A. Goulet, L. D. Murphy, and A. Panagakos. Santa Barbara: Praeger Publishing, 2016.

Stoddart, Eric. *Theological Perspectives on a Surveillance Society: Watching and Being Watched*. London: Ashgate, 2011.

The Sunday Assembly. "Sunday Assembly Presents: Retreat to the Future." www.sundayassembly.com/retreattothefuture

Woodhead, Linda. "The Rise of 'No Religion' in Britain: The Emergence of a New Cultural Majority." *Journal of the British Academy*. (4), 2016: 245–261.

Index